Ontological Security an Status-Seeking

How and why was it possible for a small state such as Thailand to challenge great powers France and Japan during the Second World War?

Putting ontological security theory into dialogue with status-seeking approaches, Charoenvattananukul uses a case study of Thailand in the early 1940s to interrogate the dynamics and logic of a small state foreign policy. During this period, Thailand's foreign policy can appear to be surprising if viewed through a lens of survival imperatives which would assume that passivity towards more powerful states is the optimal policy. As the majority of states are small and medium sized, it is very important to understand the imperatives that drive such states, especially in their interactions with great powers.

In applying these frameworks to a small state, this book makes a unique and valuable contribution to the field of international relations theory. It will also be of great interest to scholars of twentieth century Thai history and of the Pacific Theatre of the Second World War.

Peera Charoenvattananukul is a lecturer in the Department of International Affairs at the Faculty of Political Science, Thammasat University, Thailand.

IR Theory and Practice in Asia

This series will publish philosophical, theoretical, methodological and empirical work by prominent scholars, as well as that of emerging scholars, concerned with IR theory and practice in the context of Asia. It will engage with a wide range of issues and questions ranging from meta-theoretical underpinnings of existing Western-oriented IR theories to ways of theorising Asian histories and cultures.

What Is at Stake in Building "Non-Western" International Relations Theory?
Yong-Soo Eun

International Relations as a Discipline in Thailand
Theory and Sub-fields
Edited by Chanintira na Thalang, Soravis Jayanama and Jittipat Poonkham

Rethinking Middle Powers in The Asian Century
New Theories, New Cases
Edited by Tanguy Struye de Swielande, Dorothée Vandamme, David Walton and Thomas Wilkins

Critical International Relations Theories in East Asia
Relationality, Subjectivity, and Pragmatism
Edited by Kosuke Shimizu

Ontological Security and Status-Seeking
Thailand's Proactive Behaviours During the Second World War
Peera Charoenvattananukul

Going beyond Parochialism and Fragmentation in the Study of International Relations
Edited by Yong-Soo Eun

For the full list of titles in this series, please visit www.routledge.com/IR-Theory-and-Practice-in-Asia/book-series/IRTPA

Ontological Security and Status-Seeking

Thailand's Proactive Behaviours During the Second World War

Peera Charoenvattananukul

LONDON AND NEW YORK

First published 2020 by Routledge

2 Park Square, Milton Park, Abingdon, Oxon OX14 4RN
605 Third Avenue, New York, NY 10017

Routledge is an imprint of the Taylor & Francis Group, an informa business

First issued in paperback 2022

Publisher's Note

The publisher has gone to great lengths to ensure the quality of this reprint but points out that some imperfections in the original copies may be apparent.

British Library Cataloguing-in-Publication Data
A catalogue record for this book is available from the British Library

Library of Congress Cataloging-in-Publication Data
A catalog record for this book has been requested

ISBN: 978-0-367-85817-9 (hbk)
ISBN: 978-1-03-233724-1 (pbk)
DOI: 10.4324/9781003015215

Typeset in Galliard
by Apex CoVantage, LLC

For Krit and Nanthana

Contents

Figures

Abbreviations

CICN	Civilian Commanding Notebook
CUCN	Cultural Commanding Notebook
FRC	Foreign Relations Committee
FRUS	Foreign Relations of the United States
FO	Foreign and Commonwealth Office
HW	Government Communications Headquarters
IGH	Imperial Guard Headquarters
IR	International Relations
KoTo	Ministry of Foreign Affairs
LOA	Liaison Office of Alliance
MCN	Military Commanding Notebook
MoTo	Ministry of Interior
MPH	Magic of Pearl Harbor
MS	Manuscript Room of the University of Cambridge
NAM	Non-Aligned Movement
NAT	National Archives of Thailand
NATO	North Atlantic Treaty Organization
NCC	National Council of Culture
SAA	Southern Area Army
SoRo	Office of Prime Minister
SoTo	Ministry of Education
TMCM	Thailand's Minutes of Cabinet Meeting
TNA	The National Archives, London
TPMP	Thai Parliament's Minutes of Proceedings

Acknowledgements

The origin of this book was part of my doctoral journey undertaken at the University of Cambridge. This journey would not have been possible without the support of my father and mother who have tirelessly encouraged me to acknowledge the value of education. Another source of inspiration for me in this path is, believe it or not, a historical figure from the Romance of the Three Kingdoms. The genuine passion and explosive hot-headedness of Zhang Fei (張飛) remind me of the traditional Confucius values. Equally important are my two sisters who have always been playful and helpful. Second to none in terms of importance is Pichapa Indrasuta, my wife, who allowed me to study abroad. Had it not been for her decision, well-wishing intent, and patience, I would not have completed my PhD and this book. She has always been a source of emotional support for me even when I hit the lowest point in life.

I would like to express my gratitude to the Cambridge Thai Foundation for providing me with a three-year scholarship to study at Cambridge. Speaking of those involved in the formation of my research, I could not but thank Dr. Ayse Zarakol. I am a bad, if not the worst, student in every aspect, but she has been patient with my stubbornness and indifference for years. Yet, she still sees something constructive from the likes of me. I remember the last time we spoke to each other, and I asked her if my thesis could be turned into a monograph. Her answer suggested that she still believes in my potential.

Academically speaking I was supported by the two significant persons who often supplied me with necessary archival documents. One is Dr. Wasithee Chaiyakan, who believes in the best of human beings. She would not hesitate to help retrieve any archival documents or books I requested. I am greatly indebted to her. In fact, she was the first person who introduced me to the case study of this book. Another person who mattered to the archival sources of my book was Dr. Puli Fuwongcharoen. Puli is an industrious person, which is quite different from my lackadaisical research style. Seemingly insincere, he at least shared with me some uncanny details about archival sources and how to access them. I would also like to thank P'Tai, a staff from Thailand's National Archives, for advising me on several issues related to the research.

My journey would not have been possible in the first place without inspiration from Dr. Jittipat Poonkham, who gave me a reference letter twice: one for my MPhil and another for my PhD. His presence in my life in 2012 drove me towards the discipline of international relations. Moreover, I would like to give a big credit to Dr. Chanintira Na Thalang, who also wrote me a reference letter twice. And when I came back to Thammasat University, she was the first person who encouraged me to publish my thesis. She is the person who always answers my phone call whenever I need someone to talk to about academic progress.

Lastly, I would like to thank Torsak Jindasuksri. He was the person who read my theory chapter and posed challenging questions. His sharp analyses were extremely helpful to my manuscript. Speaking with honesty, I think he is one of the sharpest persons in the field of political theory in Thailand I have ever met.

Note on names and transcription

Names in this book are written according to the traditional customs. For Thai names, first names precede family names. The Romanisation of the Thai words and Thai names are based on the Royal Thai General System of Transcription (RTGS) as indicated by the Royal Institute of Thailand.

Part I

Introduction and theory

1 Introduction

Introduction

The famous Melian Dialogue, which is a tale about how a great power such as Athens annihilated a small islandic state such as Melos, is widely cited as a textbook example of how power and survival assumptions trump any other considerations in international politics. A few scholars would ask how and why the Melians prioritised their sense of pride, honour, and prestige at the expense of survival. This book project follows a similar line of inquiry. It asks how and why it was possible for Thailand to challenge both France and Japan during the Second World War. As a small country, Thailand's choices should be constrained by the survival option. The book suggests that the frameworks of ontological security and status concerns could further an empirical investigation of the selected case. This book argues that Thailand's proactive behaviours towards the two great powers were driven by the concerns for status among the Thai elites and the will to be recognised as an equal nation.

Thailand has been considered a 'small state' since the modern international system has been exported worldwide in the late nineteenth century. Its diplomacy in relation to 'great powers' is believed to naturally adhere to a principle of flexible foreign policy (Likhit 1964; Corrine 1999; Pavin 2010). A 'naturalised belief' does not always conform to reality, however. The intent of this book thus is to explore such vagaries and redirect the study of Thai foreign policy in a new direction by examining the case of Thai foreign policy from 1938 to 1944 through the lens of contemporary International Relations (IR) approaches.

During wartime, Thailand pursued a surprisingly adventurous and risk-taking foreign policy vis-à-vis the great powers during this period as exemplified by how it waged war against France (1940–41) and how it disobeyed the Japanese directions (1942–44). From 1938 to 1944, Thailand sought to assert her position to become one of the great powers on the international stage. In other words, its wartime foreign policy was determined by its desire to become *primus inter pares*. This book seeks to understand Thailand's proactive foreign policy strategy in this period, given its conventional wisdom of conducting passive and flexible foreign policy. Rather than interpreting the case study of Thailand's wartime proactive policies by employing a conventional analysis of Thai foreign policy that prioritises material interest, this book introduces the concepts of ontological security, status concern, and recognition in order to better explain Thai foreign policy. It studies how past trauma shaped foreign policy preferences and choices of Thai policy-makers during the Second World War.

The remainder of this introductory chapter presents justifications for the case study by providing a historical background of the selected case study and an overview of the gaps in the literature. The chapter concludes with a discussion of methodology and research design.

Background

Situated in the central part of Southeast Asia, the geography of Thailand[1] has had strategic implications for great powers since the country's initial exposure to the international system in the nineteenth century. A former U.S. ambassador to Thailand, Edwin F. Stanton (1954), once commented: 'because of her geographical and strategic location, Thailand is the heart and citadel of the region (72). The choices of Thai foreign policy have been limited due to its geography.

Despite Thailand's geopolitical significance, Thai foreign policy choices have not attracted much academic attention. This may be because most works on Thai foreign policy are inclined to characterise the nature of Thai foreign policy behaviours as 'reactive' as opposed to 'proactive'. By the broad definitions of Palmer and Morgan (2011; Pongpisoot 2009), a *proactive foreign policy* corresponds to a policy with an objective to transform the status quo, whereas a *reactive foreign policy* is a policy which aims at preserving the status quo. Generally speaking, Thai foreign policy is understood to be formulated in response to immediate international events and to maintain the status quo. The tradition of Thai foreign policy is usually characterised as flexible and pragmatic, but reactive. Thai foreign policy decision-makers tend to have an internalised belief that the nation should conduct its diplomacy amidst the external pressures by accommodating demands of great powers in order to maintain Thailand's sovereignty and independence. In the sphere of foreign relations, most observers see Thailand as having thus been generally 'responsive' and 'reactive' in appeasing prevailing powers to stabilise the existing status in the international system. The general understanding of the flexible position of Thailand almost becomes a cliché in Thai studies. For example, according to Pavin Chachavalpongpun (2010, 18–31), one of the most prominent scholars of Thai foreign policy, Thailand has generated foreign policies with the underlying rationale of *reacting* to international occurrences which might have an impact on the nation. To Pavin, Thai foreign policy decision-makers only break with the passive tradition from 2001 to 2006, which is the contemporary period of Thai foreign policy. Pavin's opinion about Thailand's traditional passivity is the received wisdom among Thais.

Is such a generalised explanation of Thai foreign policy behaviour valid across time and space in Thailand's history? The answer is no. Relying on the characterisation of flexibility in Thai foreign policy and thus predicting that Thailand will be merely reactive and responsive in dealing with great powers encounters an impasse when a researcher travels back in time to the Second World War period. The case study of Thai foreign relations vis-à-vis the great powers during the premiership of Field Marshal Plaek Phibunsongkhram[2] from 1938 to 1944, which is the main emphasis of this book, renders reductionist approaches to Thai foreign policy problematic.

At first glance, applying the concept of flexible foreign policy to explain Thai behaviours on the eve until the end of the war is reasonably convincing. Nonetheless, on closer inspection, it is revealed that Thailand pursued proactive foreign policies towards both France and Japan. Its behaviours, which are to be discussed in the following sections, could be considered as an objective to transform the status quo. Their policies in relation to France and Japan were not subject to preserve any status quo. In this regard, their behaviours correspond to Palmer and Morgan's (2011) broad definition of proactive foreign policy.

Thailand's war with France

Prior to the Second World War, up until 1938, Thailand pursued a political agenda of reclaiming its lost territories from colonial powers such as Britain and France. In this period, it was rumoured among the British and French diplomats that Thailand had been influenced by Italian and Japanese fascism and hence was likely to pursue a course of expansionist policies in mainland Southeast Asia (TNA-FO371/22207-F4339/113/40[3]). The irredentist tendency in Thailand gradually became substantial two years before the Thais waged war against the French Vichy government from 1940 to 1941 in order to regain territories from France. And, prior to the Thai-French armed clash which took place in December 1940, France's distrust of Thailand was more than real, and Thailand's behaviours towards France were distraught and provocative even before the outbreak of the Second World War (Thompson 1940, 248). One historian notes that Thailand's sense of irredentism was a 'dormant sentiment hidden in the heart of every Thai leader' (Kobkua 1995, 254). Similarly, Sir Josiah Crosby, the British ambassador to Thailand of the time, realised that the lost territories represented Thailand's national quest for the last 50 years (Aldrich 1988, 214). Henceforth, Thailand's aggression towards France was historically contingent.

The French and the British were worried about the tendency of Thailand's expansionist aspirations well before the war broke out. The two European powers therefore sought a guarantee towards the Thai irredentist posture by proposing a mutual non-aggression pact in August 1939, and the agreement was signed in 1940 (Sang 1944) in order to ensure Thailand's political neutrality in times of war. The French and British observed that discourses and sentiments among the Thais to reclaim their lost territories were gaining strength and thus concluded that it was in their best interest to take precaution against Thailand's opportunism. Despite the conclusion of the pact between Thailand and France, however, the Thai-French skirmish between Thailand and French Indo-China borders escalated into a war between the small Asian country and the proud major European power in 1940.

How could Thailand decide to wage war against France's Vichy government in late-November 1940? There are various explanations. A former governor of Indo-China, Alexandre Varenne (1938, 168–69), believed that Japan abetted Thailand's drive towards expansionism. Whether the Japanese succour was premeditated is no central concern of this book. However, this explanation offers inadequate grounds to understand the Franco-Thai war. If this explanation was valid, the Thais should declare war on France when the Japanese forcibly demanded military bases from French Indo-China in September 1940. On the contrary, as will be shown in the empirical chapters, the Thai government opted for diplomatic routes until the crisis was escalated in November 1940.

A seemingly even more compelling argument is that the changing structure of the international system and French weakness were the reasons for Thai leadership to conduct an opportunistic foreign policy against France. In July 1940, France capitulated to Germany and relocated the government to Vichy. The French prestige and power dropped to a new low in an international arena. This situation offered a window of opportunity for Thailand to mobilise against France and her Indo-China colonies. The undeclared war between Thailand and France actually broke out in December 1940, however. Why did Thailand not resort to the use of force immediately after the fall of France? Why would Thailand wait for five months to initiate an armed conflict? Moreover, if Thailand was naturally passive and reactive towards arising situations, why, according to archival records, was Thailand acting aggressively towards French Indo-China even before the French reached her nadir? The puzzle here is thus: 'How was it possible for Thailand, despite its inferior status in the international system, to resort to proactive foreign policy in relation to a much more powerful country such as France?'

Thailand and greater East Asian conquest

Another case in point, sequential to the border dispute with France, happened during the period of the Greater East Asia War (1941–1945). In accordance with the conventional approach to the study of Thai foreign policy, the Japanese presence in Thailand is viewed as Thailand's flexible accommodation of greater powers (Buszynski 1982, 1037). Such an understanding enormously neglects the proactive role of the Thai policy-makers in joining and turning against Japan.

On the night of 7 December 1941, Direk Jayanam, the then Minister of Foreign Affairs of Thailand, was informed of the possible Japanese invasion. He was confident that the Thais would resist the Japanese occupation by all means as he told Crosby: 'Siam would definitely put up a fight' (Direk & Keyes 1978, 62). As the Thais expected, the Japanese ambassador to Thailand, Teiji Tsubokami, sent an ultimatum to the Thai government and expected a response within an hour. Japan offered three possible choices to the Thais. The first was simply that the Japanese require the rights of passage for the Japanese troops to Burma and Malaya. The second choice involved signing a defensive military agreement of alliance between Thailand and Japan, and Japan would aid Thailand if attacked by any third party. The last proposal was a robust Thai-Japanese military alliance.

Additionally, Japan pledged to return territories that Thailand had lost to France and Great Britain in the nineteenth century (Direk & Keyes 1978, 64; Nuechterlein 1965, 73).

The Thais resisted the Japanese, and some lives were lost. Prior to any decisive agenda, the cabinet members also held a belief that by capitulating to the Japanese demands after the Thai patriots lost their lives trying to stall the invaders, Thailand's situation might be sympathetic in the Western perspective (Pensrinokun 1988, 148). Eventually, the Thai government ordered a ceasefire as the cabinet decided to grant rights of passage for the Japanese troops provided that Thailand could maintain its *sovereignty and independence.* On this matter, Pridi Banomyong, Thai Finance Minister, stressed to Phibun that the Thai-Japanese negotiation should reaffirm Japan's respect for Thai sovereignty and any co-operation should be limited (Pridi's emphasis cited in Reynolds 1988, 312).

Despite the bloodshed from both sides, Phibun and his cabinet finally drove towards the Japanese arms. On 11 December 1941, a few days after the Japanese invasion, Thailand abruptly concluded another secret military agreement to become a formal ally of Japan. And, on 25 January 1942, Thailand formally declared war on the US and Britain. In conclusion, from 1942 towards the end of the war, Thailand was formally a part of the Greater East Asian War. In 1942, the Thai army crossed the border into Burma. From the outset, Thailand's decision to join the war stemmed from Japanese pressure. Nevertheless, brilliant research by Eiji Murashima (2006), a prominent historian, contradicts the general belief that Thailand was forced by Japan to conduct a military campaign in Burma. In fact, according to Murashima, Japan was reluctant to assign Thailand's military operations, and the Burma campaign was an effort by Thai policy-makers who inexorably pushed forward an agenda to participate in the war. Although Thailand pushed forward the declaration of war against the Allied powers and co-operated as a Japanese ally, the Thai government later turned against Japan in *less than a year* of the alliance.

Thailand's wartime diplomacy and its subsequent survival from the severe punishments of the Second World War were viewed as a genius diplomatic masterpiece. The case study is often invoked to argue that bending with the tide in order to survive is a wise strategy. The flexible foreign policy approach fails to explain how policy choices and preferences were selected from aligning with and breaking from Japan. If the Japanese pressure and changing international structure factored in this case, why did the Thais formally aligned with the Japanese and why did the Thai leaders declare war on the British and Americans? And, as Murashima (2006) reveals, why did the Thais deliberately undertake the military campaign against Japan's wishes? How could a flexible foreign policy approach make sense of such choices? The optimal choice for Thailand after the course of the Japanese invasion was to pursue a limited co-operative approach. After Japan attacked Pearl Harbor, the result of the Pacific War was uncertain. As such, it would have been wise for Thailand to restrain its relationship with Japan. However, the Thais at first became an eager Japanese ally, declared war on the Allied powers, sought to be part of the Axis, and participated in the military operations in Burma. But, within less than a year, Thailand's diplomatic relations with Japan became frayed and the Thai elites surreptitiously turned against Japan.

The case study of Thai foreign policy from 1938 to 1944 thus represents a challenge to the 'flexible foreign policy' characterisation of Thailand in particular. In this period, Thailand attempted to reclaim its territories by challenging Europe's great powers such as Britain and France which were more technologically well-equipped than Thailand. From late 1941 to 1944, the time which Thailand was under the clout of Japan, the Thai decision-makers were also rather expedient in dealing with the Japanese. Phibun first pursued a proactive foreign policy towards Japan. He then decided to break with Japan abruptly. Phibun's foreign policy from 1938 to 1944, henceforth, poses a challenge to the studies of Thai foreign policy.

Conventional explanations of Thai foreign policy

As previously mentioned, the studies of Thai foreign policy have generally revolved around the received wisdom that Thailand has survived crises by adopting a flexible foreign policy strategy. This section reviews the literature on the approaches to explain Thai foreign policy and finds three competing explanations.

Flexible foreign policy approach

The dominant understanding in studies of Thai foreign policy is the 'flexible foreign policy approach'.[4] Most major contributions in this area concentrate on using this approach to explain instances in each period of time (Corrine 1999; Kislenko 2000; See examples of the works which follow the flexible approach from Kislenko 2002; Pensri 1984; Smairob 1980; Snidvongs 1960; Viraphol 1976). This explanation, as observed by Nattapoll Chaiching, has been picked up by Western scholars such as D.G. Hall (1968), Donald E. Nuechterlein (1965), and David Wyatt (2003) without questioning its tenability. Scholars who employ the flexible foreign policy explanation tend to perceive Thai foreign policy as reducible to *its conduct with external powers*. In this approach, the nature of Thai foreign policy stems from its tradition which has been characterised as 'bending with the wind', meaning Thailand conducts foreign policy on the basis of pragmatic calculations and always seeks to bandwagon with any prevailing powers in times of a security crisis, regardless of moral and reputational consequences. Likhit Dhiravegin (1974, 48) has metaphorically termed this as 'bamboo diplomacy'. The reason behind this usage is because a bamboo naturally bends towards the direction of the wind.

Consequently, Thai IR scholarship has been mostly emphasising the importance of diplomatic history and historiography of how Thailand has preserved its sovereignty from time to time (Supamit 2007, 68). The implication is that the study of Thai foreign affairs does not need to employ a variety of IR approaches to interpret international political phenomena within the boundaries of the political science tradition. In this light, Nattapoll Chaiching (2009, 4) similarly observes that most of the scholarly works on the historical events of Thai foreign affairs reproduce a conventional narrative, descriptively and repetitively explaining how the Thai elites have naturally accommodated the great power demands for the sake of national survival. One expert on Thai foreign policy commented that almost 'all textbooks on Thai diplomacy agree on the uncompromising objectives of Thailand's foreign policy [which adheres to the principle of flexibility – *my emphasis*]' (Pavin 2010, 64). The overwhelming dominance of this approach in Thai foreign policy discussion can also be further testified in the words of Chanintira et al. (2019):

> Academics have commonly highlighted Thailand's flexibility and pragmatism in its foreign policy otherwise labelled as "bending with the wind policy" and "bamboo diplomacy".
>
> (5)

The underlying notions of this approach have been clearly defined by Corrine Phuangkasem (1999, 2–3), a Thai foreign relations specialist. Corrine labels three components of Thailand's bending-with-the-wind policy. The first component refers to how Thailand would frequently accommodate the requests of greater powers which are a menace to the nation's territorial integrity and sovereignty. The second component is about how Thailand should pit one power against another power by leaning towards one side to form equilibrium and to strengthen Thailand's security. As for the third component, it is suggested by Corrine that Thailand will always befriend any prevailing or victor power. These three aspects are the Thai foreign policy hallmarks. These strategies also enable Thailand to preserve the status quo. It also cautions Thailand against catalysing discord with any greater powers. In conclusion, these features imply that the pattern of Thai foreign policy is reactive in nature and principle.

What then is the problem with the flexible foreign policy approach in relation to the case study of this book? In the case of Thailand's war with France during the Second World War, the flexible foreign policy model could not explain why Thailand became aggressive vis-à-vis France. The conflict with France was a clear discord between a great power and a small nation such as Thailand. Firstly, France was no threat to Thailand's sovereignty. Secondly, even if France was a threat to the Thais, why then did it choose not to pit one power against another? Thirdly, the Axis nations were on the rise while the Allied powers were frail. According to one of the three components of Thailand's flexible foreign policy model, it should side with the then prevailing powers. Nonetheless, the Thais opted to wage war against the French by themselves.

Nonetheless, the flexible foreign policy approach seems to grasp the situations in the case of the Japanese-Thai relations from 1941 to 1944. For instance, the fact that Thailand became a Japanese ally appears to conform to the Thai conventional wisdom of foreign policy conduct. Yes, the Thai elites accommodated the request of Japan to grant the Imperial Army the rights of passage. Nevertheless, the flexible foreign policy model partly captured the overall picture of Thai foreign policy behaviours. How could such a model explain Thailand's proactive behaviours towards Japan after they joined forces? It would be illusory to state that Japan's Greater East Asian enterprise was no threat to Thailand. And, according to the mainstream Thai historiography, Thailand emerged as one of the victorious powers after the war. However, such an account ignores how the Phibun government confronted the Japanese counterpart less than a year after they became allies.

Decision-making approach

The second dominating explanation of Thai foreign policy choices relies on what may be termed the decision-making approach. This approach probes into behaviours of decision-makers who are likely to shape policies (Herman 1972, 70–75). Although the study of Thai foreign affairs has received limited attention, there have been a few attempts to explore Thai foreign policy decision-making processes. All of the contributions in this strand follow Graham Allison's (Allison & Zelikow 1999) and James Rosenau's (1969) models.

In brief, Allison conceptualises three models: rational actor; organisational process; and bureaucratic politics. For Allison, the *rational actor model* refers to how a unitary actor, such as a government, formulates a rational policy on the basis of a rational calculation of ends and means. It is suggested that the government rationally calculates costs and benefits to optimise choices of national interest. The *organisational process*, however, is the model which suggests that a large organisation rather than a single leader is a policy input, whereas a policy is an outcome of the organisation par excellence. Instead of being a unitary rational actor, according to this model, a government consists of various bureaucratic organisations. Different organisations have different responsibilities. In order to coordinate among different units, there must be 'standard operating procedures' or rules within organisational apparatuses which allow certain policies to be executed. The optimal choice does not derive from leaders maximising interest. Nonetheless, policies are chosen on the basis of processes of organisational rules, repertories, and procedures to tackle immediate problems. The *bureaucratic politics model*, on the other hand, indicates how a foreign policy can be understood through a contest and bargain among individuals and organisations within the states. Hence, a policy is an outcome of political compromises within the states as opposed to rational choices of unitary actors or organisational rules. Bhansoon Ladavalya (1986), for example, has contributed to the studies of Thai foreign policy by applying Allison's models to explain Thai foreign policy from 1975 to 1976.

Apart from Allison, James Rosenau (1971) has famously popularised the model of 'linkage politics'. In principle, linkage politics provides a method to understand foreign policies by examining international politics and intra-national politics. Fundamentally, for Rosenau, international politics and intra-national politics are two different entities yet interdependent on one another. Simply speaking, conditions in the international environment affect the conditions of national environment and vice versa. Contributions to the studies of Thai foreign policy employing Rosenau's model can be traced from scholarly works of Charivat Santapura (1985), Corrine Phuangkasem (1980), Asdakorn Eaksaengsri (1980), Thanee Sukkasem (1982), and Naruemit Sodsuk (1981).[5]

Apropos of the usage of the decision-making approaches to Thai foreign policy, it appears that the only piece which is relevant to the selected case study of this research project has been written by Charivat Santapura (1985), who coherently applies Rosenau's internal and external factors to narrate Thai foreign policy from 1932 to 1946 in a descriptive and historical manner. By and large, Charivat's contribution is noteworthy as he concludes that the best foreign policy option for Thailand is the flexible and reactive foreign policy. On the contrary, regarding his opinion towards Phibun's premiership, he vaguely blames Phibun for personal gains in the case of Thai's irredentist war (Charivat 1985, 332). He, however, peculiarly praises Phibun for his acquiesce to Japan's invasion (Charivat 1985, 328).

There are, however, reasons why it would be inappropriate to analyse foreign policy-making through the models of Rosenau and Allison.

Although Charivat (1985) exhaustedly lists external and internal inputs, such as global environment, bilateral relationship with great powers, military capabilities, economic condition, political structure, and interest group, which could potentially shape Thai foreign policy, he eventually stresses the importance of the Thai elites, particular Phibun and his cliques, in influencing foreign policy decisions as opposed to other factors (292–295). As Charivat (1985) writes: 'In Thai foreign policy decision-making circles, the idiosyncrasies of Pibul's dictatorial and militaristic character . . . apparently dominated the whole period' (304–305). He even went so far as to comment that any transformation of the external environment did not determine Phibun's foreign policy decisions:

> As long as Pibul ruled, this second variable [changing external environment – my note] could never surpass the first in its importance. Being a dictator, once he set his mind on playing along the irredentist line he paid only slight regard to international opinion that was unfavourable.
>
> (305)

All in all, Charivat (1985) concludes that in Thailand's case from 1932 to 1945:

> [I]t goes on to emphasise the importance of decision-makers . . . as the main weight in the determination of foreign policy. Other components were of even less importance and accordingly less attention should be paid to them.
>
> (305)

As regards Allison's propositions, the period of the case study of this book also renders those three models problematic for the following reasons. Firstly, the rational model is too idealistic to explain foreign policy decisions of the Thai government during the Second World War. In this model, the government is the sole and unified rational actor of decision-making. From the outset, Allison's rational model is consistent with Charivat's description of how the Thai decision-makers were the pivots of foreign policy formulation. However, on closer inspection, there is a subtle difference. Discussing in relation to the case study, could Thailand's toughening behaviours towards the two great powers such as France and Japan be considered as rationally motivated policies? Was it worth the benefits to initiate conflicts with the two powers in the region? Rationally speaking, for the Thais, war with France was not an optimal choice. And, as it will be shown in Chapter 5, the Thai leaders understood that there was no economic value in recovering the lost territories from France. As such, risking the nation's security for fruitless territories was not rational. Similarly, Thailand's full co-operation with and defiance of Japan in less than a year would not fall into a rational category. The Thais could distance themselves from Japan so that they could later avoid being seen as a losing nation in the war if Japan fell. Worse than that, after committing to the Japanese cause, the Thais sought to defy Japan. This policy was perilous to the nation's security because Japan in 1942 became an eminent power in the war. Challenging Japan after less than six months of becoming allies seemed reckless rather than rational.

Secondly, Allison's organisational process model is not applicable to the study as well. The main period of the case was after the bureaucratic system was created for no more than 50 years. It was safe to assume that the Thai bureaucracy was in its infancy. Charivat (1985) realises this point and suggests that 'Allison's "standard operating procedures" did not exist in Thailand then as the Thai polity was not yet bureaucratic enough. Although it was true that most ministries saw their own importance rather in excess of reality . . . different leaders have different degrees of principle and conviction which proved to be more decisive' (305). Regardless of the development of the bureaucratic system of the time, the point he implies is clear: the elites were much more influential in guiding foreign policy than deriving their decisions from sets of rules, standards, and guidelines from the bureaucracy. This second reason is intricately linked to the third one.

Thirdly, the bureaucratic politics model generally explains how foreign policy is an outcome of negotiation, contestation, and bargain among different groups of players in the state apparatus. In the examples of Allison, players include 'chiefs' such as the president, secretary of state, president chief of staff, congressmen, press members, and other interest groups. Charivat (1985) believes that this model is not fit to analyse Thai foreign policy because the power was mainly centred in the executive branch, whereas the legislature's role was unimportant as it was created only after 1932 (305). Public opinion mattered only when it supported the government's agenda. Issues forwarded by any interest groups would be heard only if any members of such interest groups held key positions in the political structure (294). As Charivat (1985) concludes:

> Though competing elites, in theory, act as checks and balances and thus prevent domination by any particular faction, in a polity without democracy and regular elections, it is only a far-fetched dream. . . . Furthermore, two

> Thai characteristics, those of diffidence and respect for the elders, provide a good basis for a political bureaucracy which tends to become more and more conservative.
>
> (295)

In other words, after the 1932 Revolution, which saw the transformation from absolute monarchy to constitutional monarchy, the new regime led by civilians was undemocratic compared to the modern notion of democracy. From this interpretation, the elites were strongly unified. Moreover, a certain culture of the Thai people was also a hindrance to change. 'Diffidence' and 'respecting the elders' were the qualities that caused civil servants to be too passive and submissive to voice their opinions and agendas.

Although it could be argued that there might be factional politics even within the government cabinet, the two events from the case study suggest otherwise. For example, in the case of Thailand's war with France, Phibun received unanimous support from every sector of Thai society. There was no disagreement even among his cabinet members. Regarding the case of Japanese-Thai relations, the importance of the elites in power became more evident. Some might make a case that there was a rift between pro-Japanese and pro-Allied ministers in the cabinet. However, Thailand's leaning towards Japan was not a result of negotiation and bargain. Such a policy outcome was borne out of Phibun's decision despite Pridi's opposition. After the Japanese-Thai alliance was formed, Phibun's dictatorial style of administration materialised. He, for instance, removed any dissenters from his cabinet. Pridi was reshuffled from a key position (see Thamsook 1978). In this regard, Thai foreign policy from 1941 to 1944 was predicated on Phibun and his men.

In sum, the implication from the decision-making approach to a study of Thai foreign policy of this period is that the Thai elites, particularly those in power, were responsible for foreign policy conduct.

Descriptive approach

The third dominant framework to explain Thai foreign policy is the descriptive approach as advanced by Charnvit Kasetsiri (1974), Kobkua Suwannathat-pian (1989), Toshiharu (1985), Sumet Sukitanont (1980), and Darunee Bunphiban (1977). Apart from these scholars, other contributions are historical/historiographical works which do not straightforwardly focus on Thai foreign policy from 1938 to 1944 per se. They do, however, pay heed to bilateral relations within the timeframe of 1938 to 1944. Richard J. Aldrich (1993), for example, examines British, American, French, and Japan foreign policy strategies towards Thailand. Another thread of historical work has emphasised the conduct of Thai-Japanese relations during the wartime period. Those historians include Thamsook Numnonda (1977), Edward B. Reynolds (1988), Edward T. Flood (1967), and Somchoke Swasdirak (1981). Moreover, there are some historians such as Thamrongsak Petchlertanan (2009) and Supaporn Bumrungwongsa

(2003) whose research particularly centre on the issue of war over the territories without explicitly discussing Thai foreign affairs from 1938 to 1944.

It is quite noteworthy that all of these descriptive works follow the similar line of reasoning when it comes to the issue of Thai foreign policy-making. Their storylines downplay the proactive role of Thailand in the Thai-French and Thai-Japanese conflicts. These works begin with the implicit assumptions that Thailand's priority is survival and that the Thais should be cautiously adaptive to situations. Therefore, once the French were debilitated in the European theatre, Thailand seized the opportunity to reclaim its lost territories. And, in the case of Thai-Japanese relations, historical narratives have been projected in confirmation of how Thailand bent with the prevailing Japanese. And, at the end of the day, Thailand could successfully negotiate with the victor powers at the end of the war. Thai foreign policy analysts, for example, describe a brief history of Thai diplomacy during the Second World War without mentioning Franco-Thai war while alluding to Thailand's preservation of independence from Japan as an example of how Thailand appeased Japan to bend with the prevailing wind (Buszynski 1982, 1037; Pavin 2010, 78–80; Pongphisoot 2009, 34). Thailand's bending towards the Japanese has only been mentioned slightly as the example of how Thailand was adaptive in foreign relations (Asadakorn 1980, 48; Buszynski 1982, 1037; Kislenko 2002, 541; Pensri 1984, 195; Smairob 1980, 15; Suhrki 1971, 429). These works, as opposed to Murashima (2006), abnegate the proactive role of Thailand's gambit during the alignment with Japan.

Nevertheless, it is notable that Charnvit, Thamrongsak, and Supaporn offer an interesting direction with regard to Thailand's relations with France. These three scholars indirectly suggest that in order to understand Thailand's proactive behaviours, it is vital to probe into history and examine ideational elements such as historical memories of how injustices done to Thailand during the colonial era could influence policy outcomes. Charnvit (1974, 48), for example, illustrates how Western colonisation left scars on the Thai elites, which eventually drove the course of nationalist policies. Thamrongsak (2009, 170–184) similarly elucidates how the story of the lost territories stirred the vengeful feelings among the Thais. Supaporn (2003, 17–28) partly traces how the ideational construction of nationalist and pan-Thai thinking was accountable for Thailand's gambit in the war. In other words, although these three historians do not state their methodologies explicitly, their historical narratives suggest that past trauma was partly responsible for Thailand's aspiration during this time. However, they fall short of interpreting Phibun's foreign policy rigorously because they cover only the issues of territorial retrocession. Interestingly, a recent historical contribution by Shane Strate (2009) offers an account as to how trauma and humiliation have been responsible for the formation of national consciousness in Thailand. Strate's work, however, does not primarily focus on foreign policy during the Phibun era. He compares three periods of how the history of national humiliation has been communicated by the Thai elites without investigating how the discourse of national humiliation constructs and constitutes Thai foreign policy.

Minding the gap

A number of conclusions can be drawn from the overview of Thai foreign policy literature presented in the previous sections. First and foremost, it is obvious that the literature analysing Thai foreign policy from 1938 to 1944 is rather limited. The only complete pieces of Thai foreign relations during Phibun which examine Thailand's perspective originate only from Charivat, Kobkua, Toshiharu, Sumet, and Darunee.

Secondly, these works all tend to reaffirm the theoretical rigour of the flexible foreign policy approach, concluding that a study of Thailand foreign policy eventually boils down to how Thailand's elites flexibly adjust to catastrophes. In other words, the decision-making and descriptive approaches are simply window dressing and ultimately yield a result which is not different from the flexible foreign policy approach.

Thirdly, although there are attempts to utilise models of foreign policy analysis to explain decision-making of Thai foreign policy in different periods, certain conditions of the period of the case study of this book prevent the application of such models. During Phibun's premiership, it was the elites who ruled over foreign policy issues. At the end of the day, it was believed that the Thai elites merely conducted Thai foreign policy in accordance with the conventional wisdom of bending with the wind (Kobkua 1995, 243).

Fourthly, all of the reviewed works, with the exception of Charnvit, Thamromsak, Supaporn, and Strate, take a materialist approach and do not pay attention to the influence of ideational factors on foreign policy-making. It is undeniable that the material factors are of importance, but they cannot explain every social phenomenon. They cannot provide a satisfactory account as to how a small state such as Thailand was disobedient towards the French and the Japanese during the Second World War.

Furthermore, Thai foreign policy behaviours have been vaguely believed to be a unique phenomenon by the students of Thai foreign policy. There are scarcely few attempts to utilise other IR approaches to study Thai foreign policy. As such, what has been missing from the study of Thai foreign policy from 1938 to 1944 is an effort to develop and apply different IR approaches to reinterpret the case study. Moreover, the general absence of theoretical frameworks in the study of Thai foreign policy suggests that there are places for scholars to apply IR theories to enhance an explanation of Thai foreign policy.

In summary, there is a need to fill a lacuna by integrating approaches which highlight non-material factors to explain Thai foreign policy behaviours orchestrated by the Thai elites. The question here is whether it is possible to find alternative approaches which are predicated on the ideational reflections of the elites to explain Thai foreign policy behaviours.

The curious case of Thailand and main arguments

Posing the puzzles

Previous sections argued that 'the flexible foreign policy' explanation encounters limitations when confronted with Thailand's proactive role during the Second

World War. The primary questions and objectives driving this book can be recapitulated as follows: How was it possible for Thailand to formulate a set of foreign policies which were unusual from what it normally pursued? In the specific case of Thai foreign policy from 1938 to 1944, how was it possible for Thailand to become aggressive towards a European power such as France in late 1940? And, in less than a year, from 1941 to 1944, how was it possible to understand Thailand's proactively expedient policies towards Japan?

The flexible foreign policy approach would lead us to anticipate passivity and reactivity from Thailand even in this time period. What occurred was the opposite. Hence, we must ask: 'If the traditional approaches fail to capture the dynamics of Thai foreign policy during the Second World War, what should be an appropriate framework to rekindle a new light in the study of Thai foreign policy in this period?'

Recall that the existing approaches to the study of Thai foreign policy are predicated on material interest and structurally determined assumption, and little effort has been paid to explore the relationship between ideational elements and foreign policy-making in this period. With the exception of Strate (2009), who highlights the importance of the 'chosen traumas' and how the wartime Thai elites utilised them to justify Thai foreign policy change, no other empirical enquiry has been raised to analyse a connection between ideas and foreign policy-making. Although an effort by Pongpisoot Busbarat (2009) to inspect how an ideational variable, such as Thailand's self-perception in Southeast Asia, has influenced the formulation of Thai foreign policy in the post-Cold War period, a variety of IR applications in the case of Thailand and the Second World War period remains a subject to be discussed. The study of Thai foreign policy has rarely touched upon the ideational factor. Treating the ideational dimension and its effect on Thai foreign policy is therefore 'like questioning the existence of gods in the mind of devout adherents to a religious belief. They believe in their existence but never seek empirical evidence of how much gods influence men's daily lives' (Pongphisoot 2009, 8).

If the approaches which solely rely on material and structural ontologies do not offer a promising and well-rounded interpretation of the case study, an insight into a theoretical framework which features the ideational elements could advance a research agenda into a new academic aspect. However, ideational factors can be categorised into numerous types such as ideas, norms, analogies, identities, memories cultures, and traumas. Since IR literature has exhibited a rising trend in ideational usage, most of the aforementioned ideational characters have been widely covered in IR scholarship. Nonetheless, the treatment of the trauma and foreign policy-making through an empirical case receives scant attention in IR.

As in the case of the Franco-Thai border dispute, Sir Josiah Crosby, a British diplomat in Thailand, hinted that Thailand's traumatic experiences in relation to the West, particularly the French, in the late nineteenth century were the pinnacle of the Thai policy-makers. Similarly, the piece by Shane Strate (2009, 22–66) suggests that the Thai elites instrumentally promoted the 'lost territories' discourse to incite the Thai public hatred against France. In the case of the Japanese-Thai military co-operation, the Thai leaders declared that the Thais should not allow Japan to 'build Asia alone'. And, the Thai elites enumerated the discourse of victimisation and Asian liberation from Western influence (Strate 2009, 113–154). Furthermore, as previously noted, Charnvit, Thamrongsak, and Supaporn slightly touch upon the fact that the Thais felt repulsed by the traumatic events from the past. This suggests that the trauma of national humiliation might have influenced the formulation of Thai foreign policy in the Franco-Thai conflict and Japanese-Thai relations. In this regard, if past traumas matter in foreign policy-making, another set of questions could be postulated as follows: If trauma is crucial, what is the mechanism linking trauma and foreign policy selection? In the period under study, which specific traumatic experience had an influence on Thai foreign policy-making and to what extent?

There are a number of ideational factors which could influence foreign policy-making. This book singles out one of those factors, trauma, in order to examine its role in the construction of Thai foreign policy from 1938 to 1944.

Core arguments

This book argues that the trauma resulting from when Thailand was incorporated into the Western international system in the mid-nineteenth century was crucial in determining foreign policies of Thailand during the Second World War. Since the Thais were relatively backward by the time they were exposed to the West, they were not treated as being equal but as another uncivilised entity. In other words, they were stigmatised as inferior and excluded from the league of the civilised nations. In response, Thailand strived to attain equal status with the West by emulating Western political, cultural, and social dimensions in order to correct this stigma. In the perceptions of the Thai elites, the reason they lost considerable portions of territories to the West was because they realised they were backward and were not recognised by the international community as an equal member. Henceforth, they saw their only choice being to maximise the security and survival of their nation to gain acceptance and recognition from the 'civilised' nations. From the nineteenth century onwards, the Thais were thus concerned about their international status.

This ontological trauma of being an outcast in the international community has constantly compelled the Thais to be concerned about their international status. It was no accident that Thailand initiated political, cultural, and social reforms in various aspects since the nineteenth century. And, during the Second World War, Phibun launched a number of socio-cultural engineering programmes. The trauma of being behind the West, therefore, influenced Thai foreign policy-making. This book reveals a wide range of evidence about Thai foreign policy behaviours in order to bolster the claims that the trauma of being inferior played a part in understanding Thailand and its cases during the Second World War. In other words, for the Thai leaders during wartime, status and international approbation mattered to foreign policy-making.

Methodology, case selection, and sources

Methodology

In pursuit of the answers to the questions posed earlier, this book embarks on a qualitative study of a single case, focusing on Thai foreign policy choices formulated by the Thai elites from 1938 to 1944. The case study is divided into two minor events: the Franco-Thai conflict from 1938 to 1941 and the Japanese-Thai relations from 1941 to 1944. These two events demonstrate how trauma, status concern, and recognition matter in Thai foreign policy, while the theoretical framework explains how it was possible for Thailand to pursue an unexpectedly proactive foreign policy.

In order to provide a well-rounded answer to each case by utilising the selected IR approach, this book centres on a process-tracing method to seek answers and causalities from the two cases. According to Alexander George, a process-tracing method is 'an alternative strategy that employs a qualitative procedure that makes use of the historians' methodology of explanation' (Alexander George cited in Elman & Elman 1997, 13). Christian Reus-Smith also follows along the same line as he articulates that the process-tracing method is congenial to a project which closely works on how ideas matter in international politics (Christian Reus-Smith cited in Elman & Elman 2008, 360). The process-tracing practice will be applied to trace how Thai decision-makers had prior understandings of the world and how such understandings narrow the scope of policy options which eventually led to the stage of implementation. In this sense, as George (1979) emphasises:

> [Process-tracing method seeks to] establish the ways in which the actor's beliefs influenced his receptivity to and assessment of incoming information about the situation, his definition of the situation, his identification and evaluation of options, as well as . . . his choice of a course of action.
>
> (113)

Although there is a controversial proposition put forward by some IR scholars to see a state as a person (Ringmar 1996b; Wendt 2004), this book does not deny such a claim. Ontologically and epistemologically speaking, the states could be viewed as having the will to acquire power, the motive to survive, or even the desire for recognition. However, because this book focuses on factors such as trauma, status concern, and recognition, in order to be able to identify the state's interest in a holistic manner, it steps further to probe into the statements of the policy-makers. In an empirical sense, careful examinations of the foreign policy agents could represent the identity of the state in question.

During the periods under investigation, major foreign policy outcomes were largely determined by the elites, and the final decisions were mostly decided by Phibun (Charivat 1985, 292–311; Kobkua 1989, 3). As such, the statements of Siamese/Thai statesmen are crucial to an analysis and would take precedence over other domestic factors. The process-tracing method thus lends support to unfold the events, opinions, and ideas of the decision-makers and the subsequent outcomes which come out of policy discussion. In short, this research technique could portray how the foreign policy choices and preferences are carefully carved and selected by the influence of the status concerns. As mentioned earlier, Phibun's 'cult of leadership' rendered his rule similar to a dictatorship (Thamsook 1978, 237); this book focuses only on the speeches, statements, and memos of Phibun and his elitist circle because, according to Charivat (1985, 305), Phibun's self-opinions and the voices of his close aides would only be influential to Thailand's foreign policy during the Second World War, the period when Phibun could partly rule with an iron fist. Due to his dictatorial style of management, Phibun's cabinet members generally consisted of like-minded aides. For example, when Phibun decided to ally with Japan, he reshuffled the cabinet to remove the anti-Japanese personalities from his government. The famous example was the case of Pridi Banomyong (Luang Praditmanutham), Phibun's finance minister, who was transferred to the post of the regency council, which was a powerless position in Thai politics.

Although this book selectively concentrates on the part of Phibun and his men, it does not mean that there were virtually no other political camps in Thailand's domestic politics. The existence of different political factions in the Thai ethos could not be disputed. Nevertheless, the degree of power and influence of different political factions begs another question: Were those non-Phibun factions as influential to foreign policy-making as Phibun's cliques? The historians seem to reach a consensus that during the reign of Phibun from 1938 to 1944, his power was unparalleled until his premiership was undermined by the parliamentary system in July 1944 (Charnvit 1974; Thamsook 1978; Charivat 1985; Reynolds 1988; Kobkua 1989; Stowe 1991). Henceforth, it would be problematic to claim that the non-Phibun factions could drive the foreign policy of Thailand, not to mention that King Ananda Mahidol of Thailand, the Thai figure who could potentially compete with Phibun in terms of influence, was young and lived in exile at the time.

Some could also argue that after Phibun entered into the alliance with Japan, the 'Seri Thai movement' (Free Thai Movement), which was an anti-Japanese faction in Thai politics, should receive greater attention as an elite group that could influence Thai foreign policy. However, one historian contends that the Seri Thai movement was in fact a loosely disunified movement which was divided into different factions (Sorasak 2010). It would be quite a challenging task for a disjointed movement to influence Thai foreign policy when Phibun himself could have a free hand in domestic and foreign affairs. In fact, if other factions could be influential in Thai foreign policy, why did Phibun's successor, Khuang Aphaiwong, who was believed to be associated with some anti-Phibun and anti-Japanese factions, maintain a relationship with Japan even after the iron leader stepped down from power? This example provides evidence as to how the non-Phibun factions were too fragile to impact foreign policy-making. These are the reasons why this book scopes its research on Phibun and his elite circle only.

Inasmuch as this book seeks to employ a discourse analysis to combine with the process-tracing method, it is inappropriate to utilise a Foucauldian notion of discourse analysis because it would involve a set of different research questions. However, the book embarks on content analysis. This method generally involves a quest to analyse communication. Any materials containing messages could be subject to content analysis (Pashakhanlou 2017, 449). There are three focal principles of this method. Firstly, researchers who utilise content analysis concentrate on what has been said by relevant actors rather than on how or why such things are said (Holsti 1969, 59). Secondly, in order to generate usable and manageable data, the content analysis researchers would limit their search to themes, concepts, or words which are related to their research questions. In other words, the researchers would filter the key terms from a vast pool of available resources. Thirdly, the method would be contingent on interpretations (Rosengren 1981, 28). Research papers that are published on the qualitative basis of content analysis are typically the results of interpreting manifest and latent meanings from the statements of any actors in question (Pashakhanlou 2017, 449).

In order to be able to tell whether or not ideational factors mattered in Thai foreign policy-making, the content analysis technique employed throughout this book would mostly pay heed to private statements of the elites. The purpose is to search for smoking-gun evidence. Hence, any private statements from relevant policy actors from 1938 to 1940 as in the case of the Franco-Thai conflict, and from 1941 to 1944 as in the case of Japanese-Thai relations, would be critically analysed. What leaders state in public could simply be a façade and would not reflect their genuine ideas. Deborah Welch Larson (1985) suggests a way to tackle research questions that concentrate on ideational factors by utilising archives:

> The use of historical documents to infer beliefs raises the standard methodological problems of establishing the reliability and validity of the measurement procedures used. . . . Whenever possible, private or intragovernmental documents were used to infer beliefs. In public speeches, the source's communication goals and strategy intervene, affecting his choice of language and interfering with the analyst's efforts to discover his "true" beliefs, attitudes, or opinions.
>
> (60–61)

In summary, this book would mainly examine private statements from archival documents to infer beliefs. From this angle, there is a higher chance that policy outcomes are consistent with policy-makers' convictions.

The book specifically browses through the themes, concepts, and words which are concerned with status, honour, dignity, prestige, and reputation. Firstly, if such ideational factors did matter to the case study, there should be evidence that the policy elites confidentially discussed the issues among themselves. Because the archival sources are in Thai, the keywords that this book searches are as follows: *sathana* (สถานะ or status); *kiat* (เกียรติ or honour); *kiattiyot* (เกียรติยศ or dignity); *saksri* (ศักดิ์ศรี or prestige); and *chuesiang* (ชื่อเสียง or reputation).[6]

Although the research design of this book is primarily driven by a process-tracing method and content analysis, in order to enhance the methodological rigour, this book also adds a congruence method to test other different explanations. Yuen Foong Khong (1992) points out that the process-tracing method 'seldom establishes a direct one-to-one relationship between a given belief and the specific option chosen' (68). Henceforth, at the beginning of Chapters 4 and 5, which are the core chapters, this book would chronologically test the structural explanations and describe the choices Thailand had before pursuing proactive foreign policies motivated by status concerns. If material factors did matter, Thailand would be proactive in its early years vis-à-vis France and Japan.

Case selection

Regarding the discussion of the case selection, there are three questions that this book aims to clarify. (1) Why does this book focus on Thailand during the Second World War, especially the two key events such as the Franco-Thai War and the Japanese-Thai bitter alliance? (2) Does the emphasis on the single case of Thailand entail that the theoretical implication of this book cannot be externally valid in other cases? (3) Why does this book not embark on a comparative-historical analysis?

Although these three questions seem fairly different from one another, the answers are supposedly interconnected. Firstly, the reason why this book selects Thailand from 1938 to 1944 as a point of inquiry is because Thailand was regarded as a small state and recognised for its flexible foreign policy. Hence, the idea of Thailand acting aggressively towards the great powers would hardly be conceivable. The depiction of proactive Thai foreign policy which is contrary to a conventional expectation would feature as an interesting case. Moreover, if the case in question is likely to appear implausible, the theoretically crafted explanation would be more powerful because it could crack the puzzle of the case. Strictly speaking, the great power's aggression is somewhat imaginable and unsurprising given the historical anecdotes that have been repeatedly narrated in the world.

Secondly, by opting to solve puzzles in the single case study, this book does not aspire to establish a generalised concept or construct a grand theory which could be applicable to every case. On the contrary, this research merely undertakes the task of *interpreting* the social phenomena of Thailand on the basis of a theory-guided case study as opposed to an ambition to generalise outside this specific case. A grand theory, which tends to be superficial, is often prone to weaknesses when it is assessed against details and data of different cases. This problem is similar to how the political scientists are usually attacked for being obsessed with theoretical concepts at the expense of details, whereas the historians are criticised for relying heavily on data and narratives without building a theory that could be used to explain other similar historical instances. Thus, instead of constructing a theory of everything in social sciences, a given set of theories offered in this book should be able to explain some other cases which maintain similar properties and conditions. Focusing on the case of Thailand does not mean that the theoretical approaches utilised in this book cannot be applied to other cases. On the contrary, there are innumerable cases which share similar conditions with Thailand and might find the theories in this book useful. But one of the reasons why this book exclusively studies one case involves a methodological concern which is related to the nature of research questions and the validity of evidence.

This sequentially leads to the answer to the third question regarding the shortcoming of a comparative-historical analysis of this book. While it is undeniable that this book could compare different cases in order to display the explanatory prowess of the theories, a lightly and superficially conducted comparative-historical analysis could be counterproductive to this book's core enterprise. Because of this book's engagement with IR theories such as ontological security and the status-concern approach, which are both ideational and psychological in nature, the operation of proving a causal relationship between idea and outcome is not an easy task. Yes, there are other methodological options, and one of them might be to compare different cases to exemplify such a causal relationship. However, and strictly speaking, if a researcher compares cases without delving into declassified documents which could display genuine intentions of policymakers, there is a risk of misinterpreting the policy outcomes. Context does matter, and only in a confidential and secretive context in which the policymakers could express their true thoughts and opinions. In other words, only with access to relevant historical archives can a researcher step closer to finding truths about the case, especially when the core ontology is an idea, not material. The archival research could also lend a hand to re-interpret a different and provocative version of political and diplomatic history. If we take this rationale seriously, it implies that access to archival sources and proficiency in different languages is of paramount importance. In this regard, I closely study the case of Thai foreign policy during the Second World War because of the availability of archival documents and proficiency in the Thai language. This would enhance the credibility of the case study and improve the explanatory power of the ontological security and status-concern approaches. Moreover, embarking on a single case study does not mean that an analysis is void of a comparative dimension. As John Gerring (2006) poignantly observes, there is literally no such thing as a single case study because an analysis drawn from one case inevitably compares certain elements and differences within a given case. In the instance of Thai foreign policy from 1938 to 1944, the discussion of changes in foreign policy in each period of time through a process-tracing method involves an implicit comparison of different foreign policies of each year. Tracing and comparing changes of policy from each year help emphasise salient factors that affect and influence such changes.

In sum, this research is not a historiographical innovation to write a new history which covers every dimension of Thailand. The centre of gravity of this project is an interpretation of Thai foreign policy during the Second World War by advancing an IR approach introduced by this book.

Archives and triangulation of sources

This book primarily relies on archival research. In order to prove that ontological trauma, status concern, and recognition matter to foreign policy, it would be essential to embark on private and confidential sources. In order to enhance the credibility of the evidence, this book does not merely retrieve documents from the Thai perspective. It does, however, seeks to triangulate the reliability of the sources by utilising archival documents from the UK, US, and Japan. A brief introduction of the sources used in this book is discussed as follows.

Firstly, this book is predicated on the British diplomatic correspondence which has been registered at the National Archives (TNA) and has documented the situations in Thailand until the outbreak of the Second World War. The Foreign and Commonwealth Office documents (FO) contain records and diplomatic correspondence addressed by Sir Josiah Crosby, the British Minister to Thailand of the time. These diplomatic documents reveal an exchange of intelligence and conversation between the British and French as regards Thailand's foreign and domestic affairs. Certain parts of this book also draw on the Government Communications Headquarters (HW). In addition, some documents have been drawn from the Manuscript Room of the University of Cambridge's Library (MS).

Moreover, this book also obtains data from Foreign Relations of the United States (FRUS) which are open to the public. Additionally, this book compensates for the inadequacy of the Japanese sources by delving into the Magic of Pearl Harbor (MPH). This set of published documents consists of the documents the Americans intercepted from the diplomatic cables of Japan and which were translated into English.

Apart from the British and American sources, this book extensively consults archives from the National Archives of Thailand (NAT).[7] Archives from the Headquarters of the Commander-in-Chief of the Thai Armed Forces (BoKo-Sungsut), Ministry of Foreign Affairs (KoTo), Office of Prime Minister (SoRo), Ministry of Interior (MoTo), Ministry of Education (SoTo), personal documents donated to the National Archives of Thailand (SoBo), and records such as Thailand's Minutes of Cabinet Meeting from the Office of the Secretariat of the Cabinet (heretofore cited as 'TMCM') and Thai Parliament's Minutes of Proceedings (hereafter cited as 'TPMP') from the Office of the Secretary of the National Assembly have been utilised to serve the focal purpose of this book.

A substantial number of wartime documents have been disclosed to the public. Some sources were discovered and released several decades even before this book was written. For example, there are a number of celebrated scholars, such as Vinita (1975), Thamsook (1977), Kobkua (1995), and Murashima (2006), who profoundly study Thailand and the Second World War and utilised the archival documents from the NAT and Thailand's cabinet minutes. In order to enhance the credibility of the sources presented in this book, I draw on numerous archival accounts which are publicly available. Additionally, this book also draws on undisclosed and uncategorised sources given to the NAT by the Ministry of Foreign Affairs (KoTo 0202/61).

[8] Other primary sources are memoirs of the decision-makers of the time such as Direk Jayanam, Wichit Wathakan, Pridi Banomyong, Aketo Nakamura, Asada Shunsuke, and other related actors of the time. This book also utilises Phibun's notebooks, which are famously recognised as Military Commanding Notebook

(MCN), Civilian Commanding Notebook (CICN), and Cultural Commanding Notebook (CUCN).[9]

Although the majority of the sources in this book are archival documents, there is also an interview, for example, with a son of Wanit Pananonda who was a minister during the period in question.[10] All in all, the variety of sources shown throughout this book is primarily aimed to triangulate the credibility of the sources.

Alternative explanations?

This book's interpretation of Thai foreign policy during the Second World War could be provocative to not only scholars interested in Thai foreign policy but also Thai studies academics. Apart from a conventional explanation of Thai foreign policy, it could also be argued that Phibun's proactively adventurous foreign policy was driven by his militaristic appreciations of nationalism and patriotism, which could seemingly contradict the explanations offered in this book. However, it is crucial to clarify that the nationalist features are part of the theoretical frameworks advanced in this book. In other words, two such factors are hidden within both ontological security and status-concern approaches.

Nationalism has always been one of the defining elements of a modern-state system. The concept, at least in the context of the Thai case, is generally tied to domestic issues. For example, Phibun's social-engineering projects to improve Thai lives and cultures, which shall be discussed in Chapter 4, were often seen as a reflection of nationalist and patriotic aspirations (Thamsook 1978; Reynolds 2004). Can nationalism, which is the by-product of modernity, be considered from the angle of international affairs? How can two such prominent concepts be critically assessed along with the theoretical frameworks put forth by this book? In IR and social sciences, nationalism, national identity, and nation-building projects are seen as internal compositions of a nation. It would be axiomatically impossible to reject that a nation-state, which is a political community, constitutes national identity and that national identity per se entails nationalism and vice versa. In reality, such related notions cannot be exclusively treated as part of domestic issues. They should be studied along with the international perspectives. These concepts would be nonsensical without referring to the holistic pictures of the development of the Westphalia system, the expansion of European international society, and the crystallisation of the international system as we know it today. In other words, three such concepts are relational to international dimension. Nationalism entails national identity. National identity requires respect, admiration, and recognition from other nations. Liah Greenfeld (1995) suggests that 'national identity is, fundamentally, a matter of dignity. It gives people reasons to be proud' (487). This logic renders nationalism and national identity as inevitably *international*. Zygmunt Bauman (2000) summarised Leszek Kolakowski that the nationalists 'want to assert their tribal existence through aggression and hatred of others, [they] believe that all the mishaps of his own nation are the outcome of a strangers' plot and holds a grudge against all other nations for failing to admire properly and otherwise give its due to his own tribe' (174). In this light, nationalism and its existence are dependent on confirmation from other national communities. Without recognition from significant others, nationalism and national identity lose their meaningful essence.

In this regard, nationalism is not distinctive from the theories presented in this book. To put it in a nutshell, the senses of ontological anxiety and status concern, both of which require recognition and acceptance from others, share a similar logic with the interpretation from the perspectives of nationalism and patriotism. If the core thesis of this book is to argue that Thailand's proactive foreign policies during the Second World War were caused by the elites' ontological and status anxieties, then the assertion that nationalism and patriotism could similarly explain the events is justified because, as Christopher Browning (2015) notes, 'nationalism is driven by the community's desire to justify itself and legitimise, and possibly enhance, its position and standing' (199). What, however, sets nationalism apart from the approaches of this book is that the former is theoretically void of the discussion of how nationalism could be translated into aggressive-prone foreign policies, not to mention how it fails to address the puzzle of why a small state such as Thailand could potentially defy France and Japan. The approaches advanced in this book seek to illuminate the origins of ontological and status anxieties, which were predicated on the expansion of Western international society into Asia in the nineteenth century. Simply put, this book complements the nationalist-based explanation as opposed to contradicting it as the others might have understood.

Apart from nationalism and patriotism, there might be other psychological and ideational theories that could be employed to interpret the case in this book. For instance, the prospect theory and group-think theory could potentially come to the forefront of the discussion. The former theory might suggest that the Phibun government perceived that Thailand was in the 'loss' realm and pursued risk-taking actions to reclaim the loss in relation to France and Japan, whereas the latter theory would predict that the Phibun cabinet was tightly knit and key ministers kept reinforcing one another to act against France and Japan. Although these two theories appear persuasive, the empirical evidence in Chapters 5 and 6 suggests otherwise. For example, as a counter-argument to the assumption that the Phibun government saw Thailand in a 'loss' position, the evidence provided in Chapter 5 indicates that, contrary to the reviewer's assumption, the government saw military actions against France as a potential loss rather than a rational gain. Similarly, in the case of Nippon-Thai relations, the evidence in Chapter 6 indicates that there is no place for the prospect theory advised by the reviewer. Had the Thai government seen themselves in a loss position and acted proactively in order to recuperate a loss, as the prospect theory would anticipate, then why did the Thai leadership observe a policy of strict neutrality despite their strategic advantages in siding with either Britain and Japan?

Apart from the prospect theory, the assumption of the group-think theory is complementary to the analysis of this book. It becomes difficult to deny that a tightly knit group could influence one another in terms of ideational policy execution. Nonetheless, as Chapter 4 describes, the Thai elites after the nineteenth century tended to share a similar vision when it came to the matter of garnering recognition and acceptance from the West and other powers. The chapter also shows a trend from the era of Thailand's absolutism until a constitutional period and demonstrates how a certain concern, namely, the concern of the nation's existence in international society, had been haunting the Siamese/Thai elites. This is a core thesis of the book, which is primarily predicated on the ontological security and status-concern theory. As such, a certain element of the group-think theory has been part of my analysis all along.

While these alternative theories could offer somewhat promising interpretations which could be beneficial to each respective theory and field, it is impossible for me to initiate a dialogue with every theory in the social sciences. This is the reason why this book limits the conversation to only some of the theories, such as ontological security, the status-concern theory, a small-state work, and Thai foreign policy literature, all of which shall be articulated in Chapter 2. Moreover, one of the objectives of this book is to bring the case of Thailand, which is a small state in the context of the Second World War, to be critically assessed through the lens of ontological security and the status-concern framework in order to exemplify that such abstract theories could make sense of the least likely case of Thailand during the wartime period.

Organisation of the book

Since Chapter 1 is an introductory chapter, Chapter 2 lays out the theoretical framework of this book. The chapter begins with the state of the debate on the study of Thai foreign policy and its consistency with mainstream IR approaches. The chapter then discusses why each approach is incompatible to examine the case study and puts forth the defence of the approach undertaken. The central framework this book undertakes has been adapted from the theoretical framework advanced by Ayşe Zarakol (2011). This book modifies and applies Zarakol's propositions to the selected case study.

Chapter 3 introduces the history of Thailand and its traumatic past. The objective of the chapter, following from the framework employed in this book, is to demonstrate the process when Thailand was first exposed to the prowess of the Western powers and how the process of stigmatisation drove Thailand to correct its stigma. The chapter describes how this stigma was crucial to Thailand's nation-building. The historical description of this chapter ends in the period when the nation had undergone the constitutional revolution. The purpose of this chapter is to illustrate how the stigma was activated and reactivated throughout history. It also shows how the elites had been concerned with Thailand's international status since the nineteenth century.

Because Thai foreign policy during the Second World War is the heart of this book, Chapter 4 is devoted to establishing ideational grounds of Thai foreign policy after the end of absolute monarchy in 1932. This chapter probes into how the legacies of the nineteenth century and traumatic experiences haunted the

Thai elites even after Thailand entered into the constitutional era. It explores how Phibun and the others were concerned about Thailand's international stature even before taking the helm as the nation's executives. The chapter also shows how status anxieties shaped Phibun's actions both before and after ascending the premiership.

Chapters 5 and 6 are the foci of this project. Chapter 5 deals with the period from 1938 to 1941, whereas Chapter 6 digs into the period from 1942 to 1944. Both chapters interpret how ideational residues among core decision-makers constituted the agents and how those ideas finally guided policy orientations. These chapters investigate the discussions, speeches, and domestic policies which reflected how Thailand responded to France with war and why the Thai elites expediently dealt with Japan in a proactive manner. These two chapters proceed with the process-tracing method. The discussion follows the chronological description in order to convenience readers who are not familiar with Thailand.

Chapter 7 is the concluding chapter. This chapter concludes that in order to understand a certain course of Thailand's behaviours during the Second World War, it is necessary to investigate an issue of status concern and its influence on foreign policy choices. It also discusses the policy implications that can be drawn from this book and explains the possibility of extending this book's theories to other potential cases.

Notes

1 'Thailand' was formerly known as 'Siam'. The name 'Siam' was changed to 'Thailand' in 1939 under the premiership of Phibunsongkhram. This research intends to use 'Thailand' to denote 'Siam' to avoid confusion. However, in Chapters 3 and 4, this book uses 'Siam' until the official promulgation in 1939. The change of the name is relevant to the arguments of this book.
2 The name Plaek Phibunsongkhram will be shortened to 'Phibun' hereafter.
3 The National Archives (Kew) will be abbreviated as 'TNA' hereafter.
4 This research uses the 'flexible foreign policy approach' to refer to the notion of this explanation.
5 Although not explicit, these pieces highlight the nature of 'linkage politics' in influencing foreign policy directions.
6 According to So Sethaputra's well-known Thai-English dictionary, the translations of honour, dignity, and prestige are interchangeable.
7 Certain files from the NAT will be cited with page number if the folders are large. The page number has been sequenced by the NAT.
8 The documents within these folders were disclosed by special request. The authenticity can be verified from the NAT.
9 The original copies of these notebooks are kept at the Chulachomklao Royal Military Academy. Some soft copies, however, can be drawn from the Archival Division of Thammasat University.
10 An interview with Ananda Pananonda took place on 10 April 2016 along with Dr. Puli Fuwongcharoen, who managed to arrange the interview.

2 Ontological security, stigmatisation, trauma, and status

Ideas and the small state in realism

In mainstream IR scholarship, it is difficult to deny that realism is one of the dominant schools. Although this book seeks to contribute to the literature in Thai foreign policy-making, it also engages with the realist school and contends that this dominant IR approach and its material ontologies equally fail to make sense of the case study. Nevertheless, this research embarks on a strand of constructivism to make sense of the selected case study. This section reviews the core insights of each realism approach and explains why constructivism in IR is privileged over the others.

Flexible foreign policy and realism

As discussed in Chapter 1, there is a naturalised belief about Thai diplomacy in most studies of Thai foreign policy behaviour. Corrine (1980, 1999) has enumerated the conventional approach to the study of Thai foreign policy as entailing the following beliefs: (1) Thailand, prioritising survival, naturally appeases greater powers; (2) Thailand seeks to balance one power against another; and (3) Thailand is acute to align and realign with any predominant forces or any victors. In accordance with these truisms, the general pattern of Thai foreign policy falls under the category of a reactive-prone strategy, which means that Thailand only reacts to external events to uphold the status quo. In fact, these qualities are not exclusively unique to Thailand. Such foreign policy repertoires are what other small states were generally believed to practise when they confront great-power threats to security. What Corrine has described in the case of Thai foreign policy behaviour would be dubbed as (1) a 'bandwagoning' policy, (2) a 'balancing' policy, and (3) a shifting-alliance policy, respectively. Such policy choices have been discussed in IR for decades, and the principle of Thailand's flexible foreign policy bears a resemblance to the realist approach in IR.

It is fair to categorise Thailand as a non-great power. With regard to the selected case study of this book, it could be said that Thailand during the time was a small state in the international system (Charivat 1985, 324). Although there are approaches to analyse Thai foreign policy, it is worth discussing them in relation to the three major realist schools, namely, classical realism, neo-realism, and neo-classical realism. As such, apart from filling the gap in Thai foreign policy literature, this book could also fill the gap in one of the major schools in IR such as realism.

A classical realist such as Hans Morgenthau (1948, 196) believes that small nations owe their independence to the balance of power among great powers. He claims that a great power 'is a state which is able to have its will against a small state. . . [whereas a small state] is not able to have its will against [a] great power'(Morgenthau 1948, 129–130). Those great powers simply subject the weak under their protectorate. Hence, their foreign policy choices are limited to only guidance and orientation of greater powers. In Waltz's neo-realist edicts, small nations either choose to conform and adapt to the changing structure or perish from the map. Neo-realists presume that the distribution of capabilities among great powers, the degree of great-power competition, and the structural constraints influence small-state foreign policies. Leaders of small nations are assumed to be internally unconstrained to pursue such policies (M. F. Elman 1995, 172; Sampson 1994, 90; Snyder 2013, 20; Waltz 1979, 184–185).

Scholars who study foreign policy choices of the small states generally concur with the realists' views towards the small states. Because of the size and dearth of capabilities, the small states are not expected to partake in international affairs and conflicts (Rosenau 1974, 273). Maurice East's (1973, 563) empirical enquiry into behaviours of small and greater powers from 1959 to 1968 suggests that the smaller states are inclined to be less assertive and less proactive in the international realm. They are, however, incessantly fretful about survival and are reactive to the external atmosphere (Vital 1971, 124). Therefore, a low-profile foreign policy is preferred by the weak nations due to limited choices (Barston 1973, 16). David Vital (1971, 9), Michael Handel (1981, 261–262), Robert Rothstein (1968, 182), and Ronald Barston (1973, see the introduction), for example, find that small states would naturally depend on great powers, and in the long run, these small nations tend to either be clients or satellite states of great powers. These scholars agree that Waltz's structural dictate is the most relevant ontology in analysing small state behaviours. In other words, the crucial question of the small states is how to survive in the world under the fate of great powers. Due to the relatively small capabilities, the foreign policy of small states should be formulated in response to the great powers' behaviours because of their relative capabilities vis-à-vis greater powers. Handel (1981) summarises optimal choices of the small states in an articulate manner:

> [Small states] must always side with or placate the stronger and more threatening power at each stage of the conflict; it must switch its position when the balance changes, exactly at the moment the declining power with which it originally sided is too weak to retaliate and while the ascendant power still needs help.
>
> (186)

The realist view is that the foreign policy choices any small powers can pursue in relation to great-power threats are either balancing, bandwagoning, or shifting alliance policies because they could hardly fend for themselves. These minor powers, when facing a rising hegemon, would either group together or join a predominant power. Or, if the tide changes, they would seek to change sides in order to survive.

Drawing on the case study of this book, it could be argued that these realist-based accounts are not able to fully explain Thailand's proactive foreign policy behaviours towards both France and Japan. If international structure and survival matter for a small state such as Thailand, how can classical realism and neo-realism explain Thailand's aggressive foreign policies towards France? The Thais declared their neutral status when the Second World War broke out and remained neutral even after France was battered by Germany. To be more precise, the Thai government even signed the Non-Aggression Pact with the French government the day that Paris fell to Germany. As such, the change of international structure and survival issues were not accountable to explain Thailand's assertiveness.

As in the case of the Japanese-Thai feud, how could the two realist theories explain Thailand's co-operation with and swift escape from Japan in less than a year of their honeymoon relations? Yes, Japan's declaration of war was a threat to Thailand's survival. A bandwagoning policy therefore was conducted on reasonable grounds. But there was no convincing reason for the Thais to fully commit to Japan's cause. As it will be shown in Chapter 6, Japan genuinely wished to limit Thailand's role for strategic reasons. However, after becoming allies, the Thais irrationally challenged Japan on several occasions. Thailand's disobedience and expedience threatened its survival much more than choosing a passive and docile path.

Even if the international structure and will to survive could not make sense of Thai foreign policy during the Second World War, neo-classical realism might offer a novel adjustment to improve an explanatory power of the realist school. Neo-classical realism, a term coined by Gideon Rose (1998), mingles the systematic and unit-level factors into an analysis. The significant contributions to the neo-classical realist framework can be reviewed from celebrated scholars such as Wohlforth (1993), Brown et al. (1995), Christensen (1996), Zakaria (1998), Schweller (1998, 2004), and Lobell et al. (2009). The fundamental aim of the neo-classical realist approach is not to seek generalisation. On the contrary, the neo-classical realists attempt to explain the behaviours of specific states. The complex interactions between international and domestic factors, according to neo-classical realists, influence foreign policy outcomes (Baylis et al. 2008, 99). The neo-classical realist theory does not entirely shunt aside the force of international structure. Unlike the neo-realists, who presuppose that the international structure automatically shapes behaviours of states, neo-classical realists pose a challenge to the primacy of structure by questioning whether international structural pressure would translate into foreign policy outcomes via the influence of domestic variables. Domestic elements such as perceptions and interests of statesmen (Randall Schweller 1998, 168; Wohlforth 1993, 294, 302; Zakaria 1998, 42) and domestic-bureaucratic entanglements (Christensen 1996, 6; Randall Schweller 1998, 24; Zakaria 1998, 10–11), according to the neo-classical realists, would 'channel, mediate, and (re) direct' structural effects, which eventually would generate a foreign policy (Randall Schweller 2004, 164). Henceforth, perceptions and other relevant domestic components are intervening variables in the construction of foreign policy (Kitchen 2010, 130).

These neo-classical realist scholars might contribute to the realist research programme extensively, with the exception of Schweller (1994, 1998, 2006), who barely touches upon the application of the neo-classical realist model on small- or medium-sized states. Theoretically speaking, Schweller combines the international structure factor and statesmen's objective to explain foreign policy outcomes of any states. The states are defined in terms of the distribution of capabilities and domestic objectives. The states with more capabilities tend to be great powers, while the states with relative capabilities are ranked accordingly. The domestic objectives of the decision-makers that affect foreign policy could be divided into two categories: status quo and revisionist interest. In this regard, Schweller (1994, 101–104) roughly categorises the states into four types: lions, jackals, lambs, and wolves.[1]

The lions are the satisfied powers with great capabilities which regulate international order and guard against the rise of aggressive powers. The lambs are weak states in an international system. They possess relatively minor capabilities and have no ambition to extend their values beyond their own boundaries. Henceforth, they are likely to pursue a policy which stays aloof from great-power rivalry or adopt a bandwagoning stance. The jackals are also the weak states that have a revisionist tendency. They are keen to safeguard their possession; yet they have limited ambitions to pursue an expansionist policy by free-riding on the greater powers' aggression. The wolves refer to the ravenously predatory states. These wolfish nations are risk-acceptant and are willing to expand even when their extinction is at stake. By combining Schweller's figurative categories with the neoclassical realist account, it can be inferred that the international structure could influence how statesmen would assess the situations and react accordingly.

From these four categories, it seems that Thailand in the context of the Second World War can be considered as a jackal state for the following reasons. Firstly, it had a revisionist interest even though it possessed inadequate capabilities. As noted earlier, Thailand's sense of irredentism was dormant even before it was in conflict with France and Japan. Its will to recover the lost territories was unhidden. Secondly, Thailand's ambitions were limited to reclaim the territories only. Its aspiration was not to revise the then international order. For these reasons, the Thais could neither be categorised as lambs nor as wolves.

From the outset, Schweller's neo-classical realist framework seems to be a perfect match to analyse Thailand. Nonetheless, it encounters an impasse to explain the case study in an accurate manner. In the Franco-Thai War case, it could not explain why it took so long for Thailand to initiate war against France. Thailand had a revisionist interest even before France was dragged into the war. If Schweller's model is valid, Thailand should be expected to bandwagon with the

Nazis to attack the French colonies in Asia when the war started. On the contrary, even after France was defeated, the Thais prioritised diplomacy over the use of force.

Similarly, in the case of Japanese-Thai relations, this model fails to fully grasp the Thai government's dealing with Japan. Before Japan attacked Pearl Harbor, the Thais staunchly observed neutrality even after their victory over France. The situation of the Allied powers in Europe was devastating. For example, apart from France's downfall, Britain was weakened after the battle of Dunkirk. This was a window of opportunity for Thailand to occupy the British colonies. However, the Thai leaders were resolved to adhere to a neutral position. Although the fact that Thailand's entry into the alliance with Japan could be motivated by territorial concerns, such an explanation partly captures how Thailand behaved towards Japan. If bandwagoning for interest was crucial, how could it explain Thailand's overly assertive behaviours towards Japan even though there was no absolute guarantee of the territories to Thailand after the war? If a territorial interest was significant, there was no reason to embrace Japan to the extent of lavishing economic resources. And if a territorial reason mattered, why did the Thais confront the Japanese even before Japan became disadvantageous in the war?

If these realist theories also have shortcomings to explain the case of Thailand, there is a need to find a new approach to ameliorate the existing theoretical explanations. Henceforth, this book turns to ideational elements to add to the gap of the literature.

Constructivism and ideas

Constructivism emerges as a promising approach for understanding the foreign policy choices of the small states. Constructivism is premised upon the assumption that reality is socially constructed. National interest, therefore, is not initially given but is socially constructed (Pettman 2000). Realism and liberalism take national interest as given *a priori*. Constructivism finds origins of national interest within particular ideas and shows how such ideas guide statesmen in choosing policies and preferences from a menu of choices (Thorun 2009, 24). In other words, ideas do not naturally translate into the expected outcomes; rather they create 'permissive conditions' for state action (Finnemore 1996, 158). The choices of balancing, bandwagoning, counter-balancing, and participating in international institutions thus can only be understood by considering the intervening role of ideas.

This book seeks aids from ideational tenets in order to craft an approach that can solve the puzzles of Thailand. The integration of ideational fundamentals can, according to Goldstein and Keohane (1993, 6), help make sense of an anomaly of any selected case studies. Despite a variety of exemplary constructivist approaches in IR, the intent of this book is to decide from a pool of constructivist frameworks to unveil the puzzles of this project. In constructivism, national interest is neither given nor ahistorical. It is, however, socially constructed and historically contingent (Hopf 1998, 176). States and international structures are mutually constitutive (Wendt 1992). Without recognition by others, states may not realise their own roles and identities. In this regard, international politics is about defining interests (Finnemore 1996). The following question then is what constitutes interests? Which ideational elements define states' interests? The origin, formation, and placement of ideas are not second to others in terms of importance: How do relevant ideas come about and how do such ideas function in foreign policy-making? This book argues that concerns about ontological security and international status govern the making of Thai foreign policy of the designated period.

Ontological security and international stigmatisation

The ontological security concept steps beyond the constructivist view. 'Ontological security' refers to the 'desire of actors to have a consistent self and to have such sense affirmed by others' (Zarakol (2010, 6). For ontological security theorists, the absence of recognition does not only deprive the states of the possibility to realise their identities but also renders states ontologically insecure. The concerns about recognition, or what some scholars might call ontological security, can be the states' stimuli in international politics.

Ontological security

The concept of ontological security and its empirical application, as surveyed by Alexandria Innes and Brent Steele (2014), has been interpreted differently by scholars in IR. According to Zarakol (2010, 6), the notion of ontological security can be traced back to studies in psychology and sociology. This term was initiated by Ronald Liang who defined a person who is ontologically secure as someone whose 'sense of his presence in the world as a real, alive, whole, and, in a temporal sense, a continuous person' (Laing 1969, 40 cited in Zarakol 2010, 6). The absence of ontological security, according to Laing (1969 cited in Zarakol 2010, 6), constitutes 'a continual and deadly threat' in life.

Ontological security has later been developed by Anthony Giddens (1990, 1991), a prominent scholar in sociology. Giddens (1991, 54) introduces the concept to refer to a condition in which an individual has a 'stable sense of self-identity'. He further articulates it as 'the confidence that most human beings have in the continuity of their self-identity and the constancy of the surrounding social and material environments of action' (Giddens 1990, 92). For Giddens (1991, 38–39), individuals seek to safeguard their primary sense of safety, which is not confined to physical security. People need basic trust from others to sustain psychological safety and eschew existential insecurity. Giddens apparently stands on Erikson (1950 cited in Kinnvall 2004, 746) who implicitly suggests the relationship between identity and security. When a person encounters changes, identity functions as 'anxiety-controlling mechanisms' to maintain a sense of trust, certainty, and predictability. Therefore, rectifying a new identity would re-secure the sense of existential security (Kinnvall 2002).

The notion has later been imported into IR and become popularised in the discipline by scholars such as Jef Huysmans (1998), Bill McSweeney (1999), Catarina Kinnvall (2002, 2004), Jennifer Mitzen (2006a, 2006b), Brent Steele (2005, 2008a, 2008b), Marco Vieira (2016, 2018) and Ayşe Zarakol (2007, 2010, 2011, 2014).

Huysman (1998) begins his critique of security studies by problematising the general usage of the term security in IR, which is mainly concentrated on state-to-state military security. Security, in Huysman's proposition, should be viewed as a concept that organises forms of life. 'Security' *par excellence* orders social relations into particular security relations (Huysman 1998, 232–234). People have a fear of death. Hence, states perform security policies which mediate life and death (reducing deaths), demarcate the lines between friends and enemies (threat construction), and guarantee the degree of certainty. Such performativity of security practices does not only constitute the determinability of how states would postpone deaths from the objectified threats but also the existential security of such tasks. In this regard, the end of the Cold War, which ends the friend/enemy distinction and the central errand of the states, is reinterpreted as foiling ontological security of states and questioning the legitimacy from which they derived (Huysman 1998, 243–244). In other words, without a friend/enemy dichotomy and without the sense of certainty, the Post-Cold War states became existentially anxious about their beings. Similarly, McSweeney (1999, 2–5), puzzled by the cases of the Post-Cold War Europe, directs IR audiences to the relationship between security, identity, and interest. Indistinguishable from other constructivists who suggest that identity defines interest, McSweeney appends the conception of ontological security to the conventional constructivist scheme. Security and identity cannot be analysed independently. Ken Booth (1997, 88) implicitly suggests that identity is inseparable from security. Security that Booth has notified is clearly not physical security. He alludes to ontological security. McSweeney (1999, 157–158) amplifies Booth's opinion by explaining that once mutual interaction and reciprocal recognition, which are formative sources of collective identity, collapses, an individual becomes anxious and seeks to restore such identity to reaffirm the sense of certainty in a relationship. Ultimately, ontological security is 'a security of [a] social relationship, a sense of being safely in a cognitive control of the interaction context' (McSweeney 1999, 157). Hence, what renders an individual ontologically insecure is identity not being recognised by others (McSweeney 1999, 157). In other words, in the interaction process, if one's identity is unacknowledged, one is left existentially insecure, as McSweeney (1999) remarks, 'What is rendered insecure in a condition of ontological insecurity is fundamentally our common ties and shared knowledge with others involved in the interaction in which it occurs: our identity' (157).

Mitzen (2006a, 2006b) adapts the notion of ontological security to explain how inter-state routines can sustain Europe's 'civilising identity' and incessantly foster security dilemmas in world politics. Mitzen (2006a, 273) notes that routines and routinised activities habituate actors. Such consistent practices help avoid imbroglios and enhance a sense of existential security, as she hints that the post-9/11 American government and media encouraged their citizens to pursue their daily routines (Mitzen 2006a, 273). Routines, in other words, generate and re-generate the basis of ontological security because they constitute the system of basic trust (Mitzen 2006a, 274). Individuals, deprived of routinised activities, tend to acquire a sense of existential insecurity. Likewise, in the case of security dilemma, states can become attached to physical insecurity routines, which perpetuate hostile relations in the international sphere (2006b, 354). The preliminary logic of Mitzen (2006b, 359) is that a state has a security-seeking identity and is mutually recognised by others as such. The possibility of reneging on each other in realism sustains interactions and identities of the states. In this regard, the states reciprocally recognise the others through the lenses of competitive identity, and they conjointly cling to such identity (Mitzen 2006b, 360).

Kinnvall (2002, 2004) has later introduced the concept of ontological security to empirically discuss how globalisation, which transforms political, economic, and societal aspects everywhere, undermines the sense of certainty. It destabilises the ontological security of individuals within a nation. In order to re-establish ontological security, Kinnvall (2002, 91–101, 2004, 756) argues that the national elites, as in the cases of India's Hindu-Muslim conflict and the Israeli-Palestinian feud, exploit past traumas and glories by re-celebrating historical narratives to recreate new identities for the sake of securing existential security amidst an uncertain environment which stems from the effects of globalisation.

Brent Steele (2005, 2008a, 2008b) has comparably undertaken the ontological security approach to explain mysterious cases such as British non-intervention in the American Civil War, Belgian resistance to the German hubris during the Second World War, and the North Atlantic Treaty Organization (NATO)'s participation in Kosovo in 1999. Steele has affixed the notion of a 'biographical narrative' to relate to self-identity and ontological security. The biographical narrative is vital to self-identity. A state, according to Steele (2008b, 71), only understands itself and realises its interest through such a locus. In this connection, a biographical narrative, or what Steele (2008b, 72) interchangeably denotes as 'illocutionary discourse', shapes how policy-makers perceive events, how such events relate to self-identity, how interest should be defined, and how policies are preferably selected. Policy deviation from a state's identity renders it ontologically anxious. Practices which are incongruous to a biographical narrative often result in feelings of shame and guilt (Steele 2008b, 52–55), which could subsequently compel a state to behave according to its perception of self-identity.

Despite variations of arguments with regard to the ontological security approach, recognition from others is an essential key. A sense of stable identity is a mechanism to control anxiety, and recognition from others constitutes an inter-subjective understanding of an identity role. Although Huysman and McSweeney do not engage in an empirical quest to substantiate their claims in a systematic manner, Kinnvall, Mitzen, and Steele delve into empirical expeditions even though they contend with one another. Kinnvall and Steele disagree with Mitzen over the role of others in buttressing existential security. Mitzen (2006b, 59) accentuates the role of others in ontological security seeking; that is, a state cannot attain a sense of ontological security without a strategic partner to mutually recognise one another's identity. Nonetheless, Kinnvall and Steele highlight the influence of narratives in engendering ontological security.

Notwithstanding theoretical divergence, the mission to bridge these propositions is not insurmountable. Zarakol (2010) straightforwardly notices the discrepancies of the approaches as she puts: 'Are interactions and the international environment the main source of ontological anxiety for a state, or are the insecure interactions merely a consequence of the state's own uncertainty about its own identity?' (6). For Zarakol, the domestic and international accounts of ontological security can be synbooked. To Zarakol (2010, 7), Huysman's premises disclose a possibility to consider the impact of the international environment on ontological security. McSweeney (1999, 160) likewise echoes the discussion of the sources of identity formation and socialisation of the state actors. The states, as McSweeney (1999) notes, 'are not irreducible actors. They are an expression of the international *and* domestic. They are structure to domestic actors, and actors to international structure' (160). Similarly, Vieira (2016) points out the shortcomings of isolating the international from the domestic factors. As he argues, in the case of the Non-Aligned Movement (NAM), the member states' national self-conceptions and existential anxieties were rooted in the fact that the majority of them were newly minted independent nations. In his words, the separation of the two levels of analysis would face an impasse to make sense of the 'cases in which collective and individual self-conceptions and the ontological (in) security they generate are interdependent and co-constituted, which is precisely the case of the NAM' (Vieira 2016, 295). In other words, the issues of ontological security and identity are subject to consideration of an inter-subjective understanding, not only at the domestic but also at the international level.

As regards Kinnvall and Steele, it seems that, at face value, both scholars abnegate 'context' from an analysis. On the contrary, the difference is not comprehensive, as Kinnvall (2004) suggests that the ontological security approach cannot be separated from 'inter-subjective ordering of relations' (748), and the internalised self-notions 'can never be separated from self/other representations and are always responsive to new interpersonal relationships' (749). Steele (2008b) implicitly concedes that in the ontological security research programme, the 'the project of self-identity is neither progressive nor continuously ruptured, but reflexively, *inter-subjectively constructed* over time' (56).

In this light, empirically speaking, Zarakol and Vieira undertake a reconciliatory route of the ontological security approach. Instead of arguing whether international interactions or self-identities are the core foundations of states' ontological (in)security, Zarakol (2007, 2010, 2011) and Vieira (2016, 2018) suggest that, for some non-European states, the sources of ontological insecurity reside in self-identities and national self-conceptions which are formed by interactions with the international system. Drawing from this view, Zarakol (2007, 2011) refines her propositions by importing the concept of stigma and shame into the observations of Turkish, Japanese, and Russian policies in relation to the West. Zarakol (2010, 8) claims that self-narratives drive certain foreign policy behaviours, and such narratives are defined by interactions with international pressures in the past. Embarking on different theoretical extensions, Vieira (2018) utilises Jacques Lacan's psychoanalytic approach to focus on the ontological insecurity of post-colonial states such as Brazil. It is argued that Brazil's emergence as a post-colonial subject presented its elites with the psychological lack and the consciousness of inferiority in relations to the Eurocentric order. In other words, Brazil's self-conceptions after her independence were defined by the image of European international society. Although for Vieira, the Brazilians' self-perceived lack vis-à-vis the Europeans was race-based, the essence between Zarakol and Vieira is not drifting apart from one another. Both of them highlight the salience of how international interactions could be embedded in national self-conceptions.

This book uses Zarakol and Vieira's domestic/international conceptualisation of ontological security as a foundation to further discuss the approach employed in the study of Thailand's proactive behaviours. While the book relies heavily on Zarakol's framework, Vieira's theoretical propositions on the post-colonial states would offer an insight into the nuances and ambivalence of the post-colonial subjectivities vis-à-vis Western powers.

International society and stigmatisation

Zarakol's ontological security premises, predicated on the view that self-identities and self-narratives can be shaped by international interactions, arise from examining the exposure of non-Western states to the European modernity. In her study, the sources of ontological insecurity of the non-Western political entities such as Turkey, Japan, and Russia are rooted in their incorporation into the Western international system in the nineteenth century. The interactions between the Western powers and the non-European states result in the projection of superiority of the former over the latter in material and ideational aspects. The European model of advancement is portrayed as quintessential and is to be emulated. The Standard of European Civilisation is a prerequisite for non-European states to socialise their entry into a club of civilised members.

In order to clarify Zarakol's account, the contribution of the English School to IR serves as a perfect guideline. The English School scholars, for example, Barry Buzan (1993, 344), often examine how international societies incorporate states that do not share a common culture. He also investigates how an international society clashes with others. In fact, Zarakol (2007, 17) admits that there is a similarity between her work and the questions posed by the English school theorists. Zarakol, however, departs from the conventional English School scholars by pointing out how the expansion of European international society has left a stigmatising effect on non-European states. Such an effect renders those states ontologically insecure for years.

International society, according to Hedley Bull (2012), exists when 'a group of states, conscious of certain common interests and common values, form a society in the sense that they conceive themselves to be bound by a common set of rules in their relations with one another' (13). Mutual respect of the sovereign rights and independence of members are the heart of the concept of society. Adam Watson (1984) asserts that the expansion of European international society to other parts of the world starts in the late fifteenth century and nineteenth century. The surge of European imperialism and the material strength of the European nations astounded other international societies on other parts of the globe. This implies that the European diplomatic practices, international laws, and standards of civilisation have been exported throughout the world.

Due to the material superiority of the European powers, other non-European states, whose cultural heritage was considered backward and uncivilised by the European imperialists, were not socially and legally recognised as being equal. They were not seen as acquiring sovereign rights. Hence, the norms and institutions of European international society did not extend to include the uncivilised states (Gong 1984, 24). Following this logic, the superior Westerners, in the name of civilisation, exploited these non-Europeans by interfering in their domestic affairs. The lesser, non-European powers therefore considered it necessary to socialise their ways to become parts of the civilised entity by reforming their political structures and reconfiguring cultures along the benchmark of the civilised Western powers. These states were in search of recognition and acceptance.

According to Shogo Suzuki (2005, 141), most English School scholars select case studies in relation to how non-European states seek admission into the civilised club by focusing on how those considered uncivilised strived to gain recognition by modernising their domestic organs (see a collection of related articles in Bull & Watson 1984). Suzuki (2005, 143) also notices that the English School scholars approach the problem of international society expansion by assuming that such a process is somewhat linear and is emphasising promoting a European diplomatic code of conduct, cooperation, and toleration. Little effort has been devoted to identifying how an attempt to gain recognition by complying with the European norms can leave scars on those non-European states. On this subject, Zarakol (2007, 17) discovers that what is missing in the English School literature is the problem of becoming part of European international society from the dimension of non-European states, and the insufficient exertion to systematically discuss mechanisms that drive normative compliance and socialisation.

Zarakol (2007, 35–39) returns to a basic sociological reflection to exemplify how a dominant society and its normative system can burden those who seek membership and recognition. Firstly, the Europeans did not acknowledge the civilised status of those non-Europeans seeking status. Edward Keene (2002) has contributed to the English School's study of international societies by throwing light on European imperialism. Keene claims that a European treatment of the intra-European civilised nations differed from interaction with semi-civilised and uncivilised states. Respect of the sovereign rights and independence was therefore absent when the Europeans interacted with the non-Europeans. How did such treatments affect the non-European states? Zarakol (2011, 52) turns to Norbert Elias and John Scotson (1994) and their 'Winston Parva Study'. In summary, the study took place in villages in Leicester, which could be classified into Zone One, Zone Two, and Zone Three. The environment of Zone One was viewed as a desirable area to live, and most of the inhabitants were white-collar workers. People in Zone Two, although not as wealthy as those in Zone One, maintained a network of 'old families' and branded those villagers in Zone Three as exhibiting a working-class property. The Zone-Three dwellers were associated with dirtiness and troublemaking. In this study, it is surprising to find out that those dwelling in Zone three accepted that they were lower in terms of status and should not be accorded respect. The Zone-Three inhabitants were also ashamed of such stereotypes. In Zone Two, the old families, who long lived in this district, were blessed with the responsibility to protect the community. The so-called old families also sustained a high degree of organisational cohesiveness within their cliques, which enabled them to be able to exclude others and draw a line between 'us' and 'them'. Hence, these old families in Zone Two opted to exclude those in Zone Three from voicing their concerns and from participation in the public space. In this manner, the working class in Zone Three was stigmatised as inferior and lousy. They were ashamed by what they were labelled (Zarakol 2011, 53). The superior natives, according to Elias and Scotson (cited in Zarakol 2010, 11), characterise the Zone-Three people to make them feel that 'they are inferior in human terms' (11).

Drawing from the Winston Parva Study, Zarakol steps beyond Keene in analysing European imperialism. Yet Zarakol does not deny that the European nations treated the civilised and the uncivilised according to different standards. What she points out is that such maltreatments were accompanied by how the civilised could make the semi-civilised and uncivilised feel shameful of their existential being. These Western powers were equipped with overwhelming military capabilities and a higher degree of group cohesiveness. In this respect, the internal cohesiveness of the Western nations bears a resemblance to the old families in the Winston Parva Study. The European nations, as similar to the old families in Leicester, could effectively bar the non-Europeans from the club of civilisation because of the latter's failure to attain the required standards of the West. Strictly speaking, the Europeans stigmatised the semi-civilised and uncivilised as inferior, unworthy of recognition, and regressive.

An analogy of the Winston Parva Study has been drawn on to explain non-European elites and policy-makers when they encountered the European civilisation and were stigmatised accordingly. These non-European elites, exposing to European international society, could not but feel disgraceful of themselves (Zarakol 2011, 53). There are three rationales behind this phenomenon. Firstly, the club of civilisation was exclusive to the West because of the shared common norms, values, and culture. Second, in order to earn membership and reap tremendous benefits from Western international society, recognition from the original members was indispensable. Third, the backwardness and inferiority of the states in the non-Western international societies were exploited by the Europeans as a pretext to discard equal treatments and were justified as a reason for intervention in domestic affairs. Non-recognition from others can be considered as a source of ontological insecurity. In a nutshell, these non-European elites became ontologically insecure in relation to the rise of the West. They were not only concerned about the physical security of their states but also their status and progress in the eyes of the West. What Zarakol (2011, 59) ultimately argues is that the Western international system and the incorporation of the newcomers generated the 'Established and Outsiders'. Newcomers were excluded because of their failure to adhere to normative standards. The quest for non-Europeans to catch up with the West, therefore, was pursued in order to gain acceptance, prestige, and international recognition. Domestic institutional reforms and other strategies were implemented in order to garner attention and acknowledgement in the eyes of the West.

Stigmatisation is a two-way process. The Europeans could stigmatise the non-Europeans as inferior, backward, and childish. Nonetheless, if the latter simply feels neutral with regard to the values justified by the former, the process of stigmatisation would be immaterial and ineffective. In sociological logic, the outsiders – non-Europeans – could have a stigma if they have a common value system with the insiders because 'stigma is a shared social ground between the "normal" and those who are labelled as different as abnormal' (Zarakol 2014, 314). In other words, for the states to feel stigmatised in international society, they must first adopt the normative standards used for assessing the standardised attributes. The states can have a stigma when they evaluate their own characters as falling from expectations based on the adopted criteria and view their falling attributes as undesirable (Zarakol 2014, 314). Once the states have internalised normative ideals, escape is not an option (Zarakol 2011, 96). Therefore, the ontological security of the non-European states has been metamorphosed into ontological insecurity. In short, the consistent sense of self-identities prior to the exposure to the West had been contaminated by such stigma.

The stigmatised states that find themselves dishonourable can 'correct' their stigma in order to gain acceptance from the international community. Correcting the stigma, which was how those non-Western states underwent regime modifications in the Western image, is how to regain the sense of ontological security. On this matter, Zarakol (2011, 98) turns to Goffman (1963) who believed that the correction of stigma is possible, but a result 'is not acquisition of fully normal status, but a transformation of self from someone with a particular blemish into someone with a record of having corrected a particular blemish' (9–10). Speaking in reference to IR, once the states feel that they have fallen short of normative expectations and have felt compelled to comply with the predominant norms, they have acquired a stigma. Since the stigmatised states need recognition from other 'normal states', stigma correction or recognition-seeking through a number of assimilatory measures does not necessarily mean that the stigma vanishes. On the contrary, it means that these states feel continuously insecure about their ontological beings. They, in other words, endure the consistent sense of disquiet and feel constantly anxious about having others reaffirm their beings within international society.

While, according to Zarakol, any stigmatised states could feel compelled to correct their scars, it does not mean that the stigmatised subjects would automatically and uncritically emulate the Western powers and leave no trace of their former identities. However, the assimilating attempts of the stigmatised subjects would also involve the process of self-negotiation, the contestation of identities, and the efforts to incorporate the subjects' identities with those from the Western powers. Although Zarakol fails to tackle this point, Vieira's (2018) the ontological security account, however, helps to illuminate the discussion of this topic.

Vieira's introduction of the psychoanalytic and post-colonial approaches sheds light on how the stigmatised states became ambivalent to fully embrace and imitate the Western modernity. Key figures such as Frantz Fanon and Homi Bhabha are invited by Vieira to build the analytical framework of the ontological security discussion. Fanon's (2008) *Black Skin, White Masks* provides an analysis of how the white men (the colonisers) and the existing structure constitute the inferiority complex among the black men (the colonised). Fanon explains this dynamic as follows: 'White civilization and European culture have forced an existential deviation on the Negro . . . what is often called the black soul is a white man's artifact' (6). By interacting with the white colonisers' perceived superiority, Fanon continues, 'a normal Negro child, having grown up within a normal family, will become abnormal on the slightest contact with the white world' (111). As such, the solution of the black men is to imitate the white (3). All in all, it is because 'the goal of his behaviour [black person – my note] will be the Other (in the guise of the white man), for The Other alone can give him worth. That is on the ethical level: self-esteem' (119). As Goffman proposes, the black men wearing the white masks would be equally considered as someone who has a record of correcting scars. These white-masked black men could constantly feel ontologically insecure. Fanon's ultimate objective of his psychological analysis, however, is to destroy the inferiority complex (3). For Fanon (2008), an escape route for these white-masked black men is to move away from identifying with the white:

> Both have to move away from the inhuman voices of their respective ancestors so that a genuine communication can be born . . . Superiority? Inferiority? Why not simply try to touch the other, feel the other, discover each other?
>
> (181)

In other words, Fanon seeks to open doors to deracinate the notion of blackness as being associated with the colonisers.

In response to Fanon's call for change, Homi Bhabha (1994) suggests that the Western/non-Western interactions might not only result in how the existence of the colonised is defined in the colonisers' images. Similar to Fanon's premises, Bhabha mobilises his concept of 'colonial mimicry' to explain how the post-colonial subjects seek to reform and emulate the colonisers. The end result of assimilation is, however, 'almost the same, but not quite' (86). Speaking in relation to Fanon's *Black Skin, White Masks*, it is also 'almost the same, but not white' (89). In other words, no matter how the post-colonial subjects seek to imitate their colonial counterparts, they could never fully attain the desired stage. Bhabha recognises that the incessantly unachievable quest of emulation would produce the 'excess' or 'slippage' which is an outcome of 'the *ambivalence* of mimicry' (86). Avtar Brah and Annie Coombes (2000) summarises Bhabha as follows:

> [B]ecause colonial culture can never faithfully reproduce itself in its own image, each replication . . . necessarily involves a slippage or gap wherein the colonial subject inevitably produces a hybridized version of the "original". In other words, hybridity is intrinsic to colonial discourse itself, and consequently colonial discourse potentially undoes itself.
>
> (11)

As such, the attempted outcome of the colonial replication could be seen as only a hybridised version. Gayati Spivak (2000) concurs with Bhabha on this point: 'This is the condition of possibility of mimicry: to be different yet the same. This is the description of the hybrid: a mixture of difference and sameness' (18). On this issue, Vieira (2018) comments that despite the incomplete stage of imitation, the process in itself 'would allow them some enjoyment through the fantasy of discursively filling the existential lack/anxiety generated by colonial assimilation and acculturation' (151).

For Bhabha, the colonial hybridity opens the space for the post-colonial subjects, not only to replicate the colonial standards in order to ease their anxiety but also to resist the dominant modernity of the West. Cultural hybridity is 'a site of subaltern cultural and epistemological resistance to colonialism' (Jackson 2010, 190). The practice of mimicry has a potential to erode and unmake the colonial discourse that the post-colonial subjects strive to emulate. Bhabha (1994) reiterates such a possibility as follows:

> Mimicry . . . is, indeed, such an erratic, eccentric strategy of authority in colonial discourse. Mimicry does not merely destroy narcissistic authority through the repetitious slippage of difference and desire. It . . . therefore necessarily raises the question of the *authorization* of colonial representations.
>
> (90)

In summary, although the stigmatised states internalise certain standards, there is a possibility that they could emulate such prevailing standards in order to gain recognition along with integrating certain elements of their own cultural constructs. The extent to which the hybridised culture could defy the dominant culture is not the focus of this book. In this regard, the possibility of the hybridised version of culture in the case of Siam's formative years will be empirically noted in Chapter 3.

States, status, and recognition

Status and recognition in IR

From the preceding discussion, it appears that Zarakol's articulation of ontological security and status concern shares common grounds and similarities with the literature on recognition and status. Richard Ned Lebow (2008, 26), focusing on cultural factors such as how self-esteem and honour could result in conflicts, admits that there are similarities between the ontological security research programme and how the components such as honour and standing could be motives for the states to carve out preferences.

The essence of Zarakol's theoretical propositions, *ipso facto*, revolves around the notions of status and recognition in IR. The relationship between states, status, and recognition is not entirely a new dialogue in the discipline. One of the fundamental questions in the study of international politics is whether the states are naturally concerned about their status in the international system and whether recognition from other nations matters to any states in question. There have been numerous efforts from IR scholars to solve such puzzles. According to Jonathan Renshon (2017), there is 'the strong belief among scholars that status . . . affects outcomes of importance across international relations' (5). Similarly, policy-makers generally refer to the significance of their national status in public and private (ibid., 16). In short, there has been a consensus among scholars that an intangible factor such as status does matter to foreign policy decision-making. As previously discussed, studies of how states pursue identity recognition from others are neither ground-breaking nor innovative in IR, particularly in a constructivist strand of thought (Honneth 1996; Ringmar 1996a; Murray 2008; Muhamad 2008; Lindemann 2011). Recent publications on status-related theories similarly reaffirmed the understanding that status and recognition are inseparable (Renshon 2017; Ward 2017; Gilady 2018; Murray 2019; Larson & Shevchenko 2019).

Probing into Zarakol's scholarly account, it could be seen that status and recognition are intricately related. On the one hand, the non-Western states, which had been stigmatised as backward and had internalised the Western worldviews, would be hypersensitive to status issues. On the other hand, any behavioural changes by the non-Western states would require acceptance and recognition from the Western community. On the surface, it seems that there is a strong connection between the two concepts.

In order to further elucidate the relationship between the two concepts, it is imperative to clarify the definitions of status, which have been widely discussed in this book. Firstly, *status* entails different meanings. It could be used interchangeably with 'honour', 'reputation', 'prestige', 'standing', 'pride', and 'glory'. Carvalho and Neumann (2015) observe that, in relation to status, Thomas Hobbes used glory, Max Weber used prestige, and Emile Durkheim used pride (6–7). Secondly, not only does status involve other similar, interrelated terms, but it also insinuates relevance to the concept of recognition.

In principle, attaining a certain social status requires an inter-subjective understanding of meanings and interactions from others. In the words of Schia and Sending (2015), 'Status cannot fully be understood without considering the more fundamental quest for *recognition from* others, regardless of whether status pays off in terms of according soft power' (74). Basically, recognition of one's status implies an acknowledgement of one's identity. Renshon (2016) points out that 'status refers to the actual position or identity of a state'(521). This implicitly suggests that in each social status, there is an identity role attached to it. For example, Benjamin Zala (2017) has shown how a great power status, identity, and role should be conferred upon by both great-power peers and non-great power nations. In other words, the idea of great-power status without recognition and acceptance would be rendered unimaginable. Renshon (2017) summarises this tendency as follows: 'status is also *perceptual* in the sense that it is based on beliefs. There is no "objective" or "natural" status hierarchy' (35). Such beliefs, continued Renshon, would be easier to be considered as ' "common" or "shared beliefs," with the addendum that they are not just convergent but also shared' (36).

According to Zarakol, non-Western states that had internalised Western worldviews and had been stigmatised as outcasts tended to seek admission into Western international society by modifying their *modus vivendi*. The process of the Western stigmatisation entails a hierarchical sense in international politics. The reality that the non-Western empires sought the Western approbation equally implied that they sought a reputable status in the international system. Does Zarakol's theory differ from the literature on status and IR? Dafoe et al. (2014) propose that status should be defined as something which 'is often employed to refer to standing. Standing refers to an actor's position in a social hierarchy, and consequently what rights, respect, and patterns of deference from others they should expect' (5–6). In other words, status is chiefly 'the condition of filling a place in a social hierarchy' (Carvalho & Neumann 2015, 4).

In sum, status, recognition, and social hierarchy could not be considered separately. Each notion implies one another. Neumann and Carvalho (2015) re-emphasise such a relationship as follows:

> Recognition is what actors who are involved in status seeking are after, and in that sense the two concepts go together. The concept of status however is linked not to agency, but to structure. It is to repeat, the condition of *filling a place in a social hierarchy*.
>
> (7)

Fundamentally speaking, if a state is concerned about its status, it generally pursues a status-seeking activity in order to garner recognition. Because status-seeking 'refers to acts undertaken to maintain or better one's placement. As this is something that is done in competition with others, it is by definition a hierarchized activity' (Carvalho & Neumann 2015, 5). In short, to be able to attain better status, one is required to express certain qualities to gain acknowledgement from others. At the same time, one's status improvement could be a decline of status for others.

Following such descriptions, it seems that Zarakol's theorisation of international stigmatisation could be complementary to the literature on status and IR. If one starts with an assumption that any states care about their status, Zarakol's explanation would become more clear-cut. That is, great powers, rising powers, non-Western powers, and small powers would generally be perceived as status seekers.

As Robert Gilpin (1983, 1988), A.F.K. Organski and Jacek Kugler (1980) suggest, if proper status and prestige are denied to any revisionist, rising powers could be a motivation for international conflicts. These rising powers would engage in a status-seeking practice in order to gain their rightful prestige because, according to Daniel Markey (2000), 'prestige is the public recognition of eminence, and hence, an assessment of relative position' (55). Renshon (2017), Ward (2017), and Murray (2019) generally agree that the sense of entitlement denied to rising powers could trigger aggressive foreign policy behaviours. Such a proposition regarding status-seeking activities is similar to Larson and Shevchenko's (2019) examination of social identity theory and status-seeking foreign policy. Briefly speaking, both Larson and Shevchenko suggest that there are three strategies for states to seek desirable status, namely, 'social mobility', 'social competition', and 'social creativity'. The first strategy involves how the states emulate practices of the upper class in order to be accepted as part of the corps or clubs. The second strategy, following from the first, only starts when the states in question feel that the hierarchy becomes impregnable, so they attempt to rival and outrank those having the superior status. The third strategy, which could be optional for any states with status anxieties, is about how the states refuse to adopt the norms and values of the dominant powers and strive to thrive in different domains in order to lead in the rank creation. From the views of these status-related theorists, the status-seeking behaviours of the non-Western powers and small states would not be different from other greater powers.

In this regard, it becomes inevitable to ask whether it is necessary to elaborate Zarakol's theory extensively if one could merely start with an assumption that status matters to foreign policy behaviours. What actually set Zarakol's theoretical prescriptions apart from other literature on status and IR? In fact, starting from this assumption it is convenient to analyse foreign policy behaviours. Thailand's proactive foreign policies can be assessed along with the three strategies outlined by Larson and Shevchenko (2019), for example, Thailand's strategy of assimilation might fit with the first strategy of social mobility, whereas its proactive behaviours could be considered as the strategy of social competition. While these sets of theories might sound convincing, they fail to explain why the small states would risk their physical security in favour of social security. They barely discuss why some small states are more sensitive to status issues than others. Ward (2017), Renshon (2017), Murray (2019), and Larson and Shevchenko (2019) generally focus on the great powers such as the US, Russia, Germany, and China. While status concerns and competitively aggressive foreign policies could be anticipated from such great powers, these variations are not eminently visible in the small-state cases. The fruitfulness of Zarakol's approach, which could be distinguishable from other status-related literature, is how she highlights the importance of historical contingencies in accordance with the constructivist tradition. For constructivists, historical contingencies are essential for states to define their interests (Hopf 1998, 176). Henceforth, tracing the historical accounts in the cases of Turkey, Japan, and Russia could further explicate the reasons why these non-Western states were particularly sensitive to the issues of status and non-recognition. Similarly, tracing the historical contingencies of Thailand shows continuities and discontinuities of how past experiences could affect the anxieties of later generations.

Zarakol has developed a useful tool to analyse foreign policy. This book departs from Zarakol on three accounts. The first point is that, rather than focusing on middle power and great power as in the case of enquiry of Zarakol, this book centres on a small state such as Thailand. It is worthy of notice that Zarakol's cases can be classified as former empires, that is, agrarian great powers within their international societies. Secondly, Zarakol sheds light on the transformation of foreign policy after the major defeats of Turkey, Japan, and Russia, whereas the focal point of this book is to explain Thailand's proactive behaviours. Thirdly, despite Zarakol's theoretical richness, her work does not specify why the asymmetrical interactions between Western and non-Western states could leave psychological anxieties over a long period of time. In an effort to modify Zarakol's set of theories, this book introduces the notion of trauma to complement Zarakol's framework so that it can holistically explain behaviours of Thailand in relation to European international society. The discussion of the points of divergence from Zarakol is dealt with in the following discussion.

As mentioned in the preceding sections, the ontological security approach suggests that states can be somewhat anxious about their existential beings in the eyes of the others. Zarakol argues that former agrarian empires would learn to seek membership after the defeats. The problem therefore is narrowed down to the question about the status of the small states. Did the small states have to be initially defeated in order to internalise the Western way of thinking? And, in the case of the small states, should ontological security and physical security be considered as separate units of analysis?

For IR scholars and foreign policy analysts, abandoning the concept of material power in international politics is impractical, whereas denying other factors for the sake of power composition per se is a myopic practice. Power, especially in the case of small-state analysis, is indispensable to physical security consideration. In fact, for Zarakol (2011) and Suzuki (2009), the reality that the European states could stigmatise the non-European states and not vice versa was because of the former's military awe and the latter's cognisance of inferior capabilities. Power and physical security are the foundations of the small-state study. Where, then, is the place for ontological security? The answer is in the nature of European international society in the nineteenth century and its institutions of international law, diplomacy, and normative practice. Recall Keene's (2002) observation that the Europeans treated the civilised and the un-civilised with double standards, and the non-Western states' survival was dependent on the level of civilisation they attained and the degree of recognition they received from the members of the club of civilisation. It can be implied that, for the small states, physical security is contingent on how they could seek ontological security. In other words, physical security can only be secured if ontological security is established. Ontological anxiety-thinking about recognition by other Western European powers defines the small states' national interest and strategy. The nerve-wracking perception about physical security is only part of what defines the states' interest. Yet, despite the small states feeling physically secure, their sense of ontological insecurity is becoming a residue which persistently shapes their concerns.

As regards the small states, European international society's norms and practices such as diplomacy and international law are portrayed as a necessary means to shelter against physical aggression from threatening imperial powers. Neorealists and neo-liberal institutionalists share the belief in the logic of anarchy. Both believe that states are in a constant condition to maximise security but methods to achieve such an objective is different (Weaver 1996). Wendt (2003, 510) correspondingly claims that the states want physical security as well as recognition. Arguing along sociological thinking, Wendt points out that Self is constituted via recognition by Other in the first place. Subjectivity, therefore, hinges on inter-subjectivity (Wendt 2003, 511). In his general example, a teacher becomes a teacher only through recognition of such a role by students. As articulated earlier, non-recognition from other international entities could amount to the state of ontological insecurity. Wendt's premise with regard to how states need recognition can be evenly treated as an issue of security. In applying Wendt's idea on the previously discussed topics such as the international system and the small state, non-recognition from others can jeopardise both physical and ontological security.

Wendt (2003, 511) distinguishes between 'thin' and 'thick' recognition. The states' struggle for thin recognition means that the states seek to be recognised as legal entities within a community of law. With regard to thin recognition, rights and independence as sovereign states are accorded respectively. Nonetheless, thick recognition is about obtaining respect for differences (Wendt 2003, 511). Discussing in relation to the expansion of European international society, the small states seek recognition to enjoy the benefits of international society such as diplomacy and international law. This task should be achieved or else they, in accordance with Wendt (2003), could be treated 'like a slave or an enemy in the state of nature', and can be 'killed or violated as one sees fit' (511). In other words, failure to attain the stage of civilisation in the nineteenth century meant thin recognition was absent; hence, the uncivilised could be trampled on arbitrarily. Colonial games in the nineteenth century are apparently evident. In order to ward off such possibilities, the small states would adjust to meet the standards for thin recognition. Once the states are recognised as subjects of the community of law, the quest for thin recognition ends.

On the other side, the small states seek thick recognition as well. Respect and social acceptance are other dimensions for the statesmen interacting with the outside world. This type of recognition corresponds to the notion of ontological security (Zarakol 2007, 22). The search for thick recognition is 'open-ended and never-ending' (Wendt 2003, 512). This marks the difference between thin and thick recognition. No one would deny that physical security is essential to the small states. However, it is not always an axiomatic precondition. Wendt (2003) asserts that recognition and respect for a person render physical security 'worth having in the first place' (514). Suicide bombers and war-fighting revolutionaries,

Wendt (2003, 514) suggests, exemplify how thick recognition can be pursued at the expense of physical security. In fact, it is fair to prioritise the assumption of physical security. Nevertheless, this logical primacy is dependent on the context. According to McSweeney (1999, 153), it is reasonable to take the physical security assumption for granted if one lives in a dangerous jungle. Nonetheless, in a society, a hierarchy of human needs should be reconsidered. In a similar fashion, in international society, assumptions about the states should be contextualised rather than dryly assuming the prevalence of physical security. Because, at the end of the day, it is inevitable for IR scholars to treat the states and persons as an interchangeable unit (Ringmar 1996b).

The point, in reference to the expansion of European international society and the incorporation of the non-Western states, is that the small states were concerned about their physical survival. However, respect and acceptance are the two factors that they feel they equally deserve. Even after these states receive thin recognition, that is, when they become subjects of the community of law, they constantly worry about whether they are on par with others in terms of status. This is because, recalling Goffman (1963, 9–10), these states' remedies do not mean they acquire a normal status in the international community. It means these states have maintained a record of correcting a scar. In a nutshell, the pursuit of thick recognition, or what this book initially calls ontological security, becomes a periodic chore as Wendt remarks. How, then, could IR students make sense of the relationship between status/recognition sensitivity and foreign policy direction?

On the issue of unremitting perception of ontological insecurity that the non-European states endure, Zarakol is not without imperfection. For Zarakol (2011), the curious cases of pre-modern powers such as Turkey, Japan, and Russia puzzle IR scholarship in the sense that these states, when confronted with Western international society, did not readily perceive the necessity to conform to the European ways of life. A physical and figurative defeat, Zarakol (2011, 103–104; Mattern & Zarakol 2016, 18) argue, was a reason for them to reformulate foreign policy strategies to assimilate with the predominant international system.

From the perspective of the non-Western elites, shame and humiliation were central to their reactions towards the expansion of European international society. The civilised club of European nations barred the non-European states from enjoying equal status in international society because they shared different sets of norms and values. In the cases of Turkey, Japan, and Russia, defeat shamed and humiliated these empires. Shame can occur when one is insecure about self-identity (Steele 2008b, 13). It affects self-esteem (Giddens 1984, 55). It is 'an inner sense of being completely diminished or insufficient as a person' (Fossum and Mason 1986, 5, cited in Steele 2008b, 53). The defeat generated a feeling of shame which was associated with the sense of inferiority (Zarakol 2010, 20). It also humiliated the former formidable powers, which once were anachronistic empires. Ultimately speaking, humiliation is a process of disrespecting and de-respecting (Saurette 2006, 507). Humiliation, as discussed by Paul Saurette (2006), shatters the dignity of others by 'stripping away and revealing as false the most prized self-perceptions and most valued bases of self-respect' (507). Shame and humiliation can be seen as a metaphor and product of when ontological security is disrupted (Steele 2008b, 54). In other words, in an environment of shame and humiliation after defeat, the non-European empires suffered from a feeling of worthlessness in the eyes of the West. They realised that their values were secondary to their Western counterparts, and hence respect was not accorded. In this regard, these states, feeling ontologically insecure, shameful, and humiliated, conducted a grand strategy to assimilate with Western international society in order to correct what they perceived as blemishes so that they could earn respect from others.

A bid to gain membership into the Western club by the agrarian empires was practised to rid themselves of shame and humiliation. Such an experience would subsequently influence foreign policy-thinking of the states. In explicating the mechanism of this determinant, Zarakol, borrowing from Pierre Bourdieu (1984) and Norbert Elias (1997), brings in the concept of 'habitus' to unknot how shame and humiliation constantly guide foreign policy directions. Habitus can be defined as a 'consensus of what the world is made of' (Zarakol 2014, 318). For an individual, habitus could entail 'an active residue or sediment of his past that functions within his present, shaping his perception, thought, and action and thereby moulding social practice in a regular way' (Bourdieu 1984, 466 quoted in Zarakol 2011, 100). The modern states depend on collective memories to shape national habituses (Subotic & Zarakol 2013, 4). What Zarakol argues is that the feeling of shame and humiliation during the phase of assimilation with the European international system has been ingrained and incorporated into the nation-building process. Therefore, the stigmatising attributes and the sense of inferiority have also been combined in collective memories which structure the course of national habituses.

In short, collective memories of nations, which constitute state identities, should not be treated as if they are independent of international relations. There is a strong tendency in academia to study nationalism, national identity, and national project as if they are remotely domestic components. On the contrary, these aspects, widely categorised as domestic dimensions, intertwine with international features. As such it is no coincidence that, according to Subotic and Zarakol (2013), 'a great homology exists within domestic institutions of modern states' (5). It is the dynamism of Western modernity and the expansion of European international society which gives birth to the idea of the nation-state. The nation-state, to borrow Benedict Anderson's (2006) catchphrase, is an imagined community. However, a political entity such as a nation-state would not exist without the evolution and existence of the Westphalian system and the European global expedition (Subotic & Zarakol 2013, 5).

Generally speaking, the notion of nation-state would become nonsensical without reference to the European international system. National identity and foreign policy are inextricably interrelated, and the former element could be tainted by the stigma of the past. National identity often provides a basis for foreign policy conduct from which legitimacy derives and how its directions should be articulated (Prizel 1998, 19). Following this line of reasoning, Subotic and Zarakol

(2013) imply that, for the non-European states before the twentieth century, shame and humiliation from the inferior status vis-à-vis European imperialists have actively alarmed their elites and policy-makers. Therefore, a concern about international status has been part of the foreign policy consideration for the non-European empires in subsequent years following the entry into the Western international system. Status, acceptance, and international recognition become sources of concern for the states that yearn to correct their stigma and want to reinstitute the sense of ontological security. The sense of ontological security, in turn, is hinged on concerns for recognition from others.

Instead of utilising 'national habitus' to examine the residue of the past memory and how it influences foreign policy in later periods, this book embarks on the concept of 'trauma' to clarify the relationship between the two variables. What if experiences of shame and humiliation for being labelled as inferior are traumatic? What if the ontological insecurity feelings during the periods of incorporation into the international system have been traumatising? Would it better explain the seamlessness of how such experiences are entrenched in collective memories and national identities, and how proactive foreign policy is pursued as a result of such ideational elements?

Trauma and residues

Memory and trauma are the two related concepts. Memory is generally understood as recollections of the events in the past. Similarly, collective memory is a shared story of the past which links 'the past, present, and future in a simplified narrative' (Bell 2006, 2). Trauma is a certain type of memory which is viewed in psychology as emotional and psychic injuries. In addition, psychoanalytic studies point out that such injuries are frequently repressed and could result in certain behavioural outcomes (Bell 2006, 7). Cathy Caruth (1996) generally defines trauma as devastating events and painful memories 'in which the response to the event occurs in the often delayed, uncontrolled and repetitive appearance of hallucinations and other intrusive phenomena' (11). Trauma, which is a certain type of memory, can be personal and collective (Kristeva 1989). Personal trauma is confined to a painful memory of individuals, whereas collective trauma is expanded to include public incidents such as war, genocide, and the Holocaust which spawn collective experiences of horror (Resende & Budryte 2014, 1). Shunting aside the discussion of personal trauma, this book solely concentrates on collective trauma and how it is remembered, perceived, and translated into action by policy elites.

Not every past event is memorialised as collectively traumatic. Traumatic events are defined by the intensity of the occurrences, disability to react, and enduring effects the event reproduces (Laplanche & Pontalis 1967, 465–469). Piotr Sztompka (2000, 452) designates the character of traumatic events as follows. Firstly, a traumatic event must be rapid and sudden. Secondly, it must also be deep and radical. Thirdly, the event should be exogenously imposed upon an agent. Those who suffer from such a traumatic event do not contribute to the outbreak of the event. Lastly, an event must be perceived as mentally repulsive and shocking. It should not be something predictable beforehand. Examples of the possible traumatic events are genocide, economic depression, terrorist attack, war defeat, revolution, and assassination of political leaders. The reference to these four criteria does in no way imply that the events that meet such criteria should be traumatising for individuals. On this point, Jeffrey Alexander (2004, 1) suggests that an event becomes traumatic only when groups collectively feel that the event is horrifying and would leave marks on collective memories. In this regard, collective trauma is not a natural phenomenon. It can be treated as a product of social construction.

Collective trauma, for Duncan Bell (2006, 7), can lend support in explaining how shocking events can result in the formation of collective identity within nation-states. Collective identity or national identity of a nation-state is a story of a community which has been narrated and re-narrated over time to foster a sense of homogeneity within a specific boundary. Such a story is famously recognised as 'official nationalism' (Anderson 2006). Official nationalism narratives are the basic foundations of how the people in the community understand themselves. They are collective memories which shape how members of a given imagined community perceive the past, apprehend the present, and possibly guide the direction of the future. Collective memories are the basis of collective identities of nation-states. The constructivist trend in IR has spelt out a connection between identity and national interest (Katzenstein 1996; Lapid & Kratochwil 1996). What the policy-makers of the nation-states reflect about the national identities drives foreign policies in the international arena (Hopf 1998, 195).

Following this reason, if traumatic memories have been embedded in the national identities, they could more or less influence foreign policy-making. However, the arising concern becomes whether such a trauma is simply selected for justification by elites, or it does genuinely influence choices of policy (Becker 2014, 60). In other words, traumatising memories can be treated scholarly, in reference to Becker (2014), as an *instrumental* or *emotional* element in the social sciences.

There are empirical application examples which employ trauma as a tool to legitimise foreign policy without ruminating on how it can determine foreign policy. One of the foremost examples is Vamik Volkan (1997) who proposes the idea of 'chosen trauma' to explain how the sense of loss, suffering, shame, and humiliation in the past can be reawakened in the present time. For Volkan (1997), the chosen trauma is 'the collective memory of a calamity that once befell a groups' ancestors' (48). The chosen trauma connects the sources of suffering in the past with the present generations. Once the chosen trauma of the past has been reactivated, the group in the present generation identifies themselves with the sense of suffering their ancestors experienced from the old days. The traumatic events from the past have become alive and surreal. Oftentimes, the chosen trauma is utilised to justify policy changes (see for example Strate 2009; Kinnvall 2002, 2004; Subotic 2016).

Another strand of circles retains a doctrine that trauma, undistinguished from other ideational elements, can actually determine foreign policy directions. Brent

Sasley (2014) summarises this position as he states that if regular memories 'can shape policy, then traumatic memories have a powerful ability to influence behaviour' (139). One of the most explicit cases on this issue is the German deployment of military missions in the 1990s. Maja Zehfuss (2001, 2004, 2007), Brent Steele (2008b), and Thomas Berger (2002), for example, discuss how the Holocaust and the Nazi aggression in the past remain a contending issue and define foreign policy-making in the 1990s. Apart from the case of Germany, Robert Gildea (2002) has portrayed how the traumatic experiences of the French capitulation to Nazi Germany in 1940 influenced subsequent France's post-war leaders to restore her place and prestige among other great powers such as Britain and the US. Moreover, in the case of the British, Anne Deighton (2002) contends that the memories of Britain as an imperial power and a sense of superiority from the days when the sun never set on the British empire have contributed to foreign policy outcomes which tend to 'punch above their own weight' (100). In the case of an Asian power such as China, Zheng Wang (2014), asserts the claim that the trauma of national humiliation in the nineteenth century has remained a vital determinant of Chinese foreign policy in the twenty-first century. The historical memory of the century of humiliation explains why China reacts aggressively towards other great powers and her neighbours.

Although trauma and foreign policy can be approached in both instrumental and emotional methods, there are certain conditions for the former. It is indisputable to discredit the claim that traumatic narratives are subject to propaganda by the elites. However, such narratives are not independent of context. In broadcasting historical traumas to the public for any purpose, the members of the community must have prior entrenched memories about the traumas in question in order to be intelligible to the messages transmitted by policy-makers. Without contextual backgrounds, a promoted traumatic discourse would become incomprehensible. For instance, a foreigner living in Turkey, Japan, and Russia may not share the sense of traumatic sufferings from the past with the national inhabitants. In this regard, a collective trauma can be treated as a permissive condition. The upshot is that the exploitation of traumatic memory is not mandatory for political leaders. Nonetheless, it can serve as a tool to legitimise a policy. This is also the case for the emotional method. Strictly speaking, traumas can be a permissive condition for statesmen when they are confronted by a variety of policy choices as well.

By and large, both methods revolve around the notion of ontological security. In the case of the instrumental method, the question anyone might pose is: 'Why would policy leaders need to employ traumatic narratives to justify policy changes?' This question might be chastised for ignoring the power of the people in a democratic system. However, the enduring question is: 'Why would the elites resort to propagating such narratives instead of explaining the costs and benefits of policy changes?' The key answer to these questions is in the premises of ontological security. Volkan, which has been cited by Kinnvall (2004, 755), hints that change without mourning is unacceptable by humans.

A change requires lamentation. In times of physical loss and damage, traumatising narratives provide a comforting sentiment of continuity which preserves the ontological security of the states. They offer calmness instead of ontological calamity. Subotic (2016), for example, offers an analysis of how the chosen trauma was mobilised by the Serbs to sooth the feeling of loss which stemmed from the departure of Kosovo.

On the relationship between trauma and ontological security, the emotional method is not different from the instrumental mode. Traumatic memories can be integrated into collective memories of the nation-states (Innes & Steele 2014, 20). In this connection, the national identities, formed by traumatic experiences, could become a permissive condition for policy-makers of later generations.

In fact, there is a close affinity between Zarakol's proposition on ontological security and the notion of trauma. For example, Zarakol (2010, 4) admits that, in the cases of Japan and Turkey, the traumatic character of being stigmatised as outsiders in the nineteenth century plays a significant role in shaping national identities. This process becomes a constitutive factor which forces status-conscious awareness upon the non-Western states. They have become constantly concerned about their status and recognition from others. In other words, non-recognition from others becomes a source of ontological insecurity.

Although Zarakol avoids explicit contention with regard to the concept of trauma while focusing on Goffman's notion of stigma, the feature of trauma can be complementary. Jenny Edkins (2002, 2003) captures Zarakol's theorisation through works on trauma and world politics. For Edkins (cited in Resende & Budryte 2014), traumatic events destroy the 'expectations' and 'preconceptions of how the world function[s]' (3). The European exclusion and stigmatisation of the semi-civilised and uncivilised states bring 'to the surface existential questions' (Edkins 2002, 245).

That is, European powers' stigmatising the non-European empires as inferior did not only generate shame and humiliation, but it also reproduced traumatising memories which systematically compelled the states to question their own existence and acceptance from others. Such traumatic events became a revelation. According to Edkins (2003), traumatising events and memories 'strip away the commonly accepted meaning by which we lead our lives in various communities' (5). In a nutshell, stigmatisation also traumatises the non-Western states in question. Memories of being stigmatised by others, as Zarakol insinuates, have been traumatising. Such traumatic memories have been built into national narratives of the non-Europeans which continuously and constantly remind them to consider and reconsider existential questions. Trauma repetitively functions and endures as Resende and Budryte (2014) suggest that: 'trauma is felt, but not understood; it is memorized and recalled, but not necessarily experienced . . . it refuses to be incorporated into normality, but goes on perpetuating itself in memory' (2). To put it bluntly, collective trauma can be explored and expressed through commemorations. It has been permeated through national memories and can be invoked. It affects the formation of national identities and national interests. Yet traumatic memories can be narrated to mobilise the masses as previously discussed (Resende & Budryte 2014, 3).

Trauma, status concern, and proactive foreign policy

Following from the earlier premises, the shame and humiliation of being stigmatised as inferior have traumatised the non-European states. Such memories have been constructed into national psyches which endlessly alert the policy-makers that recognition and acceptance from others are vital to national interests and ontological security. Concerns about the international status become crucial. This argument does justice to the cases of the small states as well.

As previously discussed, the small states are less likely to pursue proactive foreign policy. Nevertheless, when they become proactive, it is irresistible to search for causes. If recognition and acceptance from others are the sources of ontological security, then the origins of existential anxiety should be non-recognition and non-acceptance in international society. Henceforth, worries about the international status which have been rooted in the states' identities can motivate the small states to formulate foreign policies which aim to gain recognition and reinforce the sense of ontological security.

The trauma of being stigmatised as inferior or trauma of ontological insecurity can permissively guide how the states respond to external pressure. Karin Fierke (2007) notes that trauma 'provided the foundation for consolidation of collective identity, which led to a projection of military power and the emergence of [a] regional or international security dilemma' (132). This mechanism functions when the experiences of social sufferings such as defeat, shame, and humiliation are fabricated into collective identities which open a possibility for military operations (Fierke 2007, 135). However, Fierke (2007, 135) is careful to forewarn that not all traumatic experiences result in military projection. But they are a necessary condition to make military projection possible. There are numerous examples with regard to how traumatic memories are not translated into related policies. In this light, trauma can be comparatively treated as a constitutive factor which renders certain courses of action possible.

Instead of depicting an extreme connection between trauma and military projection, it is more fruitful to substitute 'military projection' for 'proactive foreign policy'. Recall that a proactive foreign policy is modestly defined as a policy which seeks to adjust the status quo. And non-recognition from the past, as extensively discussed, is a gauge of ontological security which remains fluid among the policy-makers. It can be adduced that the trauma of ontological insecurity can influence the outcome of proactive foreign policy.

As previously pointed out, there are similarities between the ontological security approach and the IR projects on status and standing (Lebow 2008, 26). Lebow (2010, 171) also found out from the dataset that there is a convincing relationship between standing and international conflicts. For instance, out of the 94 wars that he examines, 62 wars were caused by states' concern about standing, which was 58 per cent in total.[2] Similarly, Jonathan Renshon (2017) introduces a statistical model to test how the perception of status deficits could lead states to seek higher standing by waging war. Concentrating on the cross-case historical comparison, Graham Allison (2017) also finds that the concerns for status of the ruling and rising powers could breed inter-state conflicts. In his words, those wars are generally about,

> "the rising power syndrome" and the "ruling power syndrome". The first highlights a rising state's enhanced sense of itself, its interests, and its entitlement to recognition and respect. The second is . . . the established power exhibiting an enlarged sense of fear and insecurity as it faces intimations of "decline".
>
> (44)

In sum, the proposition that a concern about status is a source of international conflicts is nothing pioneering. What this book seeks to tackle is how to understand the proactive behaviours of the small states, especially in the case of Thailand during the Second World War.

If status dissatisfaction could motivate the states to undertake war-prone behaviours, would it be applicable to the case of Thailand? Would it be more illuminating also if we modify the aforementioned theories by substituting the 'conflict category' with 'proactive behaviours'? Instead of replicating the findings by viewing the relationship between standing and conflicts, what if this book steps back and sees how the concern about status could generate proactive behaviours in the case of Thailand? On this topic, the small non-European states that were stigmatised have been ontologically anxious about their status and recognition from others. They have been seeking to pursue a foreign policy of stigma correction in order to reinforce the sense of ontological security and enhance international status. Therefore, if the small non-European states feel that they are stigmatised as outsiders, unequally treated as inferior, and traumatically insulted, they prospectively tend to craft a proactive foreign policy to adjust their positions. As Joslyn Barnhart (2016) and Steven Ward (2017) argue, states that are humiliated, disrespected, and denied status claims could potentially engage in proactive behaviours to alter what they perceive to be the seemingly unjust status quo.

In conclusion, the concept of ontological security is the basis of the approach utilised in this book. The experiences of being stigmatised as an outsider are also traumatic. The sense of ontological insecurity non-Western elites of the nineteenth century perceived vis-à-vis European international society was similarly disquieting. Such traumatising memories have been built into the national identities which become a source of foreign policy determinant in subsequent periods. The statesmen of later generations are thus hypersensitive to their nations' international status. Signs of non-recognition and non-acceptance from others result in a proactive foreign policy to amend the position on the international stage. This book employs this approach to interpret the case of Thailand during the Second World War, which appears in the following chapters.

Notes

1 In Schweller's (1994) article, he categorises the states into four types only. However, in his book published four years later, he expanded the categories into eight types to include the medium-sized states (Schweller 1998). For convenience purposes, I intend to discuss the four types only because Thailand during the Second World War could in no way be considered as a medium power.
2 The findings suggest that standing accounts for 58 per cent of the war, whereas standing, security, revenge, interest, and others account for 18, 10, 7, and 7 per cent, respectively (Lebow 2010, 114).

Part II

The origins of Thailand's sense of ontological insecurity

3 Latecomer

Siam and the quest for civilisation

As a small state in Southeast Asia, Siam encountered a threat from Western imperialism. The case of Siamese foreign policy in the nineteenth century has been commonly cited as the ingenuity of a small country to survive European colonisation. What has been largely missing from the Thai historiography and IR discussion was how the Siamese elites were anxious about their admission into the club of civilisation. This chapter reviews the relations between Siam and the West through the analytical frameworks of stigmatisation and ontological security discussed in the previous chapter. It explains how Siam started to develop its sense of status concern and how such awareness became part of the trauma. The point is to show how the export of European international society rendered the Siamese elites' ontologically insecure about their inferior position in the international hierarchy.

Sources of self: Siamese kings and gradual adaptation

The early nineteenth century marked the apex of colonialism and the expansion of the European powers throughout the world. It was the beginning of what Eric Hobsbawm famously called 'the Age of Empire'. Siam was no exception in its interactions with the West. Although the contact with the West began in the sixteenth century, the communication between the then Ayutthaya Kingdom and the West, namely, the Dutch, the Portuguese, and the French, did not incorporate Siam into the international system. It was the nineteenth-century encounter with the West that marked Siamese assimilation, acculturation, and socialisation with Western international society. Being a latecomer to the modern international system, as Jean-March Coicaud (2015) views, 'must have been humbling, intimidating and a source of much psychological trepidation' (232). This section addresses the source of Siamese Self, which anxiously originated from the interactions with the Western powers, and highlights how Siam, being a latecomer, engineered changes and transformations in order to gain recognition.

Confrontation with civilisation

Before the Europeans sailed to Southeast Asia in the nineteenth century, Siam was a state under the tutelage of the Sinic-world order. Its main economic partner was the Chinese empire (Viraphol 1977). In the early nineteenth century, the Siamese also began to accommodate the economic demands of the European powers such as Britain. The Siamese-European trade was kept at a minimum level (Kullada 2004, 25). The beginning of the watershed interaction between the West and Siam began during the reign of King Nangklao, or generally known as King Rama III (1824–50).

In 1824, Britain steadfastly expanded into Burma, and it was rumoured in the Siamese court that they would similarly advance into the Malaya Peninsular (Wyatt 2003, 152). Faced with a possible threat, Nangklao consented to negotiate an agreement in 1825 with Henry Burney, the British delegate. In 1826, the British and Siamese concluded the Burney Treaty which symbolised the conciliatory tone between the Western power and the agrarian kingdom. The nature of the treaty was the political settlement between the influence of Siam and Britain in Burmese and Malaya territories (Tej 1977, 50). The agreement was related to the economic dimension as well. Firstly, the treaty outlined foreign conduct with the West, particularly the British. Secondly, the economic provision clearly stated that the British could trade with Siam without a third-party intervention (Tarling 1960, 46). The treaty brought about a 50 per cent increase in trade with Singapore (Wyatt 2003, 154). Later in 1833, the Siamese correspondingly concluded a similar treaty with the Americans. The economic terms were not much different from the agreement with Britain.

Despite the interaction in the 1820s-1830s and the augmented prosperity from the treaties, Nangklao did not perceive the necessity to adjust his kingdom to conform to the normative standards of Western international society. It would not be until the 1850s that the Siamese elites felt ashamed of the country's status and progress in comparison to the West. David Abeel, a Western missionary, recorded that Siam possessed 'shameless indecency of language and dress' (cited in Baker & Pasuk 2014, 39). For him, the moral and political condition of Siam was 'a dark one' (ibid., 29). F.A. Neale, an Englishman, similarly described Siam as 'at best semi-barbarous . . . an oppressed and cringing people, . . . wrapped in the grossest ignorance and superstition, lost to all sentiment of moral virtue' (cited in ibid., 29).

Although the Westerners held a derogative view towards Siam, it did not translate into Nangklao's willingness to conform. A striking instance was the issue of map-making technology. Neale described his audience with Nangklao when the Siamese court proudly presented the map drawn by the locals under the Siamese conception of cartography. The map showed the Burmese-Siamese boundaries in which there were only two kingdoms surrounded by oceans, and the image displayed Burma as demonic and Siam as saintly (Thongchai 1994, 34). Upon seeing such a cosmological map, Neale later noted that,

> We were, however, very nearly outraging all propriety by bursting into fits of laughter, and very painful was the curb we were obliged to wear to restrain our merriment.
>
> (Neale cited in ibid., 34)

For Neale, the cosmological map was a ludicrous matter, but for the Siamese, it was a matter of pride as he continued the description: 'The inclination to smile, too visibly depicted in our faces to be mistaken, was, happily, by His Majesty, construed into delight and admiration at the beautiful work of art' (ibid., 34). In short, the Siamese had not yet internalised the values and standards of the West and were satisfied with their own knowledge (see also Zarakol 2014).

The expansion of European international society into the extra-European territories was frequently accompanied by violent practices in order to civilise the barbarians (Keene 2002, 98–99). As John Crawfurd, a British envoy to Siam in the 1820s, commented, the two gunboats 'would destroy the capital without possibility of resistance from this vain but weak people' (Baker & Pasuk 2014, 39; Tej 1977, 50). The fact that the Europeans were materially superior was demonstrated in front of the Siamese's eyes when the British expanded into Burma in the 1820s. It became more obvious in the 1840s when the Chinese empire was defeated in the infamous Opium War. Before the subjugation of China at British hands, the Middle Kingdom was regarded by the Siamese as powerful. Such an outrageous event reaffirmed the material supremacy of the West at the expense of exalted regard of the Chinese (Terwiel 2011, 137). As a result, King Nangklao distanced his kingdom from China. This was evident from 1844 to 1851 which saw only one tributary mission from Siam to China (Terwiel 1991, 42).

Nevertheless, a distant relationship between Siam and China did not mean that Nangklao acquiesced to the Western demands and culture. On the contrary, he increasingly acquired an anti-Western attitude and pursued an isolationist policy (ibid., 43) He imposed trade restrictions on sugar with the Western partners. Exports of sugar had dropped dramatically from 240,000 piculs to 80,000 piculs (Vella 1957, 127). The Siamese court also refused to purchase steamers from the well-known British merchant, Robert Hunter, who once received favours from the king. And in 1844, Hunter was expelled from the kingdom. Despite Hunter's threat to push the issue to the British government and to introduce some warships to resolve such matters, the king became more inimical towards the West (ibid., 129). The subsequent events were vividly projected to the world when the Siamese court declined revision of the British and American treaties in late 1849 to 1850. Joseph Balestier, an American representative, and Sir James Brook, the British delegate, failed to convince Siam to repeal economic terms from the former treaties (ibid., 131–140).

When did the Siamese become ashamed of themselves? And when did they feel an impetus to be recognised as an equal? In order for the Siamese elites to become ashamed of their values, they first had to learn to judge such values from the European perspective. In other words, they should internalise the values of the Europeans which they assessed as more superior. In a metaphor, the Siamese elites should 'eat the fruit of knowledge' so that they became able to judge that they were in a naked state (Zarakol 2014, 321). Such dynamics took hold after the death of Nangklao.

King Mongkut and the enlightenment

Despite all measures against the West, Nangklao would never deny that the Westerners were far more advanced in material terms. Before he passed away, he cautioned that there might be further conflicts with the Westerners. He bemoaned that 'Whatever they have invented, or done, which we should know and do, we can imitate and learn from them' (cited in Barmé 1993, 19). In 1851, his brother, Mongkut (1851–68) assumed the throne.

King Mongkut, or King Rama IV, was known as an illustrious character in *The King and I*, a romantic fiction between the Siamese king and Anna Leonowens, the British teacher to Siam. Mongkut was widely known for his scientific and modern mind. He was ordained as a monk before becoming king. During his monastic years, he spent his time learning Western languages such as Latin, French, and English. Modern knowledge such as science, mathematics, geography, history, and astronomy became his interests during his monkhood (Chakrabongse 1960, 179–182).

He became one of the first leaders of Siam to present the notion of 'civilisation' or 'progress' to his people. Becoming 'civilised' meant being recognised by the Westerners as possessing certain attributes worthy of recognition. He deeply regarded the fact that Siam was 'half-civilised and half barbarian', but he also held a strong urge to transform those uncivilised aspects to conform to the civilisation standards (Charnvit 2000, 120). The quest to become civilised and the struggle for recognition had been a formative feature of Mongkut as he once revealed to his audiences:

> Those who do not wear jackets are as much as being naked altogether. Their torsos might be blemished by skin troubles or they might be heavily perspiring, in both cases it was utterly disgusting. In all countries which are great powers men wear jackets and are properly dressed. People who do not dress properly are uncivilised or they are primitive savage tribes. Henceforth you will all wear jackets when attending my audiences.
>
> (Chakrabongse 1960, 183)

Mongkut's opinion clearly implicated the anxiety and shame of being recognised as uncivilised. Moreover, he adopted a dichotomy of being civilised and savaged to contrast the stage of progress. He had eaten the 'fruit of knowledge' and fully realised that his state remained backward in comparison to the world. Hence, recognition from the West became the sources that could complete Siamese conceptions of Self. Without Western acceptance, Siam would be anxiety-ridden of its existence.

According to Walter Vella (1955), Mongkut equated his reign with 'Western' and 'enlightened' elements (333). Why was that the case? It was because Mongkut judged his kingdom from European standards and pursued policies in order to fulfil the normative benchmark. Due to the desire to be recognised, not as inferior, but on par with others, he directed the state towards reforms. The driving reason was a status concern amidst the Western powers as Thongchai (2000), a renowned Thai historian, argues:

> Siam could no longer confirm . . . its meaningful existence by claiming the lineages to the traditional cosmic origins. In order to survive, not from colonialism but from indignity and inferior existence, and to remain majestic, Siam needed a confirmation according to the new ethos of civilization that it measured up to other leading countries. The desire and anxiety to keep up with the world, not an escape from being colonized, was significant in itself. (534)

In other words, Siam could not be recognised as equal if it refused to admit that it remained in a regressive stage. To be ontologically secure and fully registered in Western international society, Siam should catch up with the standards of civilisation. This became the basis of Siamese foreign policy in subsequent years.

Immediately after the death of Nangklao, Mongkut informed the British following the failure of the Brooke mission to observe the re-direction of Siamese foreign policy. He also offered gifts to the American counterparts to re-establish relations with the Pacific power (Wilson 1970, 351). The Siamese elites opened more trade with the West and allowed a certain degree of freedom of movement to foreign residents (Terwiel 1991, 43).

In 1855, Mongkut prepared for the arrival of Sir John Bowring to restart negotiations with the West since the reign of Nangklao. In preparation for Bowring's visit, the king and his people only expected that the concessions with the British would not amount to the loss of Siamese prestige (Gong 1984, 208). The result of the Bowring mission became a cornerstone for Siam's conduct in foreign relations. The by-product of the meeting was the Bowring Treaty which granted free trade to the British. In the economic clauses, import duties were confined to no more than 3 per cent, and export taxes were capped at 5 per cent (Wyatt 2003, 168; Lysa 1984, 57–59). As regards the stipulations on international affairs, the British consul was established, and British residents in Siam would be exempted from the Siamese jurisdiction (extraterritoriality). Similar treaties with foreign powers such as the US (1856), France (1856), Denmark (1858), Portugal (1859), the Netherlands (1860), and Prussia (1861) were inked in subsequent years (Wilson 1970, 362).

Above all, the significance of these treaties marked the formal integration of Siam into the international system. Although Siam became part of the new diplomatic corps as a new sovereign, it was stigmatised by other members as underdeveloped. The Western powers maintained the two modes of interaction with the semi-civilised or uncivilised states. Instead of upholding the practices of sovereign equality, toleration, and international law, Siam was not bestowed such privileges. Apart from the effects on fiscal autonomy and land rights (Larsson 2008, 8–11), one of the most irritating problems for the Siamese was the exercise of foreign extraterritoriality according to the Bowring Treaty and other resembling agreements. The imposition of the extraterritoriality was a symbol of unequal relations imposed by the West. Because of the belief that the Siamese legal system was barbarous, granting Siamese jurisdiction would risk the possibility of cruel and unfair justice. Fundamentally, it was how the Westerners imagined Siam and the rest of Asia as backward, inferior, and semi-civilised (Hobson 2004, 224–231). Similar treatments occurred in semi-civilised states such as Japan and China during the same time. In order to change the existing condition, Mongkut could either opt to adhere to the traditional *modus operandi* or correct the stigma by fulfilling the standards of civilisation to garner proper recognition.

The king circumspectly chose to correct what he felt was a flaw. He abolished the custom of barring people away from any royal visit occasions. For Westerners requesting royal audiences, they were allowed to stand in front of the king instead of prostrating and crawling (Chakrabongse 1960, 192). As an admirer of Western civilisation, he discerned the significance of learning from the West. Therefore, foreign teachers were employed to instruct Mongkut's sons in English, science, and literature without any attempt to convert them to Christianity (Terwiel 2011, 167–168). As regards the issue of the abolition of slavery, he even hinted at such a possibility because the practice of slavery would amount to embarrassment (Kullada 2004, 36). According to Anna Leonowens, an English teacher to the court, Mongkut sought to 'doubtless without hesitation, abolish slavery' (Baker & Pasuk 2014, 49). Although this plan was not implemented during his reign, his intent and shame from sustaining the slavery system were apparent. This scheme was later materialised by his son, Chulalongkorn.

Apart from other changes, one of the most famous reforms that Mongkut had spearheaded during his reign was the forecast of the eclipse in 1868. Traditionally, in the Siamese cosmology, an eclipse was a phenomenon in which Rahu, a black evil, strived to devour the moon and the sun from time to time. And in order to ward off the devilish Rahu, the people would be required to generate loud noises to drive evil from the moon and the sun. Such a belief was local and non-scientific which traversed the knowledge of the Western world. Mongkut himself understood the absurdity of the story due to his interests in science and astronomy. He therefore utilised modern tools and knowledge to calculate the timing and whereabouts of the 1868 eclipse and informed his fellowmen through the spectacles of science. His perspiration was perceived by other Siamese to be incredulous (Chakrabongse 1960, 212). After the eclipse was proven to be accurate, the Europeans who participated in the eclipse expedition praised Mongkut for his modern mentality (ibid., 213). Shameful and angry at the backwardness of his Siamese subjects, he criticised those disbelieving in his modern method for adhering to old techniques and theories with regard to the subject of astronomy (Thongchai 1994, 47). The king later passed away within the same year.

Throughout the reign of Mongkut, as opposed to Nangklao, Siam was more open to the West. Although the signing of the treaties with foreign nations would be disadvantageous to Siam in socio-economic aspects, it was a driving force which reminded the Siamese of their place and status in Western international society. The Siamese elites desired recognition as an equal country vis-à-vis others. Hence, the king partly introduced Western modes of life to Siam. From this period, it would be impossible for Siam to define their place without any reference to the West.

Chulalongkorn's civilising missions

Mongkut's keenness on Western civilisation had paved the way for his son's colossal reforms of Siam in the nineteenth century (Vella 1955, 334). After the death of Mongkut in 1868, Chulalongkorn (1868–1910), Mongkut's son, ascended the throne while he was 15 years of age. It was during the reign of Chulalongkorn that Siam underwent modernisation along the Western contours and encountered crises in foreign relations. The memory of this era would mark and mould Siamese foreign policy.

For Chulalongkorn and other princes, flexible diplomacy was inadequate to avert Western hazards. Showing a civilised identity was of paramount importance in order to counter the civilising missions from the Westerners. Prince Prisdang, a minister to Paris during the reign of Chulalongkorn, reflected his thoughts after being consulted by the king. In order to manage foreign threats, Prisdang wrote,

> Siam must be accepted and respected by the Western powers as a civilised nation. Hence there is no choice but to bring about a new government modelled after the Western pattern, or at least after Japan, the only country in the East following the European way.
>
> (an archival document cited in Murashima 1988, 84)

Henceforth, the strategies employed by the king were domestic reformation to garner approbation from international audiences. In other words, Siamese physical security was interrelated to ontological security. Without proper acknowledgement from the West, Siam could be penetrated by foreign interventions in the name of Western civilising missions. This foreign policy thinking propelled Siam to assert itself proactively in the politics of recognition.

At the beginning of the reign, Chulalongkorn was a young king without genuine power. It would not be until 1873, when he became 20 years old, that Siam would undertake his reform projects. During the five years of interregnum, Sisuriyawong (Chuang Bunnag), administered Siam as a regent. Under Sisuriyawong, Chulalongkorn was encouraged to travel to foreign countries to experience modern techniques of administration. It was observed by David Wyatt (1969) that Chulalongkorn himself did not want to be seen as a barbarian (41). This was marked by certain changes during the first trip of the young king in 1871 to Singapore and Batavia. Western-style accoutrements were introduced and familiarised among the staffs. European etiquettes and manners were imposed on the royal consortium (ibid., 41). His visits to key infrastructural places such as schools, hospitals, railways, post offices, and the likes, and his observations on customary practices of the West astounded and inspired him to proceed with reforms (Atthachak 1995, 131).

Upon his second coronation in 1873, Chulalongkorn, in order to exhibit Siam's civilising attributes, replaced the tradition of prostrating the king and officials with 'standing, bowing, and lifting the hat' (Vella 1955, 336). The royal decree of the proclamation rationalised the change on the basis of ridding the country of oppressive practices. The enforcement was decreed in order to follow other Asian nations which began to abolish the prostration (ibid., 336). He ventured to establish the State Council and the Privy Council, which were patterned after Western models to work on the law-making process and to offer personal advice to the king respectively (ibid., 336). One of the immediate tasks of these two councils was to deracinate practices which drew opprobrium from Western attitudes, such as corvée and slavery. According to the 1874 order, anyone born as a slave from 1868 would be freed and could not sell himself or herself as a slave (Baker & Pasuk 2014, 51). Later, the 1905 Slave Abolition Act completely terminated slavery in Siam.

The king sought to construct an absolutist state by centralising power from locals, nobles, and tributary suzerains. He initially formed the Finance Office to collect tax-farms which were formerly disseminated to 17 treasurers. This strategy strengthened the power of the king and his networks at the expense of other lords. By 1892, the king's treasury amounted to 15 million ticals circa (Siffin 1975, 53). Following the fiscal reform, he steered other modernisation programmes such as initiating post and telegraph services, constructing railways, and establishing institutions for training bureaucrats modelled on Western education such as the famous *Suan Anand* and *Suan Kulab* schools (ibid., 52–58).

In 1892, governmental organisations, which were predicated on the Western prototype, were reconstructed. Major Ministries were founded and identified as the Ministry of Justice, Ministry of Defence, Ministry of Education, Ministry of Foreign Affairs, Ministry of Finance, and Ministry of Interior. Map and survey units were formed to demarcate the boundaries of Siam. The king further gripped the power of the state by dispatching commissioners to former tributary areas such as Luang Prabang, Nong Khai, Khorat Ubon, and Phuket in order to administer to the locals on behalf of Bangkok and to draw a clear line and limit of sovereignty. Such an administrative structure resembled the British-style governance in India (Baker & Pasuk 2014, 53).

Chulalongkorn also favoured the services of Western advisors. As mentioned in the preceding parts that the king sought the great transformation of Siam through key reforms, he therefore entrusted the Western technocrats with several tasks relating to modernising the nation (Thongchai 2011, 28). Additionally, Chulalongkorn's sons were sent to study in Europe to familiarise themselves with Western culture. One of the notable figures who studied in Europe was Vajiravudh, who was to succeed his father's throne.

All in all, the Siamese elites and the emerging intelligentsias of the time unanimously agreed that Siam should attain the stage of civilisation. The petitions from the intellectuals to the palace expressed their will to see the re-configuration of the Siamese political system into the parliamentary mode of governance. For them, this was the practical option for Siam to progress and become civilised (see collections of petitions and responses from Chai-Anan & Kattiya 1989; Barmé 1993, 21). Such hope was unpretentious and not only driven by colonialism (Thongchai 2000, 532). As opposed to the intellectuals, the king and his coteries desired civilisation with the maintenance of the court's status quo. Their status anxiety was intricately tied to an economic dimension. The Ministry of Education that originated during the reign of Chulalongkorn stepped into publishing textbooks to preach necessary values. In a series of textbooks called *Thammacha-riya*, ideal norms such as cleanliness and proper manner were to be strictly followed. The contrasting example of backwardness stressed in the official textbook was 'negroes' who were associated with uncivilised aspects by the Siamese (Kullada 2004, 87). The central cause of the underdevelopment of the Africans was their repulsion to interact and adapt with the outside world (ibid., 87).

Scar of the semi-civilised Siam

Despite great efforts by the Siamese to display modern dimensions of Siam, its international status within the orbit of Western international society was confined to semi-civilised status. According to Michael Herzfeld (2002), a nation with a semi-colonial or semi-civilised status would similarly prefer a set of policies which was an 'aggressive promotion of their claims to civilisational superiority . . . that almost always [is] disproportionate to their political influence' (902). This was the case of Siam in the nineteenth century. While the nation's material capabilities were in no way parallel with other European imperialists, Siam oftentimes self-perceived that its key reforms would reposition the status of the country to an acceptable level. The traumatic event, which had enlightened the Siamese elites, was the *1893 Paknam Crisis.* The incident has been uncomfortably recognised by the Siamese as *RorSor 112* even until today.

The 1893 crisis stemmed partly from the fruit of knowledge that the king and other courtiers had eaten. It was worthy of notification to state in this place that Siam sternly delineated its boundaries through Western-imported mapping technology. In the context of the late nineteenth century, the British carved out their sphere of interest in Burma and Malaya, whereas the French hinted at the possibility of expanding into Indo-China, namely, Cambodia and Laos, which were considered by the Siamese elites as their tributary states. Siam was once ashamed of its primitive awareness of cartography. It realised that modern-mapping knowledge was pivotal not only to plea against the French claims but also to function as a symbol of modernity. Modern-mapping technology, in other words, would become the only grammar comprehensible to the West when it came to territorial issues (Thongchai 1994, 121).

The mapping competition between France and Siam in the left bank of the Mekong River had begun since 1884 when the Siamese dispatched topographical surveyors to the Laotian areas (ibid., 124). Both the Siamese and French presented numerous maps to assert rights and sovereignty over Laos and Cambodia. Eventually, the French and the Siamese decided to form a joint committee to settle the questions of boundaries. The Siamese Foreign Minister, Prince Devavongse, even proposed an international arbitration to settle the disputes (Battye 1974, 315). In short, the Siamese strived to behave in a European manner.

Nonetheless, sporadic border clashes and conflicts between the two governments escalated the Franco-Siamese tensions. The Siamese claims to its sovereign rights over the areas of Mekong resulted in numerous incidents such as arrests of the French agents and citizens along the disputed regions (Terwiel 2011, 210).

In addition, the Siamese aggressively ventured to annex areas in Laos across the Mekong River before the French (Thongchai 1994, 109). In response, Auguste Pavie, a French diplomat and surveyor, recommended that the French government demand the most out of Siam and even establish a protectorate status over the country (Terwiel 2011, 211). In other words, France did not consider Siam as an equal partner in the first place. Hence, there was no ground for military restraint when it came to dealing with Siam. In short, Siamese acting as Europeans was not European in the eyes of France.

Why did the Siamese elites punch above their weight? In the late nineteenth century, Britain and France struggled for colonial supremacy in the world. The international context was permissible for Siam to manoeuvre the two European powers against one another. The situation was advantageous to the Siamese strategic calculus. Nevertheless, instead of bending with the wind, Siam derailed. The Siamese elites mistakenly assumed that other nations recognised them as a civilised country. Noel Alfred Battye (1974), a historian on military reforms during King Chulalongkorn's reign, concludes that,

> Until 1893, it seems, it had been reasonable for Siamese to believe that the West would respect the integrity of earnestly progressive Asian countries. Chulalongkorn believed that Siam had much progress on her own that other nations had nothing to gain by imposing themselves over her politically. Nevertheless, in the name of "civilisation", and progress . . . there was intervention and trespass.
>
> (401)

In this regard, Siamese leaders thought that both Britain and France recognised them as an equal nation. Hence, the Siamese stiffened its stance against the French while actively siding with the British. In each conflict with France, the Siamese reported and consulted the British until the outbreak of the 1893 crisis (Thongchai 1994, 108–109, 2011, 26).

In April 1893, the French increased pressure on Siam to retreat from Laos and Cambodia by dispatching two gunboats to intimidate the king at the delta of the Chao Phraya River. Rather than succumbing to threats, Chulalongkorn warned that any foreign vessels barging into the inner part of the river would violate the Franco-Siamese Treaty and should be propelled accordingly (Terwiel 2011, 211). At the same time, as a matter of preparation, Siam mobilised its forces to defend the territorial integrity (Battye 1974, 338–355). The Siamese elites calculated that the British would intercede for them. On the contrary, the British speculated that the French would resolutely engulf the areas along the Mekong. The British correspondence at the time revealed that Britain would position herself as neutral because Siam was too weak and should accommodate the demands of France (Jeshurun 1977, 51).

In July 1893, the French gunboats barged further into the inner part of the river. The Paknam Fortress opened fire on the French vessels without success. France pursued a strategy of naval blockade in the Chao Phraya River, and the Siamese Grand Palace was held at gunpoint. The nation was demoralised and was near the verge of pandemonium. Hence, Chulalongkorn sued for peace. Siam withdrew its claims on the left bank of the Mekong River. Chantaburi and later Trat provinces of Siam were to be under French occupation, and Siam was forced to de-militarise the areas from Battambang and Siemreap. It was also obliged to pay three million francs of indemnity to the French government.

In summary, the defeat was both a shock and humiliation to the Siamese elites. The 1893 crisis, according to Shane Strate (2009), was a 'symbol of the country's disgrace and a constant reminder of Thailand's inferior relationship with the West' (201). Originally, the Siamese upheld the idea that they were on par with the West, but the outcomes in 1893 shattered the most prized illusion that they had about their status. After the crisis, the king became ill and lost weight. He even lamented his mortified life (Battye 1974, 369). Before the settlement of the conflict, he informed Prince Devavongse that he felt like a 'frog in a coconut shell', which was a Thai-language metaphor referring to his assumption that he grasped the dynamic of global politics, but he was utterly incorrect (Krairiksh 2008, 422).

After defeat and humiliation

Siam's encounter with the West from Nangklao to Chulalongkorn formed the foundation of national identity. Firstly, it became unimaginable to find its place in international society without adaptation and recognition from the West. Secondly, despite Siam's best efforts to engineer reforms, the 1893 crisis was marked as a critical moment which would constantly remind Siam of its inferior position vis-à-vis the West (Strate 2009, 201). The Siamese were 'permanently scarred by 1893' (Battye 1974, 396). After the shocking defeat, Siam's prime task was to gain recognition even further because it realised that misrecognition could result in another 1893. This section therefore traces a historical account of Siam's quest for status and recognition from Chulalongkorn to the 1932 Revolution. It shows how status concerns continued to be central to Siam's foreign relations.

Siam seeking position

After the defeat of 1893, the learning curve of the Siamese elites had improved steadily. They realised that they should secure recognition and reception from the Western nations. The Siamese became more proactive. Firstly, the king and his aides-de-camp decided that they should visit Europe. The trip was not planned to maximise physical security of Siam. It was, however, a voyage to maximise ontological security of Siam in the international sphere. The conventional version of Thai historiography hails the trip as a diplomatic success, guaranteeing the independence of Siam. It should be noted that the French and British had earlier in 1896 agreed to situate Siam as a buffer zone between them in 1896 (Jeshurun 1970). As such, the trip was in no way affecting the imperialistic policies of any Europeans.

Chulalongkorn's European tour was in fact anticipated to enhance the standing of Siam. The records of the British foreign correspondence could substantiate the motive of the king and his trip. After the defeat, Chulalongkorn's aide, Prince Svasti, informed the Earl of Rosebery of the proposal of the king's European visits. Rosebery suggested that if Chulalongkorn wished to study European institutions, his visits should be incognito. Svasti immediately 'dismissed the possibility of the king's coming incognito' (MS-Scott-UL1.55.9). According to the document, Rosebery fully understood that 'there would be a want of dignity in any such visit just after Siam had suffered so cruel a blow as she recently had to endure' (ibid.). Strictly speaking, a secret state visit was not desirable among the elites. It was envisioned to attract a conspicuous spotlight from the European leaders to reinstate their sense of ontological security. Deep down, the elites acquired a sense of inferiority when comparing themselves to the West. This was evident in how Chulalongkorn described his visit to Europe: 'Coming to Europe this time is the right thought . . . our country is backward from the perspective of the West' (Krairiksh 2008, 84).

In both European tours in 1897 and 1907, the king lavished the resources on ostentatious items such as Swedish local porcelains, relaxed in Sanremo, Italy, which was the then a modish destination of the European nobles, and invested heavily in Western-style artworks (Peleggi 2002, 32–39). Conspicuous consumption was a strategy for the Siamese courtiers to manifest the civilised identity. The strategy was similar to Peter the Great's efforts to emulate Louis XIV's grandeur fashion in court (ibid., 42). Chulalongkorn and Peter, despite differences in time, resembled one another in conditions. They both sought status and recognition from the West by modelling reforms on the dominant *modus vivendi.*

Furthermore, in order to enhance its international status, Siam participated in the World's Fairs in 1889 (Paris), 1893 (Chicago), 1900 (Paris), 1904 (St. Louis), and 1911 (Turin). The events were international exhibitions for nations to project the zenith of Western evolution and exotic elements from the colonies and semi-civilised nations. The nature of the fairs was to situate the developed and underdeveloped within hierarchical order. The motive of the Siamese government with regard to the fairs was to show its national profile (ibid., 144). Why would a showcase of a national profile be significant? Thongchai (2000) analysed that participating in those world fairs would enhance 'recognition and elevate their status in the eyes of the world' (540). Siamese presence in the fairs would ultimately place the Siamese elites on par with other nations (Peleggi 2002, 145). In order to garner acknowledgement, Siam decided to present the technological advancement within the nation by exhibiting modern aspects of Siam such as railways, roads, telegraph facilities, and other relevant portraits which could possibly demonstrate Siamese maturity (ibid., 174–175).

Siam frequently wanted to be part of the exhibitions. Nevertheless, the elites were predictably apprehensive about recognition from Western nations. In the Fairs, Siamese exhibition areas were normally sited among non-colonial states or other semi-civilised countries such as Haiti and Caribbean-located nations (Thongchai 2000, 541). The government once protested in the 1900 Paris World's Fair when their exhibition area was placed among the colonies. The elites were distraught about how the Paris organisers classified the independent Siam with inferior states (ibid., 541). Despite great efforts exerted by the Siamese, there was no substantial indication that Siamese participation in the fairs had transformed the views the Western powers held towards the semi-civilised status of Siam. Anyhow, Siamese exhibitions received a number of awards, and they became jubilant of their minor successes in the fairs (ibid., 542).

Siam and the great war

In 1910, Chulalongkorn passed away, and his son, Vajiravudh, succeeded the throne. Like his predecessor, King Vajiravudh (1910–1925) was constantly perturbed by the status concern. In the first seven years of Vajiravudh's reign, the core foreign policy objective was to overturn the unequal treaties with foreign powers (Oblas 1974, 99). In fact, the existence of the unequal treaties signified an inferior position of Siam. Hence it was a source of paranoia. An attempt to negotiate the treaty revision had governed the Siamese relations with the foreigners in Vajiravudh's reign. From 1907–10, before Chulalongkorn's death, Siam had mostly secured the consent of the US to revise the extraterritorial clauses. Nevertheless, the Great War in 1914 had brought the process to a halt (ibid., 100). The First World War beseeched Siam to question its position in foreign affairs. How then should the small nation react to the global crisis?

Vajiravudh initially declared neutrality in August 1914. As an Oxford graduate, he naturally favoured the British. However, as a small state surrounded by the colonies of the Allies, Siam's move should be wary. On the one hand, the British and the French were notorious in imperialistic records. On the other hand, the Germans and other Central Powers had not been embroiled in any territorial conflicts with Siam. They were even more amicable to the Siamese than the Allies (Vella & Vella 1978, 102). This was a lucid account. The best possible solution for Siam was to pursue a course of strict neutrality.

In April 1917, the US declared war against the German and the Austro-Hungarian empires. The American entry into the Great War reshaped the context of the globe. Prince Devavongse, the foreign minister, cautioned the king earlier that the Central Powers had shown no sign of belligerence towards the Siamese. Hence, there would be insufficient grounds to justify the declaration of war. Shortly after the Americans pledged to join the war, Siam reinstated its neutral intention (ibid., 106). Despite pressures from the British, French, and Russian ministers in Siam, Devavongse suggested that he believed 'from the start the Allies would win, but see no good reason for Siam to join in' (ibid., 107). This partially implied that the changing international situation had no direct effect on Siam's stance. On the contrary, Vajiravudh searched for a different goal. He considered Siam's options to participate in the war.

The king was anxious about the status of Siam in the post-War settlement. Remaining neutral would exclude Siam from the family of nations after the war. The pride and prestige of Siam would also be overshadowed. Therefore, entry into the war was the covetable option because it could enhance the respect of the nation and could appeal to repeal the unequal treaties (Likhit 1964, 59–60). Prince Charoon, the Siamese minister to Paris of the time, happily expressed his feeling that participating in the war would be 'our real opportunity of raising the Status of our beloved country' (cited in Hell 2007, 25) Siam eventually declared war on 22 July 1917. On this decision, one of the Siamese aristocrats noted that 'our rulers . . . have tried so hard to elevate Siam to be on par with other nations. Such an intention has been achieved completely on Sunday of 22 July 1917' (Atthachak 1995, 204). In other words, it was the concern about status as opposed to the international structure which determined the king's wartime objective.

After the war declaration, Siam dispatched an expeditionary force of 1,300 men to participate in the war. The king conveyed messages to the military men who were assigned to travel to Europe that 'this was a highly important chance . . . to show other nations which we once feared. But now we are walking uphill. . . . In this time and the next, Siam shall rise to be on par with other nations' (ibid., 205). From the evidence of the official documents at the Thai Embassy in Paris, it was recorded as follows:

> Regarding the Thai soldiers in the war, despite being the first time in Europe, they effortlessly tried to preserve the dignity that the Thai soldiers were the battalions fighting should to shoulder with the Allies . . . not the colonial people who were recruited by the colonial masters.
>
> (Manij 1979, 173–174)

In short, the decision to join the war stemmed from the concern about the status of the nation. One of the observers from the *Saigon Opinion* commented that Siam's participation in the war had ignited 'a certain degree of combativeness in order to reach the level of civilisation of the great Western powers' (cited in Vella & Vella 1978, 125).

The yields in terms of status were immense. When the war ended, Devavongse ordered Charoon to ascertain that Siam's place in the peace talks was to be guaranteed. He was convinced that the Western powers might neglect the presence of Siam due to the perceived backward conditions. Devavongse's disquiet could represent Siam's concerns for status and recognition from the victor powers (Hall 2007, 27). At the end of the day, Siam earned its place at Versailles and became a member of the League of Nations. The Siamese elites became ecstatic. Devavongse cherished the success 'that the nations forming the League are to be equal in every respect' (cited in ibid., 29). Whether his view was myopic, his motive was clear: the entry into the war was due to an ideal aspiration to be recognised as one of the equals.

The 1932 revolution and foreign recognition

On 24 June 1932, a group of revolutionaries who called themselves 'the People's Party' forced the then Siamese king, Prajadhipok, who succeeded Vajiravudh's throne, to adopt the constitution which limited the power of the king and transferred the political authority to the people. Within the day when the coup d'état was staged, the People's Party became concerned, not only for domestic affairs but also for the status of Siam in relation to other great powers such as Britain, the US, France, and Japan. They were anxious about non-recognition of the foreign powers which could readily translate into external intervention. The telegram from the British Legation to London described how Pridi Banomyong (Luang Pradit), the brain power of the coup-makers, explained how the situation would not affect the foreign residents in Siam and how treaty obligations would be accordingly observed. The incumbent Foreign Minister of Siam, Prince Devawongse Varothai, was informed by the revolutionary movement to address foreign legations and to apply for 'recognition of the new Government' (TNA-FO371/16261-F5917/4260/40). In addition, according to the British intelligence of the time, the Siamese elites 'should therefore take whatever steps were necessary to prevent intervention' (TNA-FO371/16261-F5917/4260/40).

Since the transformation of the Siamese political landscape, there had been concerns for recognition by external powers as indicated by Phraya Srivisar, the People Party's new foreign minister, who sought acceptance from the British by describing the situation to Malcolm Delevinge of the British Home Office that King Prajadhipok's approval of the new constitution was an assurance that the king would remain as head of state. Because the revolution was entirely an internal affair, the question of foreign recognition would be irrelevant. However, the concerns about the status of Siam on the international stage loomed large (TNA-FO371/16261-F5846/4260/40). Cecil Dormer, the British minister to Siam of the time, similarly noted that the Siamese new rulers were steadily disturbed by the fear of non-recognition which could result in foreign intervention due to political disturbances (TNA-FO371/16261-F6564/4260/40).

Four days after the coup, the People's Party held the first parliamentary assembly of the nation. The so-called Six Principles of the People's Party[1] were promulgated which revolved around a guarantee of equal rights and security of the citizens (TPMP 1/1932, 28-June-1932, 6–7). However, it was striking to note that the very first priority of the Six Principles was a task to struggle for independence in politics, judiciary, and the economy of Siam. According to Nakarin Mektrairat (2010, 76–118), a prominent historian on the 1932 revolution, one of the significant causes of the revolution was the transformative sense of the Siamese middle classes who believed that the modernisation of bureaucracy and the revision of the unequal treaties with great powers were two significant factors. The existence of the unequal treaties, which granted the extraterritorial rights to foreign residents in Siam, was a sign of Siamese inferiority within the international system. It also implied that Siam was not accepted as an equal nation on the international stage. Hence, one of the first foreign policy priorities of Siam in the constitutional era was to seek revision of the unequal treaties. In this light, the new elites sought a display of the 'New Siam'. For them, the New Siam should be 'able to run her household without foreign interference' (Vinita 1975, 112).

After the day of the revolution, the interim government proclaimed the Provisional Constitution. The People's Party had meticulously exhausted almost six months to draft the Permanent Constitution for Siam which was scheduled to be sacralised on 10 December 1932. On 9 December 1932, one day before the official proclamation of the Permanent Constitution, the drafters of the law discussed for the last time the speech of the party, which was composed to deliver to the king. The discussion reflected the concerns of the elites with regard to Siamese international relations in the constitutional era. On the prepared manuscript, the constitution was legalised for the purpose of 'developing [Siam – my appendage] to be on par with foreign countries'. Chaophraya Wongsanupraphan objected to the aforementioned sentence. He believed that 'various countries', for the sake of linguistic beauty, should replace 'foreign countries'. Pridi protested and reasoned as follows:

> The phrase "various countries" . . . could implicate several countries which could be more developed than us or lesser than us. Hence, I may change it to "civilised countries".
>
> (TPMP 46/1932, 9-December-1932, 659–662)

Although the issue of wording was of minor importance, it partially revealed how the party's leaders sought to position Siam in international relations.

The new regime believed that the constitution should be legitimised and sacralised. Hence, the revolutionaries implemented copious legitimising campaigns to justify their coup and draw co-operation from the ancien régime.[2] For the revolutionaries, the constitution was equated with a sign of modernity and civilisation, whereas absolutism was associated with anachronisms. Since the constitution was promulgated on 10 December 1932, the national celebrations ensued in the following years. And in each annual celebration of 10 December, it was described that the decorations, architecture, and festival environments were aimed to display Siam and progress. It was, according to a prominent architecture historian, a celebration to express a 'scene of modernity' (Chatri 2009, 179; cited in Puli 2013, 137). The message of Constitution Day celebrations was clear: It was 'intended to guarantee that everyone who visited the Constitution Day celebrations would return home with the vivid impression that Siam had now become a modern and civilised nation' (ibid.). Drawing on this issue, it implied that the Siamese elites were obsessed with status and the idea of civilisation in international society of the time. Henceforth, the civilisation and progress were utilised as a justificatory claim for the legitimation of the constitution.

Conclusion: hybridised Siam

Since the period of King Nangklao, Siam confronted a dominant mode of legitimacy: Western recognition. This chapter has described how the Siamese elites, since their exposure to the West, learned, adapted, adjusted, and conformed to the emerging international system. Some might argue that the Siamese strategic alarm in relation to the West was purely survival, and no one can deny the survival motivation. This chapter complemented this existing assumption, however, by showing the images of how the Siamese elites were not only concerned about physical security but also ontological security.

The Siamese leaders from Nangklao to Prajadhipok had been constantly anxious about recognition and respect from the West. And in order to fulfil such objectives they pursued reformative policies and other proactive policies, not merely for the sake of survival but also for receiving Western approbation. The chapter shows how the desire for recognition was not alien to Siamese elites. It was the experiences from these periods and the desire for recognition that subsequently governed how later generations of Siamese should behave in the realm of foreign policy.

Although the main purpose of this chapter is to trace how the incorporation of Siam into international society had defined the Siamese orientation and how the Siamese leaders responded to their ontological anxiety by emulating Western powers, it did not mean that the Siamese elites abandoned their own identity entirely. It is imperative to note the nuances of seeking ontological security in this place. Bluntly put, adaptation 'is an act of appropriating or salvaging, and this is always a double process of interpreting and creating something new' (Hutcheon 2006, 20).

The first point to consider is that Siam was never fully colonised by the Western powers. Nevertheless, by striving to emulate the West, it could be considered as a semi-colonial nation (see Anderson 1978; Chaiyan 1994; Lysa 2004; Loos 2006, 13–24). As such, it was no exception to the post-colonial analysis. Secondly, Siam's quest for civilisation was predicated on the desire to be recognised by the Western powers. Although the Siamese elites sought to replicate the West, it was impossible for them to fully become the West. The outcome of Western adoption was a hybridised version of Siamese civilisation. Thongchai (2000) captures this point as follows: 'the Siamese quest for *siwilai* was a transcultural process in which ideas and practices from Europe via colonialism had been transferred, localized, and hybridized in the Siamese setting' (529).

There are various aspects of how the Siamese elites selectively hybridised their local culture with the discourse of civilisation. One of the examples was the case of the Siamese leaders' attempted colonisation of Patani, the southern province of Siam. In the late nineteenth century, Siam pursued its own colonial policy in competition with the British domination of Malaya. Viewing the Malay Muslims as backward and barbaric, the Siamese elites attempted to colonise them in the name of civilisation (Loos 2006, 81). There was no substantial interest for Siam in Malaya. By civilising the locals, Prince Damrong wrote, it 'would appear to the eyes of the world that Siam is absorbed with progressing along the path of prosperity with full strength' (cited in Loos 2010, 84). While it was true that Siam followed the British system in administering the colonies by dispatching governors and establishing Islamic family courts, Siam's Buddhist traits were translated into practices of the state power (Loos 2006, 94–95). This was different from other

Western colonial powers which maintained a secular policy of non-interference in religious practices of the locals (Loos 2010, 86). For instance, Chulalongkorn donated the money to the local Buddhist temple to be a centre of training officials who would work for the Thai state. Moreover, such a religious site was marked as a place for the locals to drink the water of allegiance to the Siamese king, a Buddhist ruler. Muslim officials were forced to perform such a ritual, which was forbidden by the Islamic precepts (ibid., 87). This sectarian practice was merely one of several dimensions of the nation's hybridised creations.

As Bhabha (1994) theorises, the hybridised culture, no matter how it eases the anxiety of the stigmatised states, could function as a site of resistance. This could be demonstrated by the case of Vajiravudh's anti-Western discourse in the domestic domain. As the first Siamese king who was educated in the West, Vajiravudh ironically cautioned against imitating the West entirely. In the early twentieth century, the civilisation project was a success to the extent that imitating the West had also became a popular craze (Jackson 2010, 200). Vajiravudh wrote a scathing piece under his pen name, Asvabahu, to criticise the trend of replicating the West. In *the Cult of Imitation*, he explained:

> Imitation in thought, speech, or deed is a characteristic of a slave (*that*) and so is antipathetic to *Thai-ness* (*khwam-pen-thai*). Being free (*itsara*) or *thai*, means that we can choose to think and do as we please.
>
> (cited in ibid., 201)

The king also blamed those wishing to become extremely civilised for 'turning their backs on everything that belongs to the old order of things' (cited in Copeland 1993, 38). They were similarly accused of 'having forsaken the principals of Buddhism in order to adopt the vulgar mannerisms of lower-class foreigners' (ibid., 28).

Although the Siamese elites sought recognition and acceptance from the West by the strategy of emulation; they did not imitate the West to the extremity. There were certain hybridised components which stemmed from the nation's indigenous values such as Buddhism. Despite such hybridised conditions, the chief goal of the Siamese elites was to obtain approbation from the international community, as this chapter has described extensively.

Notes

1 The Six Principles of the People's Party can be enumerated as follows: 1) Securing independence in politics, judiciary, and the economy; 2) Ensuring the matter of national security; 3) Improving the economy and job security of the Siamese; 4) Protecting the equality of the citizens; 5) Guaranteeing rights and liberties; and 6) Providing public education for all Siamese.

2 See an example of the works on constitution and legitimisation from Puli (2013) For a similar analysis see Subrahmanyan (2015).

4 Interest, status anxiety, and status-seeking

Prior to discussing the empirical cases of the book, it is imperative to define the national interest of Siam of the time. This chapter contextualises the background of Phibun's government. It traces interests, anxieties, and aspirations of the nation since the 1932 revolution. The chapter argues that apart from survival consideration, the Siamese elites, Phibun particularly, were concerned about status and recognition from foreign powers. The starting point of discussion begins from the time when Phibun rose to power as prime minister. The objective is to establish the ideational ground to which Phibun adhered. The chapter demonstrates how status anxiety and existential insecurity influenced Phibun's actions and policies.

Trauma and status concerns

Traumatic experiences are not the composites which are independent of context. They are historically contingent. The study of Shane Strate (2009) points out how the Thai government enlivened the 'loss of territories discourse' in order to legitimise the foreign policy of territorial retrocession. On the one hand, while such an argument is valid, it can be critiqued for over-determining the role of traumatic memories as merely a tool for political leaders. On the other hand, trauma could also be considered from an emotional dimension (Becker 2014). In order to supplement Strate's finding, this section is devoted to inspecting a general belief and behaviour before the ascendancy of Phibun as prime minister. It shows how trauma and status concerns were part of national memories even after the nineteenth century. The purpose is to show that the traumatic histories remained relevant almost 50 years after Siam's encounter with the West.

Institutionalising trauma through textbooks

The preceding chapter described how Siam's dealings with the West in the nineteenth century formed the basis of Siamese's anxiety-laden Self and psychological trepidation. Since the central focus of this book is on the twentieth century, the question is whether the traumatic experiences, which guided Siamese elites during the nineteenth century, continued to be relevant to policy preferences in the twentieth century.

After the 1893 incident, which stripped Siam of its status delirium, the Siamese elites were constantly reminded of their inferior place in international society. Western powers stigmatising Siam was traumatic and left an imprint on the nation's collective memory. In order to show that the residual effects of the traumatic experiences were pertinent to the twentieth-century context, it is necessary to trace how such memories were carried forward. Zheng Wang (2014), introducing techniques to investigate the relationship between trauma and foreign policy in the case of China, suggests that scholars should direct attention to history textbooks and analyse the official historiography which has been institutionalised in Chinese education. In a similar vein, analysing Siam's standard textbooks on history from the era of Chulalongkorn to the constitutional period could reveal how shameful remembrances remained relevant to the twentieth-century context.

The 1893 incident was a traumatising scar for Chulalongkorn and his successors. Following the dishonourable defeat, the Siamese elites prior to the 1932 revolution became seemingly oblivious to such a humiliating episode. The traumatic event was a constant reminder of how stigmatisation due to misrecognition could backfire on the nation's physical and ontological security. As seen through Siam's history textbooks, the Siamese leaders deliberately omitted the history of how the 1893 incident tarnished the royal dignity of Siam. The early history textbooks described how Siam merely seceded the territories to the French and British without mentioning how Siam was intimidated by force and coerced to exchange the lands for peace (Thamrongsak 2009, 140). The 1893 trauma was unspeakable for the Siamese rulers. As Karin Fierke (2004) explains, trauma 'is more of a "dislocation" accompanied by an inability to mourn or speak of the trauma' (472). Although the history of humiliation was silent, it did not refer to a state of absence. Névine El Nossery and Amy Hubbell (2013) suggest that 'traumatic experience may be unspeakable, but it is not necessarily unrepresentable' (1). The Siamese case, likewise, is not different from others.

Although the history of subjugation to the West was blurred, the objective of becoming civilised was deeply entrenched in Siam's textbooks. For the Siamese, survival was hinged upon military capabilities and recognition from others. In *Phumisat Lem Song* [Geography Volume 2][1] (Thepphasatsathit 1904), Siam's early and influential textbook distributed throughout schools even after the Second World War, the relationship between becoming civilised and reaching a great-power status was attentively articulated (155–177). First and foremost, the Siamese royals understood that the miscalculation of the 1893 decision stemmed from their inferior status in the Western international system. As discussed in Chapter 3, Siam became increasingly status-sensitive following the 1893 episode. Becoming civilised, for the Siamese rulers, was a prerequisite of gaining acceptance from the West. Being civilised, according to the textbook, was the equivalent of being 'developed' (ibid., 158). The contrasting example of being uncivilised was Africa, where there were only barbarians and it would never become civilised in comparison with others (ibid., 157).

The message conveyed to readers was to civilise Siamese students: 'It was a duty of every student to behave in a civilised manner so that our country in the future would be as civilised as other countries in the world' (ibid., 163). The underlying logic was a reference to Western international society. For example, it was mentioned in the textbook that the Europeans were once barbaric, as in the case of the Africans. Siam, likewise, could become as civilised as the Europeans (ibid., 169).

The purpose was hidden with an incentive to enhance the national status: 'If countries have citizens with the civilised attributes as a foundation, such countries would be strong . . . because these citizens would not be a stooge to anyone' (ibid., 162). Drawing on this issue, the content of this textbook reflected the true intent of the Siamese. Since Siam's encounter with the West in the nineteenth century, it had been almost impossible to behave without any reference to the Western mode of living. The quest for self-identification of Siam, in this case, the quest for civilisation and recognition, had been embedded in the Siamese's worldview even before the outbreak of the Second World War.

It would not be until the 1930s that the history of the 1893 incident and other stories related to the lost territories appeared in Siam's textbook, *Prawattisart Sakol* [International History], which was composed by Luang Wichit (cited in Thamrongsak 2009, 147). And, after the 1932 revolution in Siam, the historiography of Siam's lost territories and the ideas of Western colonialism became clearer. As Wichit justified his history, writing: 'It was deep-rooted in the lives and minds of the Thai people, and it was an issue that we need to know the truth. Before, we dare not write or say about it. . . . But now . . . it is time to completely respect justice and truth' (ibid., 151–153). Although the traumatic history was not institutionalised until the 1930s, it was more likely that the Siamese leaders deeply and collectively remembered such traumatising memories. The details of such memories and anxieties will be discussed in the following section.

Aspirations of the Siamese

The Siamese elites were constantly concerned about their status among other powers. Their fervent attitudes with regard to the recognition as being independent and equal with others were second to none. The only viable option for Siam to avoid humiliation from others was to become one of the great powers. Such routes could not be achieved without recognition from others. Although the ambition of the general Siamese was notable, the crucial element was how the policy-makers perceived and interpreted the situation. The question was how Phibun and his cliques projected the vision of Siam to the world before coming to power. The perceptions of ontological insecurity with regard to the Siamese status were obvious. Firstly, they were ashamed of being recognised as a colony as opposed to an independent nation. As such, a struggle for recognition was strongly desired by the elites. Secondly, the memories of the loss of the territories were a provocateur and symbol of stigmatisation from the past. The sense of inferior position in the international system was historically tied to the lost territories. In other words, because Siam was not accepted as equal, their territories were ceded and sovereignty was trampled. These became sources of stimuli for Siamese redemption.

Phibun himself was no exception to the senses of grudge and inferiority. He and many of his fellow revolutionaries were awarded scholarships to receive education in Europe. As elite military and civilian personnel, the People's Party members including Phibun were exposed to progress, modernity, and civilisation in Europe. In the memoir of Prayoon Pramornmontri (1975), Phibun's confidante, when they were students in Europe, Phibun was harassed by the French border official. Prayoon recorded how the French official, after inspecting Phibun's passport at the immigration bureau, mistakenly thought that Siam was part of the French colonies; hence the quarrel ensued between the two nationals. The French officer mockingly responded that Siam 'was either a leech or dog flea, how can I recognise it' (103). Phibun, feeling vindictive and shameful, replied: 'Be cautious, some day the very leech and dog flea would annihilate the whole French nation' (103).

In addition, Prayoon (1974) himself also described how the British similarly intimidated him. His experience was written down as follows:

> When we visited foreign nations, firstly, we would be astounded by the progress of other countries which make[s] us rethink about the state of our homeland as to why it was left in tatters. . . . Moreover, we could not but feel offended for being insulted as a colonial slave. . . . When I arrived in London . . . I was grouped together with other blacks. I informed them that I am the First Lieutenant of the Siamese army which is an independent entity. But the British official was indifferent and smeared that if the Siamese were the British subjects, you would be satisfactorily treated. I felt numb and deeply hurtful.
>
> (3–4)

Not only Phibun and his colleagues encountered similar misgivings, but one of the conservative elites who was educated at Oxford such as Seni Pramoj experienced stigmatisation as well. For example, in his personal files documented when he arrived as Siamese minister in Washington in 1940, he noted that it was important to disseminate the information about Siam to the American public. The rationale was simple:

> From my observation, while I studied in England, most of the Westerners did not recognise Thailand, even if they knew, they mistook it as a colony of either France or Britain. This reason is enough for us to find ways to spread information about Thailand so that they know that Thailand is the only independent country in the Far East.
>
> (NAT-KoTo-0202/61-Washington-38/233)

The perception of Siam as a colony was painstakingly wounding for the Siamese elites. It rendered them existentially anxious. Phibun's son brilliantly captured the sentiment of the elites as follows: 'The backward nation is just like this. Its citizens were unavoidably insulted. . . . If they visit other countries, they would be humiliated by the white men as if they were colonial subjects.' (Ananda 1975a, 69).

Apart from the views of the elites, there were also widespread public sentiments in response to being excluded from the club of civilisation. They believed that the status of great power could secure the acceptance and place within the international system. After the revolution, a number of public letters from the Siamese were submitted to the government to voice concerns and opinions from below. Some of them were foreign policy recommendations for the People's Party, which were noteworthy because they were related to Siam's place in the world and the necessity to project power.

For example, a letter dated 25 December 1932 by Kum Srisuwan orderly addressed that '1. Siam is lesser than others. 2. Siam will be progressing. . . . I write to the People's Party to consider an option for Siam to expand the territory to the former areas' (NAT-SoRo-0201.25/109). Within the correspondence, Kum particularly specified that Siam must rescue other members of the Thai race who were under the tutelage of the colonial powers. The correspondence also hinted that in order for Siam to rise, territorial expansion was a prerequisite. In a similar vein, a letter in 1935 composed by Phraya Winaisoonthorn described how the people of the 'Thai race' resided in the territories ceded to the Europeans. Hence, Siam could find an opportunity to 'unify the Thai race living beyond Siam into a single country. Thailand then can become a greater power. A small country will become a great power' (NAT-SoRo-0201.25/772). This petition was seriously considered as it was forwarded to the meeting on 20 June 1935. In the same manner, a former Member of Parliament, Samarn Suchatikul, wrote to the government in June 1940 that Siam must annex French Indo-China and British Burmese and Malaya. If Siam incorporated those territories, 'we will have around 50 million populations . . . and will become a great power in less than five years' (NAT-SoRo-0201.25/821). Such a proposal was rubber-stamped by the Ministry of Defence for consideration. Such attitudes were reaffirmed when a member of parliament from Lampang Province enquired of the cabinet in the National Assembly whether they had considered an option to retrocede the lost territories back. The then premier, Phraya Phahol, politely replied that Siam adhered to the peaceful principles of the League of Nations which sought to pacify international conflicts. Hence, the question was dropped (TPMP 20/1934 [1935], 14 February 1934[2]).

In the publications of the time, there was a lot of discussion about striving to become a great power. For example, there were widespread copies of the book called, *Siam RorSor 112* (Khana-Yoowasarn 1934) which called for Siam to orchestrate its own 'Anschluss'. The resolve to initiate the Anschluss was amalgamated with the idea of parity and non-intervention from the Western powers. The book reasoned as follows:

> Had Laemthong [the Indo-Chine Peninsular – my note] had Anschluss, there would be no chance to write about RorSor 112. India was fallen under

> the protection of foreigners because there was no Anschluss. China was plagued by the power and sovereign rights of foreign intervention due to the absence of Anschluss.
>
> (1)

'Anschluss' represented the idea of uniting people from the same race together. Only through Anschluss could Siam be strong and be on par with others, hence the question of foreign intervention could be crossed out. The other relevant monthly journals of the time which spearheaded similar ideas were *Yuddhakos* and *Nawikasart*. In *Yuddhakos'* August 1938 issue, the journal published a lecture script in which Colonel Payom Chulananda discussed how other Europeans were afraid of Siamese Anschluss (TNA-FO371/22207-F10005/113/40). Such a strand of thought reflected how the Anschluss could be a building block for Siam's great power status and a stepping-stone to salvage the traumatic pasts of the nineteenth century. On this matter, an Indo-China French weekly newspaper reported that Siam was 'the frog who wished to puff himself up to equal the cow in size' (TNA-FO371/22207-F4660/130/40). The article accused Siam of pursuing the German, Italian, and Japanese paths in projecting power. In *Nawikasart*, one of the authors justified the reason for naval defence spending. To him, sturdy naval capabilities could preserve sovereign rights, maintain independence, and enhance the national status. Mighty vessels could elevate status and garner equal recognition from others as the author recalled that,

> Anyone educated in Europe and America might have understood that there was a slight chance that we would be insulted, mocked, discriminately suspected, and randomly labelled with different names. The solution in naval policy is to orchestrate warships to express our might in ports of foreign countries in order to show the world our ways of living, capabilities, power, and independent status of our nation and people. . . . Large naval vessels are considered in the world as elevating the status of a nation [Welt Geltung – Sense of worthiness to live in the world]. If we have powerful vessels, our national status will be higher.
>
> (Damri 1938, 870–871)

Hence, it was apparent that within Siamese society, the elites and other public figures exhibited a sense of resentment in relation to Western stigmatisation. As a result, foreign propositions were forwarded to correct the sense of inferiority. Stigmatisation often functions as a pretext to power projection.

Phibun's pre-premiership visions

The anxiety of the elites and their will to power before the onset of the Second World War was evident. The aghast emotion vis-à-vis the European powers was not mere rhetoric. It was translated into action as well. This was no more evident than in the case of Phibun's path to power in which he posed a tough stance against the British and French. In fact, the French and the British both realised Phibun's arduous position as indicated in the British correspondence. The Quai d'Orsay and British Foreign Office were concerned about the possibility of Siamese designs which could endanger the interests of the two European powers (TNA-FO371/22207-F7178/113/40). In 1938, French Minister Paul Lepissier revealed the intelligence to British Minister Sir Josiah Crosby with regard to how Siamese secret agents fomented anti-French activities in Indo-China and along the borders (TNA-FO371/22207-F10006/113/40). This was scouted by the French secret agents whom Crosby dismissed as unreliable and non-sensical (TNA-FO371/22207-F10430/113/40). Whether the war against the French was planned two years in advance, what was quite undisputable was the restless sense of the French counterpart. Such fear was palpable even prior to Phibun's ascending premiership.

Phibun had risen to political power following his heroic subjugation of the counter-revolutionary royalists in 1933. He became Minister of Defence in 1934. As a statesman of the small nation geopolitically situated between two powers such as France and Britain, he was expected to undertake a reconciliatory approach in relation to great powers. Nevertheless, his proactively toughened stance against the two European powers was manifested even before he became prime minister of Siam. This section investigates Phibun's proactive stance as Minister of Defence until the day he resumed power as Premier.

Phibun, undistinguished from others in terms of status concerns, wanted Siam to gain recognition as an independent power by others. For the nation to be respectable, he preferred a hard-line approach to express his aspirations. This was the basic guidance of his proactive foreign policy in subsequent years. Since the concept of status is inter-subjective, proactive behaviours to acquire status symbols are vital to recalibrate the perceptions of the others (Larson et al. 2014, 11). In Phibun's case, it was how he initiated the two prominent programmes which manifested his imperious behaviours. Such programmes were military consolidation and a strong stance towards the British and French. In other words, Phibun, as a policy elite of a small nation, punched above his nation's weight even before becoming a leader of the state.

Phibun believed that Siam would 'advance proportionately as its military advanced' (Charivat 1985, 97). His foreign policy and military thinking were unsurprisingly entwined with the desire to gain respect from others in international society. In one of his speeches, he praised Japan for becoming an emerging great power because of a large expenditure on arms. He also compared the successful cases of others with Siam as follows:

> On the Thai nation, any patriots would truly understand. One of the examples is how the Thai farmers once exported produces to others easily. But now it is not as smooth as before. We cannot do much but begging [sic] for them to buy our products. On the contrary, if we were Japan, France, and Java, we can export the products easily because these nations were respected and befriended.
>
> (Srikung 15 May 1937)

This reflected how Phibun interpreted the dynamics of international politics of the time. Abnegating the prowess of military capabilities was impossible. However, for Phibun, military modernisation was aimed not only to defend any encroachments but also for gaining respect and recognition from others.

As Minister of Defence, he sought to enhance military strengths. For example, on 31 March 1937, Phibun delivered a radio speech in which he remarked how the British and Japanese would eventually clash with one another and how the latter would strategically occupy Siam as a geopolitical base to launch an attack on the British colonies (NAT-[2]-SoRo-0201.4/18; TNA-FO371/21052-F2269/14/40). This was indeed a justificatory claim to enlarge the military budget. Such a tendency could be reaffirmed by his 1934 scheme to sell stamps, organise sports exhibitions, and plan donation campaigns in order to raise funds for military purposes (NAT-[2]-SoRo-0201.4/13).

During his tenure as defence minister, he brought about a number of military reforms. For example, he sought alteration of the Conscription Law in order to improve the living standards of the conscripts (Charivat 1985, 117). He negotiated deals to purchase five warships from Japan and three sloops from Italy (Srikung 2 September 1937). By dint of catching up with modern warfare of the time, he ordered four 320-tonne class submarines from Japan. Naval primacy could be marked as a sign of status symbols. Edmand Delage, a foreign observer, remotely and exaggeratedly commented that 'Siam has become an emerging naval great power' (translated in Suraphan 1978, 138). For the navy, sea ambition could be justified on the grounds of preventing infringement upon the nation's prestige. In order for other nations to respect a neutral country, strong naval capabilities was a prerequisite (Sub-committee of Maintaining the Military of the Naval Unit 1937, 3195).

In addition, in 1935, he established a military organisation for the youths called *Yuvachontaharn* which was modelled on Germany's Hitler Youth Movement, and it was rumoured that Prayoon, Phibun's aide, was encouraged to study such methods from the Third Reich (Stowe 1991, 93, 100). Phibun was implicit in his vision. On the one hand, he wanted Siam to become militarily robust so that the nation could progress proportionately. On the other hand, he also yearned to display how Siam was not an ordinarily backward colony but was equivalently cognisant of the values upheld in the international community. One of the reasons to form the youth organisation was notable. For Phibun, *Yuvachontaharn* would 'ground the foundations for the Thai nation and give birth to the new Siam. The new Siam needs *morality, culture, independence, and security* [my italicisation]' (Prachachat 4 November 1938). In short, the 'Phibun Youth Organisation' signified that, firstly, Siam would conform to international norms. Secondly, Siam maintained its own culture, unlike other colonies. And, thirdly, for the preceding reasons, it was an independent sovereign nation which deserved equal treatments.

Why were the military improvements so crucial? Did the facts that enlarging military expenditure, purchasing four additional submarines, acquiring six warships, and forming military youths could deter the surrounding powers such as

British Burma and Malaya, French Indo-China, and Japan? One of the naval officers admitted that Siam 'as a small nation and is still backward in capabilities could not shake other countries. That is, our independence is ultimately our peace' (Sa-nguan 1938, 2555–2556). It could be equivocally interpreted that despite a certain degree of military improvement, the Siamese capabilities could barely coerce other nations. The military spending from 1934 to 1938 was 26 per cent of the fiscal budget (Chai-Anan 1971, 154). On average, the Siamese spent roughly 26 million ticals a year (TNA-FO371/21052-F1496/164/40). On this matter, Phibun cited the relative expenditure between Siam and other powers. For instance, he confessed that in comparison to Britain, France, Germany, and Japan, the Siamese defence budget was rather minuscule (Thaimai 24 March 1936 [1937] cited in Suraphan 1978, 142, 144). It could imply that the Siamese buildup was a status-seeking measure. Given the fact of the time that the European powers loomed large in Asia and Japan became militarily stronger, Siamese preparations for a defensive war amounted to an impossible task. Phibun briefly summarised his intention as follows:

> When I was in a foreign country, I was asked about my nationality. When I told them that I came from an independent nation, they did not really care. On the contrary, when they saw another Eastern person and asked about the country of origin. That person replied that he was from Japan. That was all. I saw them converse on an equal and shoulder-to-shoulder basis. What set the Japanese apart? I think military capabilities were important. They made a country reputable and rendered our face important.
>
> (Publicity Bureau 1940b, 42)

In other words, military capabilities were not only a defensive tool but also an instrument to transmit a certain message. In this case, they were a means to promote the national status.

Another indicator of how Phibun desired equal recognition was his anti-Western attitudes. Phibun was notorious for stirring up troubles in foreign relations with Britain and France. The British Minister to Siam, Josiah Crosby, noted that after the 1932 revolution, the 'anti-occidental feeling' was intensified within Siam. Crosby analysed in his memorandum to London that it was,

> due in part to the overbearing attitude assumed in [the] face of them by so many of those who belong to the white races; but even more than that it is due to a consciousness of their own inferiority to the white man in many respects. I will not venture upon an opinion as to whether this inferiority complex is well grounded in itself. . . . The fact remains that the complex is there with its unavoidable reactions.
>
> (TNA-FO371/22214-F10000/1391/40)

Crosby further amplified that one of the responsible factors was the ruling elites 'who have acquired that easy familiarity with the West which comes from long residence in occidental countries' (ibid.). In other words, this was what was mentioned earlier regarding the anti-Western sentiments developed during the formative years of the Siamese elites. The anti-Western feeling, for Crosby, contributed to the jingoism which 'enhanced self-assertiveness which is the characteristic of the new Siam [referring to Siam after the 1932 revolution – my note]' (ibid.).

An act of valour against the Europeans, for Phibun, represented intransigence vis-à-vis those with equal status. His defiance was consistent with Crosby's description. In 1937, the British protested against the articles published in the Siamese naval journal, Nawikasart, and requested censorship from the government. In the May 1937 issue, there were articles which discussed how military improvements were important for the nation. In a letter to the editor, the author noted how military might was 'now the motto of civilised countries. . . . Let all the Siamese support the defence plan of the government' (NAT-KoTo-80/325). Moreover, the British complained about the map printed on page 1405 of the journal. The caricature pictured a sleeping Siam while arsenals from British Burma and French Indo-China were directed towards the Siamese (ibid.). Pridi, the Ministry of Foreign Affairs of the time, forwarded the messages from the British representative to Phibun.

Upon receiving the dispatch, Phibun, as a defence chief, issued a secret memorandum on 14 June 1937 in response to the British reprimand. The secret Ministry of Defence document clearly stated that:

> It is necessary to embolden the spirits of the citizens and pointed out the significance of defending the nation. . . . Thus, writing and explaining to the citizens in a straightforward manner is important. Beating around the bush would not be working. We should announce further that 1. Being a colony is awfully distressful. 4. With regard to the map with surrounding foreign armies, it naturally concerns us. . . . Had Britain and France did not increase the capabilities, there would not be such a map. These two nations are the causes and it is wrong to blame others. . . . The Ministry of Defence . . . has considered and concluded that we can reply in a straightforward fashion. . . . Because this is how we feel, and if we answer otherwise, they would not believe us anyway.
>
> (ibid.)

This was unexpected from the elites of a small state. Instead of apologising instantly and humbly, Phibun refused to compromise with the British. He diverted blame to the European powers. This was because of his realisation that if Siam was viewed as an equal sovereign, unaccommodating the British demand was judicious. Besides, military matters and public opinions were confined to internal affairs. Hence, Phibun found no grounds to issue an apology. Pridi had to intervene to solve the problem on behalf of Phibun by raising an excuse that Phibun's comments did not pertain to any bad intention (TMCM 4/1937, 12-May-1937).

Apart from the feud with Britain, France was another power to which Phibun would show no sign of weakness. As mentioned earlier, the French and British were anxious about how the Siamese would resort to an irredentist war, and such a tendency became tangible for the border peoples in Siam. According to one secret document in July 1938 from the Defence Ministry, it was reported that the French fomented seditions along the border, which was the North-Eastern part of Siam, and the Siamese residents in the areas lost morale accordingly. The document expressed grave concerns and possible counter-measures to execute in response to the reported situation (NAT-SoRo-0201.35/1).

Phibun suggested to the prime minister that the Siamese government should organise events to boost morale through a cunning plan. Eventually, the cabinet agreed to launch a propaganda scheme to inform the local residents that Siam was not inferior to others. In a circular dated 23 July 1938, the cabinet outlined the strategy to mitigate the anxiety of the people through pictures and films which glorified the supremacy of the nation. It was stated in the document that the Publicity Bureau should 'proceed through speeches and pictures such as pictures from certain films that portrayed the mastery of the army, navy, and air force in order to pacify the Thais' (ibid.). Such a technique was primarily aimed to signal a message to the two audiences: the Siamese residents and the French. Firstly, it was meant to inform the Siamese that their nation was not second to others. Secondly, and by the same token, the move transmitted the message to the French that Siam would not conciliate with any powers. However, the strategy was not an endeavour to subdue the French. It was fundamentally driven by the status concern. This was shown in the ultimate part of the document which cautioned that the propaganda and speeches 'should not escalate into defamation and hatred of other countries' (ibid.). Such a statement reflected how the Siamese elites did not prefer to be recognised as inferior. They also did not seek to escalate inter-state tensions into armed clashes.

Phibun as prime minister: seeking status

In December 1938, Phibun was elected by the Assembly to become Siam's premier. He had been widely recognised for initiating a number of nationalist programmes to re-engineer Siam. The fact that he populated a variety of social renovating enterprises was generally regarded as his nationalist wishes without any reference to international implication. Nonetheless, upon closer inspection, Phibun's social reforms targeted both the internal subjects and international audiences. Such political and social enterprises were often neglected from the explanation of the courses of proactive foreign policy. This section contextualises Phibun's first two years as prime minister (1938–1940) in order to establish how the concerns for status resulted in a certain course of foreign policy.

A child becoming an adult

In his policy statements delivered to the parliament when he became premier Phibun mainly focused on upholding the Six Principles of the People's Party. This was unquestionably a tussle to achieve independence in the areas of politics, the economy, and judiciary. In foreign affairs, he pledged to enhance relationships with other countries (TPMP 3/1938, 26-December-1938). In the first cabinet meeting, the centre of gravity was an agenda to revise the existing unequal treaties with every nation (TMCM 1/1938, 20-December-1938).

Phibun understood that there was an incoherent tendency between the Foreign Ministry and Defence Ministry. Oftentimes, it was thought that, at the outset, the former strived to compromise whereas the latter sought to jeopardise the foreign relations. He clarified such administrative conflicts in the cabinet meeting as follows:

> Military theory is dependent on bluffing. What the Ministry of Defence has done was to help the Ministry of Foreign Affairs. . . . Some interpreted that the Foreign Ministry tries to revise the treaties but the Defence Ministry obstructs the process. But for the sake of success, we need to bluff to show that we have power just like Hitler, for example. In fact, we do not follow Hitler because we have done bluffing before Hitler's campaign in Czechoslovakia. We shall not proceed to that extent. We need help. We want to succeed in revising the treaties.
>
> (ibid.)

It was clear that Phibun's ferociousness against the foreign powers stemmed from the will to settle the unequal treaties with foreign powers in order to be on equal footing. Generally, it could be read as a dual-track strategy. What was reflected was his ideational foundation to gain recognition from others through resolving the existing unequal treaties. Such foreign policy thinking could also be grasped from the conviction of Phibun's reputable advisor, Prince Wan (1943):

> The initiation of relations with the Western civilised nations was limited by the extraterritoriality, which jeopardised the national independence. Ultimately, we modified the civilisation to complement the Thai culture in order to get entry into an international community.
>
> (8)

In other words, the Western approbation was a pre-condition of the government to further other foreign policy initiatives.

The negotiations with 13 countries to revise the treaties had been initiated, at least, according to the British records, since 1935 (TNA-FO371/19379-F2639/2639/40). In order to reach status parity, complete independence should be attained. The treaties were the remnants of the unequal treaties signed in the late nineteenth century, which incorporated Siam into the international system. The agreements basically preserved clauses which maintained extraterritorial rights for nationals of foreign powers. For instance, foreign consuls could withdraw its citizens from the Siamese court. Moreover, in the existing protocols, Siam could not raise taxes and tariffs beyond a specific rate (Charivat 1985, 100–102; Vinita 1975, 116–117). In other words, these stipulations were symbols of unequal status and non-recognition. If Siam were accepted as an independent sovereign, there would have been no such unequal treaties. Seni expressed the sentiment in his private memo that the existing treaties should be revoked because they represented a 'substance form of inequality' (NAT-KoTo-0202/61-Washington-38/233). As such, the treaty revision 'was a major matter of prestige' (Stowe 1991, 92).

Although the treaty negotiations began prior to Phibun came to power, the abolition of the unequal agreements with foreign powers was finalised on 13 February 1939 (TMCM 10/1938 [1939], 13-February-1938 [1939]). It appeared that Phibun suggested that the cabinet accolade Pridi and other relevant officials who accomplished the mission with medals (ibid.). A foreign observer noticed that after the conclusion of the new treaties with other powers, Siam was 'putting in a stronger and more sovereign position in the eyes of the world than she had ever assumed before. . . . Siam now enjoyed genuinely full and equal rights as an independent country' (Coast 1953, 10–11). For Siam, the treaty revision elevated the status of Siam into the spotlight of the civilised nation. Crosby noted that the significance of the treaty revision negotiations marked 'the recognition of her right as a member of the Family of Nations to negotiate with the various Treaty Powers on a basis of entire equality, full autonomy and complete reciprocity' (TNA-FO371/24751-F3326/19/40). In this regard, Phibun decided to celebrate the historic event on 24 June 1939, which was then the national day of Siam.

The evidence, which indicated that the Siamese elites were concerned about the status of the nation, could be interpreted from the ceremony of the national day in 1939. After the 1932 revolution, 24 June of each year was marked as a national day. Nevertheless, the annual national day had never been celebrated before 1939. Therefore, 24 June 1939, which was proclaimed the Celebration Day of the Nation and Treaty Revision, was, for the first time, set to become a national festivity (Somsak 2004b). In preparation for the ritual, the government's propaganda on the virtues of the treaty revision reflected the thoughts of the elites. For example, a song was composed to sanctify the accomplishments. Part of the lyrics was '(after treaty revision), Siam become civilised. Thais should help Thais and there will be prestige. . . . We are free and equal, not more or less, in comparison with other nations' (NAT-SoTo-0701.23.1/6, 145). Phibun also announced that because Siam improved every dimension to conform to the standards of international society, 'other countries respect Siam, and every nation was willing to revise the treaties to unshackle us. Thailand have [sic] complete independence in areas of justice, politics, and economy' (ibid., 324).

There were also a number of similar propaganda projects to inform the citizens of the success of Siam. On the celebration date, it appeared that the government publicly sacralised 13 treaties to covey the messages that Siam attained independence. But most importantly, the government initiated a project to rectify a monument in commemoration of the admission of Siam into the club of equality. The monument, according to the Phibun cabinet, would be located in Paknam (ibid., 324), which was the place where the French gunboats coerced the Siamese to accommodate their demands in the nineteenth century. It was a historic site which signified the inferior status of Siam in the international system. The construction of the so-called 'Independence Monument' in this area was an attempt to overcome this traumatic past. This tendency could be verified by a letter forwarded to the prime minister which articulated that the construction of the monument at Paknam was related to 'human psychology significantly. . . . It was unarguable that the Independence Monument at Paknam was to show to other foreigners to think about our independence' (NAT-SoTo-0701.41.1/26). For others and the navy, it was also an honour and prestige in the eyes of the world (ibid., 11).[3]

At the ceremonial location, the government invited foreign diplomats to witness the sacralisation of the new treaties. Siamese consuls around the world organised ritualistic events. In Paris, a Thai minister, Bahiddhas, had stated that the consent of the foreign governments to repeal the treaties was the 'indication of the status of the nation which displays credibility. This is because of our 4–5 years of mission [reforms] which illustrates our progress in front of their eyes' (NAT-[2]-SoRo-0201.97.3/7). A Thai minister to British Malaya viewed that the treaty revision was meaningful for foreign policy because it 're-calibrated relations with other nations on the basis of equality' (ibid.).

Although the 1939 national day symbolised the maturity of Siam, it did not imply that the Siamese elites were no longer concerned about recognition and status. Srisena, a Thai minister to Tokyo, offered indicative words of encouragement:

> In the national day, I beg you to help expand our nation. We have built ourselves for almost 1,000 years. . . . We need to help each other . . . to become as great as other powers in the near future. . . . If we carefully consider further, we can see that the civilisation and culture of our nation were needed to be modified in order to be on an equal footing with other civilised countries. (ibid.)

Srisena's remark was noteworthy of analysis for two points. Firstly, Siam was constantly worried about its place among others. Secondly, for him, in order for Siam to be recognised as equal, or at least to attain equality, certain cultural standards should be practised and adjusted to impress other nations. This was consistent with Phibun's thoughts. In Phibun's 24 June 1939 speech (Publicity Bureau 1940b), he hinted that: 'We live in the world with other nations, we must conform accordingly' (30). By this, Phibun meant that his nation should modify many aspects in order to receive status recognition as he mentioned: 'If we consider it seriously, it can be seen that our civilisation and culture should be improved and enhanced so that we can be on par with other Western civilised nations' (34). He justified his view by comparing it with the sense of patriotism: 'If our love of this nation from now on is not equal with others', our nation cannot be independent along with other nations in the long run' (39). In short, Phibun implied that without proper cultural modifications in conformity with international standards, there would be no recognition from other civilised nations. And Siam could not survive eventually. Such a statement reflected the sense of ontological insecurity and shame from the Siamese elites.

In order to surpass such shortcomings, Phibun aimed to launch social-engineering projects to transform the face of Siamese society. Such grand programmes were famously known among Thai specialists as 'Ratthaniyom' or 'State Conventions'. They were generally associated with the nationalist policies of Phibun (Charnvit 1974; Thamsook 1977). However, beyond a simplistic nationalist claim, the formation of the State Conventions could also be interpreted as the Siamese elites' sense of existential anxiety and the motivation to be recognised. Phibun remarked in his national day speech that,

> The government prepares to announce and invite Thai people to follow certain practices in the near future. . . . We call it "Ratthaniyom". It is the practice which should be traditional mandates of the nation. . . . Ratthaniyom is similar to the manners of how the civilised should do. . . . Same as we have heard stories from the civilised countries.
>
> (Publicity Bureau 1940b, 39–40)

It was doubtless to say that the State Conventions could be read as a product of nationalist fervour. However, such a nationalist sentiment stemmed from the sense of ontological insecurity in the eyes of the others. During the stage of infancy, the justificatory rationale of the State Conventions was the reference to the standards of civilisation and acknowledgement of international society. The emulation of the standards of civilisation was a continuous attempt since the 1932 revolution (Nakarin 1989). It is argued by Nakarin (1989), a prominent historian, that the People's Party believed that the human revolution should also follow the political revolution (244–251). Similarly, for Phibun, politics, economy, and society did not constitute a civilised nation. Culture, however, was an indicator that a nation could step along with foreign powers (259).

Culture was a tool to manifest the status of a nation. It was a means to guarantee physical and ontological security. The two components were intertwined. Considering the fact that the European powers expanded influence throughout the globe and Siam was the only state which maintained independence in the region, in order to safeguard against the physical threat, recognition as a civilised nation became crucial to prevent justifications that Siam should be a target of civilising missions. Phraya Anumanrajadhon, one of Phibun's advisors, suggested that culture was a cradle of respect. In order to be respected, an internationally acceptable culture was a significant foundation (ibid., 260). The new Siam of Phibun should acquire a dignified culture in the eyes of the world (Thamsook 1978, 40). Additionally, the dire international situations such as the Sino-Japanese war and the imminent outbreak of the European war of the time were complementary factors which determined the policy directions. As Kobkua (1995), an expert on Phibun, noticed that because the war loomed large, 'the need for reform became more urgent as Thailand had to achieve the same cultured society status as the allied countries' (111). Hence, the implementation of cultural reforms during the period was indicative of how the elites were anxious about the nation's place in the world.

Siam becoming Thailand[4]

The State Conventions were the means for status mobility in the international system. From 1939 to 1942, there had been twelve State Conventions issued for the citizens to follow. Although there were 12 prescriptions, certain Conventions should be brought to light.[5] In June 1939, the government had formed a committee to discuss the socio-cultural engineering programmes (NAT-SoTo-0701.29/5). Phibun rationalised the formation of the committee as follows:

> The dress of the Thais is mostly disordered and distasteful for others . . . such dismay could be a window for foreigners to claim that the Thai nation is underdeveloped and immoral, and not deserved to attain complete independence like other nations. . . . Hence, in order to correct the flaws, we should convince the Thais through the State Convention style.
>
> (TMCM 11/1939, 5-June-1939)

The committee was thus formed and given a task to correct 'flaws' and 'blemishes' from Siamese culture. Scot Barmé (1993), a specialist in Luang Wichit who was Phibun's trustee, explained that,

> [the flaws and blemishes] were defined as the unsightly dressed and undisciplined social behaviour of the population . . . which made the country seem "unprogressive" to foreigners and therefore unworthy of retaining independence.
>
> (144)

In other words, these cultural projects were not domestic, they were exogenously driven, to be presented to other nations. Backward and childish elements of the society should be re-moulded.

The first State Convention was to change the official name of 'Siam' to 'Thailand'. According to Wichit, one of the reasons to rename the country was to celebrate the treaty settlement (NAT-SoTo-0701.29/4). It was also a symbol of the new Siam which became truly independent (Barmé 1993, 147). For Wichit, 'Siam' was a misnomer given by the Ancient Cambodian Kingdom (Somsak 2004a, 84). Phibun, for example, proposed that one of the reasons to change the name was because 'during this time, most of the foreigners do not recognise Siam, if we change the country's name, we can take a chance to popularise our country' (TMCM 4/1939, 8-May-1939). Other relevant State Conventions such as the fourth, sixth, seventh and eighth proclamations, which were primarily based on saluting the new national anthem, inspiring people to build the nation, and revising the lyrics of the national song, were promulgated to present the new face of the nation. Charnvit (1974), a well-known historian, comments that such conventions were decreed 'in an effort to create a psychological feeling that the country was entering a new era' (39).

The name-changing scheme implicated the intention and subtly defined the national interest of the government. It was meant to correct inferior scars that the elites had long adopted. This could be interpreted as follows.

Wichit purveyed the idea that the Thai people should be classified on a racial basis. He was captivated by a Thai map shown by the École Française d'Extrême Orient, which portrayed the areas from Southern China, Burma, Laos, and the Golden Peninsular, where there had been inhabitants of the Thai-speaking people (Barmé 1993, 148). In the cabinet meeting, Wichit indirectly purported the idea that by calling it 'Thailand', it would cover those Thai-race peoples scattered beyond the Thai borders (TMCM 4/1939, 8-May-1939; and see selected transcripts of the cabinet minutes from Somsak 2004a, 81). He proudly announced in one of his radio broadcasts that the Thai-race peoples were 'independent because they regard themselves as Thai, which means a great nation and no stooge to anyone' (ibid., 85). The word *Thai*, in the Thai language, refers to being free and independent. However, Wichit further insinuated that freedom and independence could be maintained if a nation became another great power. And, in order to expand, manpower was crucial (see Wichit's speech on this substance in Murashima 2005, 346–347). He addressed the public that Thailand had a population of 13 million circa. By including the Thai-race peoples residing in China, British Burma-Malaya, and French colonies, there would be 36.5 million people approximately (ibid., 84). He, in a closed-door cabinet meeting, offered Phibun a map which covered the areas where there presumably were Thai-race inhabitants (see Figure 4.1). This at least signified his genuine intention with regard to the stigma correction. A historical observer put that the new name signalled 'to the "Thai" living outside its borders that the country represented the foundation for a "Great (er) Thai Kingdom"' (Ferrara 2015, 115). In this connection, the third State Convention was edified to discourage the Thais from dividing the 'Thai people' into sub-groups.

The ulterior motive of the first State Convention was to define the territories where, if possible, Thailand could incorporate the peoples in order to achieve the great power status. This intention was reflected when Wichit suggested that the name of Thailand in Chinese character should be written as *Daguo* (大国) instead of *Taiguo* (泰国). Despite his confession that *Daguo* might be inaccurate in historical terms, he justified that the pronunciation of *Daguo* bore a resemblance to the name of the great family in Southern China and further admitted that such characters had a good meaning because they referred to 'a big country' and were often used for a complimentary purpose (TMCM 72/1939, 27-December-1939).[6]

The great power aspiration was rife during the time Phibun came to office. One of Phibun's mottos was that if 'if we do not want to be a lackey, we need to become a great power' (Manit 1997, 96). Such a tendency to project power

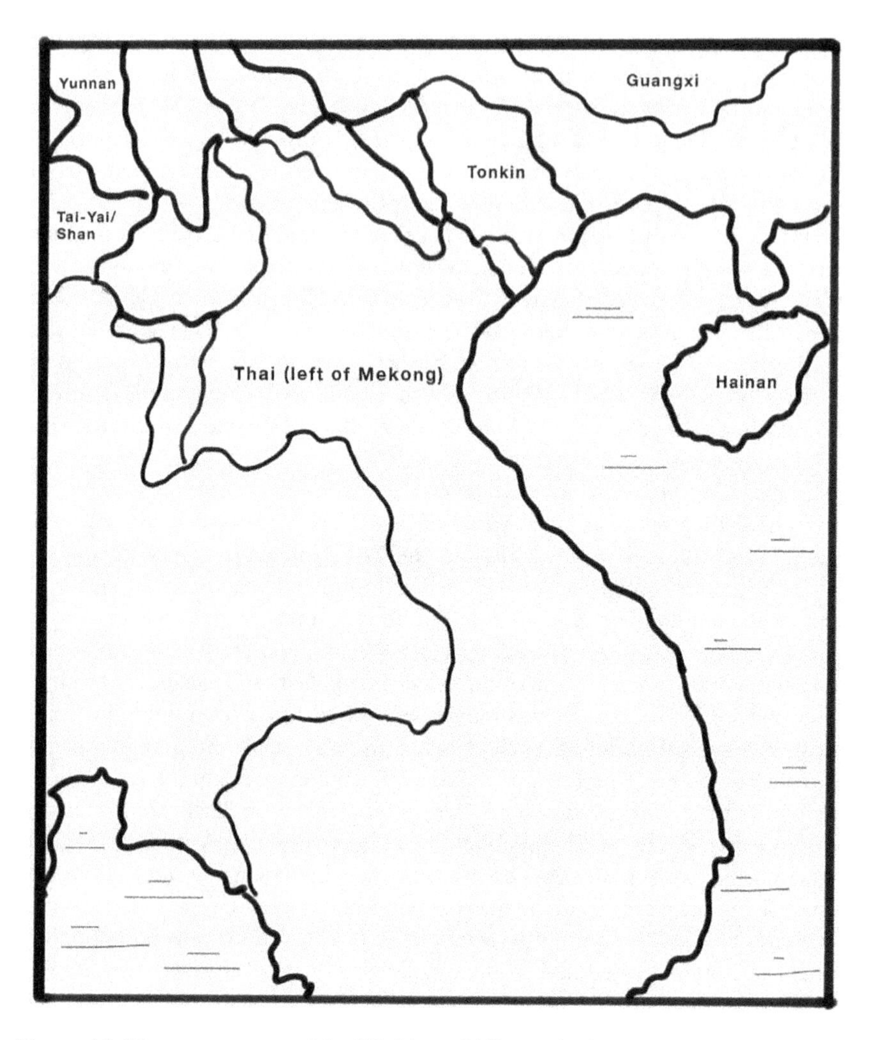

Figure 4.1 The map presented by Wichit to Phibun which covered the Thai race in Mainland Southeast Asia[7]

was later emphasised by him in an interview given to reporters, which Phibun requested for content reservations:

> For any countries in the world, there are two choices: It is either becoming a great power or suffering as a lackey. There is no choice for a middle ground. What was meant by a great power does not mean a super great power, but the sixth or seventh-ranked power, which means we can preserve ourselves. . . . I predict that in the future, there are only two choices of either depending on ourselves or becoming a subject of others. Being under the

> control of others can vary into different methods, that is, it can be direct and indirect. But they are the same. . . . Small nations in Europe will be governed by others. It is an inescapable era.
>
> (NAT-[2]-SoRo-0201.92.1/6, 4–5)[8]

In short, achieving a great power status was indispensable for Phibun. The pursuit of great power status was, at least in Phibun's philosophy, to avoid being a subject of powerful countries. He in no way wanted Thailand to be seen as a lackey. From this point, it could be insinuated that a name-changing course and other correction enterprises were aimed to show others that Thailand was not lost in history but was worthy of recognition.

Dresses and duties

Although the name-changing practice was to cast an independent display to the world, the elites constantly felt that the Thais and their ways of lives could be misconstrued by others as anachronistic (NAT-SoTo-0701.29/4). Prior to the celebration of the 1939 national day, Phibun was aghast at the public unruliness during the New Year day. The clearest case was how the people tossed rubbishes at the pageant beauties (NAT-[2]-SoRo-0201.45/7; TMCM 11/1939, 5-June-1939; Nakarin 1989, 256). Such boisterousness was worrisome for the elites. In order to establish a sense of existential security, Phibun's government further regulated socio-cultural practices.

One of the notable initiatives was the tenth State Convention on attire. According to the government declaration, the Thais were not expected to appear in public without proper clothes on top. The countrymen, moreover, should dress properly in a Western fashion (Barmé 1993, 156). Wearing hats by men and women should be habitually practised. Long trousers, as opposed to shorts, became a central mode of the outfit. For women, the imitation of the Western clothing style such as putting on gloves, wearing skirts or blouses, and seeking a pair of high-heeled shoes became a mandate (ibid., 157). Indecent clothes were stigmatised as uncivilised. The government was thoughtfully determined over the measures on attire to the extent that they ardently enforced civil servants to dress properly as a leading example for the people (see circular order numbered 1847/2484, 7-June-1941; 2338/2484, 1-August-1941 in Office of Prime Minister 1990). The elites genuinely believed that the transformation of how the Thais dressed could uplift the status of the nation to 'the equal of civilised nations' (NAT-SoTo-0701.29/1; also cited in Barmé 1993, 157).

Phibun also claimed that both China's Sun Yat-sen and Turkey's Kemal Ataturk had similarly undertaken the dress policy adjustment (ibid., 158). According to the eleventh State Convention, the Thais were encouraged to behave in a Western-civilised manner. The Thais should obtain social etiquettes, for example, bathing in public was strictly forbidden (see in detail from Kongsakon 2002). The government also accentuated this point to the civil servants. One of Phibun's circular orders, for example, expounded how mannerisms should be ingrained into the habits of the Thais. The order raised an example of how the English would be bashful if they were accused of not being 'an English gentleman' (circular number 1075/2483, 3-May-1940 in Office of Prime Minister 1990). Therefore, values such as helping children, prioritising elders, or supporting people with disabilities (twelfth State Convention), queuing in a line, and other similar civilised etiquettes should be strictly followed (ibid.).

The programme was intensified when Phibun's cabinet ratified the 1940 National Culture Maintenance Act manner and the 1941 Royal Decree Prescribing Customs for the Thai People (Act and Decree translated by Kobkua 1995, 115). Basically, the two legal papers were passed to punish anyone who failed to become civilised in appearance and manner. The essence of the laws, as explicated by the official document, was

> to understand that in preserving national prestige, the Thais should practise it so that we are seen as a civilised nation and a nation that has equal dignity as other developed nations. . . . And, in particular, the dress should be re-ordered, changing the usual demeanours. . . . The Thais should not dress in a way that damages the national honour.
>
> (NAT-[3]-SoRo-0201.55/8)

Any policy often produces dissenters. This was no exception. There were inevitably arising criticisms against such transformative policies (NAT-[3]-SoRo-0201.55/7). However, Phibun's response was to construct a series of reasons to sustain his vision. The reason given reflected his existential apprehension vis-à-vis foreign nations. It was stated in the 178/2484 official circular that,

> Once the Thais adopted the lousy and barbaric culture, it would incur deplorable feelings in front of the eyes of the global people who have higher culture. For example, the Africans have a despicable culture. They dress improperly, merely using leaves to cover their parts. Their houses are untidy and full of diseases. They sustain their lives by catching animals. As such, they could not be independent, and ultimately, the countries with higher culture would intervene . . . citing the cause of peace for other nations in the world, which eventually they will lose independent status, or become colonised.
>
> (ibid.)

As regards the quest to be on an equal footing with a civilised nation, cultural engineering programmes were intricately tied to status concern and recognition. For the government, backward behaviours would not earn Thailand a civilised status. The elites would be ashamed of his nation as suggested by the circular:

> If we dress like a savage, when foreigners see us, they will insult and try to help us dress, citing the purpose of enlightening us with a culture. . . . If foreigners look down on us, it will be a cause for us to be difficult in establishing relations with other nations. As an easy example, suppose we put on

> silk pants to dine with British diplomats, it is believed that we would not be invited again, and cannot befriend other British.
>
> (ibid.)

Phibun gave a complement to the reasons in this circular and wrote in his handwriting that 'these should be published' (ibid.). It could be conjectured that for Phibun, progress, culture, and status should be developed altogether.

Conclusion

Since the 1932 revolution, the elites generally possessed a continuous sense of ontological insecurity. The policy-makers who had been educated abroad similarly experienced how the European powers barely recognised their proud nation's existence. They were anxious about the nation's status and possible repercussions. For them, the struggle for recognition was necessary. Hence, in order to overcome the sense of inferiority in relation to the club of the civilised powers, Thailand's great power aspiration was widely advocated, and Phibun's reception of the idea was evident.

Phibun's ideational precept was coherent even before he had stepped into premier office. As defence minister, he had commenced a range of policies such as increasing military expenditure, promoting defence reforms, and concluding lucrative arms deals. He also reacted negatively towards the British and French despite apparent relative limitations in material capabilities. Once he became prime minister, his status concern remained intact and became an impulse for him to undertake a number of initiatives such as the State Conventions. The celebration of the 1939 national day symbolically marked the new era of the nation. It implied that Thailand had risen. The event redefined the national identity and interest of the nation. The name-changing arrangements and socio-cultural modifications mirrored the government's ontological insecurity, desire to gain recognition from others, and status-seeking behaviours. For Phibun, in order to overcome the sense of ontological insecurity, Thailand must garner recognition and seek status. It must achieve equal status with foreign powers, and, in order to reach those ends, other nations should recognise it as such.

These descriptions ground a foundational context for an analysis of Phibun's foreign policy. The status anxiety of the elites became an integral element which shaped subsequent foreign policy choices of Thailand. In other words, a concern about status played a constitutive role in the cases of Thai foreign policy towards France and Japan. These cases will be discussed in the following chapters.

Notes

1 *Geography Volume One* was very influential. It was first published in 1902, and the copies were estimated to be almost three million. Although there was no exact record of *Geography Volume Two*, it would be safe to assume that this textbook series was widespread and powerful in Siam (Thongchai 1994, 184–185).

2 Before 1940, Thailand's new year began in April, which was the traditional calendar. Hence, in this case February 1934 is February 1935 according to the international calendar.
3 See further technical discussions from the navy from the Fine Arts Department document within the same folder numbered 1231/1939, dated 6 July 1939.
4 'Siam' is substituted by 'Thailand' hereafter.
5 The twelve Conventions can be enumerated as follows:

    1 State Convention on the Name of the Country
    2 State Convention on Prohibiting the Thais to act as a Foreign Agent
    3 State Convention on Calling Thai Peoples as 'Thai' without Categorising them into Northern Thai, Southern Thai, or Muslim Thai
    4 State Convention on Saluting National Anthem
    5 State Convention on Domestic Consumption (Economy);
    6 State Convention on the Lyrics of the National Anthem
    7 State Convention on Encouraging the Thais to Build the Nation
    8 State Convention on Revising the Word 'Siam' to 'Thailand' in the National Anthem
    9 State Convention on Civic Duty of Citizens and Proper Usage of the Thai Language
    10 State Convention on Proper Dress
    11 State Convention on Guidance of Routine Lives of the Thais
    12 State Convention on Helping the Children, Elders, and People with Disabilities

6 In the cabinet meeting, Wichit's objective was later dismissed on the linguistic ground because '大' must be employed as an adjective. The examples from the minute were '大日本' (great Japan) or '大中国' (great Middle Kingdom). Therefore, Thailand should have its own character before employing '大' (TMCM 72/1939, 27-December-1939).
7 The original copy was prohibited from taking a photograph. Somsak (2004a) similarly floundered, so he searched for a similar map. I drew the map based on Somsak's figure.
8 The collection of these documents, titled 'Interviews with Prime Minister', was an interview with Phibun. Oftentimes, Phibun felt compelled to leak his genuine opinions and requested the interviewers to sweep them under the carpet.

Part III

Thailand's two gambits

5 Beating goliath for prestige

Thailand's war with France

The eruption of war between Thailand and the French in Indo-China was a major issue for Thailand in late 1940. The development of the policy of neutrality of Thailand during the initial stage of the Second World War to the Franco-Thai conflict involved large-scale movements of the Thai masses. The flexible foreign policy approach generally outlines how Thailand rarely becomes proactive in foreign affairs. As such, a small nation such as Thailand challenging France is commonly unintelligible. This chapter illustrates how Thailand's war with France was brought about because the Thai policy-makers were concerned about Thailand's international status vis-à-vis the great powers. The chapter demonstrates that Thailand's proactive foreign policy stemmed from the nation being stigmatised as inferior.

Structural opportunities and the choices of Thailand

Phibun was obsessed with the standing of his nation even before becoming premier. The context before the clashes broke out between Thailand and France was the commemorative event which characterised the complete elimination of the unequal treaties with the foreign powers and festive elation. This section traces the development of Thai foreign policy from the early months of Phibun's premiership until the conflict with France became intensified. It shows that Thailand, during the outbreak of the Second World War, was nothing but a small state with a limited revisionist aim. It had some territorial ambitions and great power aspirations. Instead of balancing or bandwagoning with any greater powers such as Britain, France, or Japan when there were structural changes, the Thais first chose to adhere to neutral diplomacy. As this chapter illustrates, the status concern was eventually a catalyst for war, but, initially, Thailand did not exploit aggressive policies even when the opportunity presented itself.

Observing strict neutrality

On 1 September 1939, Germany blitzkrieged Poland. The event sent shockwaves throughout the world. Two days later, France and Britain declared war on Germany. Adolf Hitler's ambition to engulf Europe was responded to by a united coalition between Britain and France to counterbalance Germany. The two empires were preoccupied with European affairs rather than colonial enterprises, but the situation made it mandatory for Britain and France to mobilise men from their colonies to deter the Germans. The development of European politics at the time presented a great opportunity for Thailand to launch an attack on either France or Britain, or to demand territories. Instead, the Thais declared a neutral stance.

Thailand aspired to become a great power. Nevertheless, for them, the road to status and recognition in the early days of the war should not involve overt aggression. Before the outbreak of the war, the influential newspapers of the time such as 'Tai Mai' and 'Bangkok Times' similarly echoed views that Thailand's commitment to neutrality would be difficult to maintain. More or less, the colonial rebellions in the British and French empires would affect Thailand's neutral position. Perchance, if the Japanese sought the Far East domination, she would, according to an analyst, need the aids of Thailand (TNA-FO371/23595-F4252/1850/40). From such an observation, taking any side was not a favourable option, whereas upholding neutrality would be equally impossible. How should the elites cope with the policy dilemma?

It is necessary to juxtapose the case of Thailand into context. The European war broke out three months after Thailand had announced its new status to the world. As discussed in the preceding chapter, the national day on 24 June 1939 was an audacious occasion which marked the transition of the nation from child to adult. Therefore, there was a sense of self-esteem and pride among the Thais. For example, the song was composed to describe how the 'Thais would walk along shoulder-to-shoulder with foreigners' (NAT-SoTo-0701.23.1/6, 73).

Even though a number of socio-cultural schemes of Phibun mirrored the great power aspiration and status recognition, it did not readily translate into Thailand's territorial aggrandisement. One of the Italian diplomats of the time secretly suggested to Direk Jayanam, the then Deputy Minister of Foreign Affairs, that since Siam had changed its name to Thailand, 'it means that [the Thais] have a nationalist idea. You have to think of waging war or will suffer like Czechoslovakia' (NAT-[2]-KoTo-1.1.5/6). In short, Thailand was encouraged by another fascist nation to embark on a course of aggression. Direk, however, responded that,

> Thailand now is different from the past. It is awakening. The reason we enhance military capabilities was not to fight against anyone. We befriend anyone. . . . But we need to improve our country because we have been slumbering for a long time.
>
> (ibid.)

From Direk's statement, it was safe to assume that Phibun's military improvements prior to the war were aimed to enhance the status of the nation. There is other evidence which indicates that Thailand's intention was bereft of opportunistic ambition in 1939. The private conversation between Paul Lepissier, the French Minister to Thailand, and Phibun in August 1939 revealed the anxiety of the French and the foreign relations posture of Thailand. Lepissier teased Phibun about the rumour in Indo-China of the secret agreement between Thailand and Japan which resulted in the crackdown on Chinese in Phibun's domestic policies.[1] Phibun snickered, denied such a rumour, and clarified that it was all 'internal affairs and nothing relevant to politics' (ibid., 34). Similarly, Josiah Crosby, the British minister envisaged the possibility of the Anglo-Japanese war and the violation of Thailand's neutrality. He mentioned to Direk that the British should purchase more fleets in Singapore to monitor neutrality in Southeast Asia. Direk reported that he 'concurred with the British Minister' (ibid., 24). This was at least a portrayal of how the elites were untiring to remain neutral in the early periods of the European war.

In this regard, following the eruption of the war, Thailand formally declared its neutral status (NAT-SoRo-0201.33/12). The following question was whether Thailand's policy of neutrality was genuine. Was it a mere façade to assure other powers? According to the British records, firstly, Phibun had issued a Royal Proclamation for the Thais to uphold neutrality. The message was clear: 'All Thai authorities and subjects, and all persons residing in Thailand are ordered and commanded to observe strict and impartial neutrality in and the said state of war' (TNA-FO371/23596-F11457/1860/40). Secondly, he secretly informed Crosby that his own 'countrymen had no reason for coming into the war' (TNA-FO371/23595-F10315/1860/40). Thirdly, the government prepared the navy and air forces to secure the nation's neutrality in case there was an imminent attempt to invade Thailand. Crosby noticed these three points and presented his observations to the British government. Additionally, the document concerning the Convention Respecting the Rights and Duties of Neutral Powers and Persons in Case of War on Land concluded by the family of nations in 1907 were circulated among ministries in order to prepare for a common understanding among the officials (NAT-SoRo-0201.33/11; NAT-SoRo-0201.33/14). The Thai Premier also delivered a statement beseeching his people to act neutral towards foreigners (NAT-SoRo-0201.33/28).

The implication of the policy of neutrality could be subject to different interpretations. Despite Thailand's great power aspiration and Phibun militaristic tendency to invest in military capabilities, Thailand turned towards neutrality. Before becoming a leader, Phibun had acted in an uncompromising way towards the European imperialists. He similarly boosted arms spending as defence minister. The message of his daunting deeds in relation to the policy of neutrality was obvious: Phibun's defiant behaviours were a result of his outright denial to be identified with an inferior identity by others. Hence, when the war in Europe exploded, the government did not seize an opportunity to revise the status quo by force. This was evident in Phibun's opinion when the European war started:

> [Regarding the war between Britain-France and Germany – my summary]. . . . Joining with any side would not bring us any benefit. Before, we fight for reputation. But now, we have everything that we need such as independence in judiciary and tariffs and the treaties with foreign powers are on an equal basis.
>
> (TMCM 47/1939, 2-September 1939)

The statement suggested that Thailand's interest was primarily defined by its concern about status and recognition from foreign powers. Following June 1939, the Thai leaders were content with how their nation was accepted as one among equals. Henceforth, taking sides in the European war would not contribute to Thailand's status and recognition. As a result, the Thais opted for neutrality.

Negotiating the non-aggression pacts

After Thailand declared neutrality, Britain and France approached the Thai government for Non-aggression Pacts. Such military agreements would be a guarantee for the European powers of Thailand's commitment to inaction in the time of turmoil. In fact, the British and French counterparts had never fully relied on Thailand's stance. A British diplomat had speculated since 1936 that Thailand's neutrality would be bound to break down into hostility against the British empire (TNA-FO371/22215-F5586/2113/40). Hence, both powers had sought the Non-aggression Pacts with Thailand even before the explosion of the European war (TNA-FO371/22207-F10968/113/40). Since 1938, the Thais were offered such treaties to ensure peace and stability in the region. They, however, turned down the offer for fear of antagonising the Japanese (ibid.).

As a test case for Thailand's stance, the context of the European war and the imperial mobilisation from the colonies presented a window of opportunity for Phibun to justify the nation's territorial expansion. In September 1939, it was wired to Phibun that partial mobilisation was conducted in French Indo-China along the Thai borders (NAT-SoRo-0201.35/2). Trenches along the Thai-French areas were built, and the Indo-China governor instructed the locals to report to officials if any Thais crossed into the French-controlled territories (NAT-[2]-SoRo-0201.86/45). More infantrymen were reinforced later in June 1940 (NAT-[2]-KoTo-2.4.1/76). Similarly, the Thai consul in Singapore reported to the head office that there was also partial mobilisation in Penang, British Malaya. Moreover, one battle fleet and 12 submarines were deployed to station in the Southeast Asian colonies from Hong Kong (NAT-[2]-SoRo-0201.86/91). Furthermore, 3,000 aeroplanes were stationed and more troops from India were to be reinforced in the Malay Peninsula (NAT-[2]-SoRo-0201.86/88). Additionally, the Thai nationals in Malaya were surveyed to have an aversion towards the British (ibid.). These conditions were preferable and yet unfavourable to the Thai elites. The defensive movements along the borders of French Indo-China and British Malay could be perceived as a threat to national security. Nonetheless, with both empires' preoccupation with the European affairs, the Thais had a justificatory cause to wage a defensive war either against the British or the French.

Once the war in Europe became critical, Britain and France wished the conclusion of the insurance treaties with Thailand more than ever. Thailand was in a position to bargain heavily or to rebuff the bids from the Europeans. There was little doubt that the Thais would prefer to negotiate provided that certain diplomatic exchanges could be settled. Although both the British and the French were suspicious of Thailand's intent, the Thais fully understood the power differential between itself and other great powers as Phibun had warned his cabinet:

> In reality, it is difficult for a small country to invade a bigger country. France's objective to sign the Non-aggression Pact with us was to demonstrate that she has a proper moral value. This is to tell other countries that she would not bully a small country.
>
> (TMCM 74/1939 [1940], 10-January-1939 [1940])

For the Thais, the pacts signified an abstract value. Phibun personally informed his cabinet that the propositions from the European powers to ink the mutual non-aggression agreements were the symbolic gesture of recognising Thailand's status:

> These treaties [Non-aggression Pacts] are our objective. Because we are a smaller country than they are, their willingness to conclude the agreements with us means that they honour us.
>
> (TMCM 12/1940, 11-June-1940)

To reemphasise the matter, the Phibun regime recently declared itself as an equal nation to the world in June 1939. It was not surprising that status and standing were central to Thailand policy-makers. The pacts had both material and symbolic meanings for the Thai elites. The Thais surmised that the French and British did not have to offer an agreement in order to seek a security guarantee from a small country, but the pacts would reassure Thailand's physical security along the borders and symbolise the recognition of Thailand's status.

The questions for the Thais were as follows: How should they respond and what should be included in the Franco-Thai bargain? In the nineteenth century, Thailand had ceded territories to France and Britain. Burma and Malaya were ceded to the British, whereas Laos and Cambodia were relinquished to the French. Although there was an irredentist sentiment among the Thai elites, a policy of territorial aggrandisement was not a prerequisite because it would violate the principle of absolute neutrality. However, Thailand had been informally acknowledged by the two European powers as a buffer state since the nineteenth century. Instead of demanding the whole lost territories from Britain and France, the Thais, as a matter of diplomatic quid pro quo, called for border delimitations with both Western nations to resolve the lingering issues, which were the historical remnants of the unequal treaties with France.

In fact, the Thai government had identified the delimitation problems with British Burma and formed a committee to seek preventive measures in 1935 (NAT-SoRo-0201.20/2). They wished to delineate the borders with France and Britain on the basis of 'deep-water channel' or 'thalweg'. In 1938, the British counterpart expressed goodwill to settle the boundary issues according to the principle of thalweg along the Burma-Thai borders (NAT-SoRo-0201.20/3).

Similarly, Thailand had proposed to redraw the Franco-Thai boundaries by holding the deep-water channel in 1936. The French, however, were reluctant to reciprocate (Thamrongsak 2009, 184). It was inevitable for the Thai elites to feel that the British prized their relationship and status much more than how the French downplayed Thailand's sense of honour.

Hence, the Thai cabinet was readily prepared to agree to the British concessions. Direk suggested to the cabinet that an issue with the British was not as concerning as with the French because the former was willing to settle the border questions. He concluded that 'in dealing with France, if she proposes to negotiate, we should get along with them. But, a common understanding for us should be two issues: 1) the Pact and 2) the thalweg. These two should be inseparable clauses' (TMCM 74/1939 [1940], 10-January-1939 [1940]). Wichit and Phibun were more than straightforward: 'Had the French dismissed the thalweg proposition, we should reject the agreement' (ibid; TMCM 73/1939 [1940], 3-January-1939 [1940]). Instead of compromising with France to ensure a matter of national security along the borders, the Thais were inexorable in their aims. The reason for Thailand's determination was also a concern about standing. Crosby (1945), who had been part of the negotiations among the three nations, described that the islets in the Mekong along the Franco-Thai borders were,

> of no intrinsic importance, but many of them, little more than sand-banks, were united to the Siamese mainland at the season of low water. . . *it can be readily understood that their subjection to French jurisdiction must have proved embarrassing to the Siamese* [my emphasis], upon occasion, from the administrative point of view; for instance, a criminal escaping from Siamese territory to one of these immediately adjacent islets became immunes [sic] from arrest by the Siamese police.
>
> (117)

The frontier ambiguity was embarrassing for a sovereign nation. For a small country that was seeking respect for its stature from the international community, the application of the international law was of absolute necessity to express a sign of sovereign equality, unlike how the colonies and semi-colonies were treated. Thailand after 1939 was different from other colonial protectorates as they officially proclaimed:

> The existing border demarcation does not conform to the principle of international law and justice. But it was determined by the French arbitrariness. According to the international law, if the frontier is close to the river, the deep-water channel should be marked as a border. The British-Thai delimitation has been based on this principle for a long time.
>
> (NAT-[2]-KoTo-2.7/29)

On the subject of the frontier revision, as a Nippon-Thai historian, Edward Thadeus Flood (1969, 309), noted, the French would 'agree to redress some long-standing injustices on the Franco-Thai border including the thalweg issue' (309). For the Thai elites, this implied that the European power acknowledged injustices committed against them in the past and signified that the new phase of the Thai nation garnered adequate international recognition. In brief, the process of frontier readjustment between Thailand and France represented whether the European nation would regard the status of Thailand. The existence of the boundary ambiguity had been a source of shame for the Thais. Resolving the lingering boundary issue would mean receiving respect from France.

The British and French fully realised that the Thais reserved a number of options to move and Thailand would be better without the presence of the Western powers (TNA-FO371/23596-F11460/1860/40). Yet the Thais sought a path of tranquillity amidst an incentive to exploit a window of opportunity. In order to avoid an accusation of colluding with Japan, the Thai government extended the signing of the pact to the Japanese as well (Direk & Keyes 1978, 14). This move reshaped the calculation of the British because they were anxious about the Japanese influence over Thailand. In this regard, the British encouraged the French to accede to the Thai assertions or else they would solely sign a contract with Thailand at the expense of the French entanglement (TNA-FO371/23596-F11516/1860/40). For the Quai d'Orsay, the Thai requests were seen as 'frank and brutal methods' (TNA-FO371/24751-F2819/19/40). In contrast, Lepissier, the French representative in Thailand, even sympathised with the Thais. For him, the Thai demands were 'just and reasonable' (TNA-FO371/24751-F3326/19/40). On this matter, Lepissier personally understood the historical values attached to the deal from the Thai views.

In March 1940, the French resolved the matter by yielding to the Thai request and proposed to appoint a representative to discuss technical issues (TMCM 83/1939 [1940], 13-March-1939 [1940]). However, France introduced one condition prior to the ultimate terms. France, with the concurrence of Britain, wanted Thailand to incorporate another clause which stipulated that the British could revoke the pact if the French were merely threatened or fully invaded (TMCM 1/1940, 15-April-1940). The emerging proposition implied that if the Thais planned to invade France, the British could act as a force of deterrence. For the Thais, signing the pacts was an honour. As such, Phibun conveyed a message to Prince Wan, his advisor, that 'if they want us to agree with the invasion deal, we can go along, but we need to govern the islets' (ibid.).

There were two points for Thailand to consider. Firstly, the European proposition of the Non-aggression Pacts was considered an honour for the Thais. However, as a matter of quid pro quo, Thailand regarded the chance to negotiate as an opportunity which could enhance their standing as well. Henceforth, the border revision was the fulcrum of the negotiations. Secondly, if the French failed to adhere to the Thai claims, then the Thais would be more than willing to renounce the Franco-Thai Pact. Simply put, they would prefer to gain nothing at the expense of an unsatisfying outcome.

In summary, the Thais wished for the adjustment of the frontiers along the Mekong with France as a condition for further negotiation. The proclamation in June 1939 marked the era when Thailand redefined its identity and interest; that is, the Thais anticipated the French to recognise them as an equal, sovereign nation. As a result, they demanded an exchange from France and would not finalise the agreement unless their claims were accepted. Prince Wan (1943), the government's advisor, summarised this point as follows:

> Thailand has a modern form of governance and becomes a country with complete independence. We therefore try to adjust borders justly and improve international relations for peace and enhance co-operation on an equal basis. This is the principle that can preserve perpetual peace.
>
> (79)

Because the Thais felt that British Burma and French Indo-China were their former territories bequeathed to the imperialists, the Celebration Day of the Nation and Treaty Revision in June 1939, which redefined the national identity as an equal nation, generated an immense implication for Thailand's foreign policy direction. As an equal, sovereign nation, border alteration should be considered fair and square by both parties unlike the period of imperialism. On the one hand, concluding the pact with France would guarantee Franco-Thai peace along the borders, particularly for a small country such as Thailand. On the other hand, the Thais decided to prioritise the question of frontier modification at the expense of safeguarding national security even though the border adjustment scheme was of minor material value. In other words, the Thais were fully prepared to select the choice of breaking the deal, which would not be beneficial at all.

The conflict of passion

What factor compelled Thailand to become proactive towards the French? This section illustrates how misrecognition and disrespect to Thailand's pride resulted in the small state rising against the great power. It also portrays the interplay of a feeling of ontological insecurity and foreign policy formulation in the case of Thailand's preparatory measures against France.

Phibun's proaction: extending the demands to France

The French were reluctant to satisfy Thailand's objectives of border revision. However, they were desperate for insurance so that when the tide in Europe turned against them, the Southeast-Asian colonies would not be in peril. In early June 1940, the development in Europe was unfavourable to both France and Britain because the Allied forces were vanquished by the Germans whereas Belgium surrendered. Additionally, on 10 June 1940, Italy declared war on France and Britain. The situation tipped the balance towards Thailand to withdraw from the Non-aggression Pacts. It was not deranged for the British and French to foresee the possibility of Thailand retracting its contractual commitments. Therefore, the French and British worried that Phibun, who absconded to the South of Thailand, 'might perhaps delay indefinitely signature of non-aggression pacts' (TNA-FO371/24751-F3326/19/40).

Contrary to what the Europeans fretted about, the abrupt change by the Thai counterparts, the Thai cabinet was more than resolved to sign the pacts with the three powers on the same day. On 5 June 1940, the cabinet meeting unanimously agreed that the three pacts should be signed on 12 June 1940 (TMCM 11/1940, 5-June-1940). Although the Allied powers were in a disadvantageous position, the pacts were ritualised on the designated date. It was noted by the local newspaper that Thailand had 'a long record of strict observance of treaty engagements' (Bangkok Times 12 June 1940). The conclusion of the treaties, as observed by the paper, was 'considered as a further application of the policy of equal friendship' (ibid.). For the Thais, the finalised deals were a sign that the status, prestige, and rights were honoured because the French accepted the deal and the pact was signed. Crosby viewed that June 1939, which pinpointed Thailand's new period in its history, was of utmost importance. Hence, the Non-aggression Pacts between Thailand and the Western great powers 'may be judged of equal significance with other agreements [the revision of unequal treaties]' (TNA-FO371/24751-F3326/19/40).

Almost a week after the proclamation of the pacts, France fell to Germany and the Vichy government was established as a neutral entity. The change of the regime in Central Europe did not affect the terms negotiated with France. One of the Thai Members of Parliament enquired about the revocation of the pact due to the annihilation of France. Direk replied that the change of government would not 'affect the treaty signed. However, it will be completed after the process of ratification' (TPMP 4/1940, 18-July-1940). One former member of parliament submitted a policy letter to the Prime Minister's Office to encourage the government to invade French Indo-China and reclaim the lost territories. The letter was dismissed as 'absurd and should be dropped' (NAT-SoRo.0201.25/821). The Thai cabinet, even a month after France succumbed to Germany, focused on the preparation of treaty ratification and frontier adjustment with the contractual partners (TMCM 18/1940, 17-July-1940). The premier even consoled his people to forget about the hatred against France: 'I beg you . . . to forget that past and think of it as only a bad dream' (Direk & Keyes 1978, 20).

By dint of the mounting ambiguity in the Franco-German armistice, the former Grande Empire formulated a diplomatic chicanery strategy to delay the discussion about the border demarcation with the Thais. The French representative was not appointed to settle the technical issues regarding the frontier question. Worse, the Vichy government pressed for the treaty to come into force without proper ratification between the two nations. Henceforth, the French demeanour fed on the sense of mistrust held by the Thais. The Thai government therefore became apprehensive about the French reneging on the border arrangements (Flood 1969, 311–312).

For the Thai policy-makers, France's move was seen as disrespectful and insulting. Since the phase of negotiating the pact, the French played down the significance of the Thais by exchanging semi-official letters between the two nations instead of official pledges. Such practices were considered an insult to the Thais (Charivat 1985, 148; TNA-FO371/24751-F3326/19/40). Once again, the French expediency previously mentioned irritated the Thai leaders. As Phibun secretly revealed his grudge to the reporters:

> This [French tactics – my note] is a disease of a liar. Ultimately, it won't end. I adhere to the principle that, in diplomatic negotiations, one cannot prevaricate. Or else, what would be the value of the international law and international credibility? . . . If official agreements are untrustworthy, we should not stay in this world. Let's go to live in hell.
>
> (NAT-[2]-SoRo.0201.92.1/6, 7)

The Thais were agitated by how the French did not apply the principle of international law and did not entrust credibility to the Thais. In the context of the mid-twentieth century, there were only the colonies, which were not accorded proper treatment on the basis of international law. Phibun's indignation could be translated to the fact that the identity of the Thais was not recognised by the clubs of the sovereign powers. As Michelle Murray (2014), a scholar investigating the problem of recognition in IR, observes:

> If a state's identity is not recognized, however, it suffers disrespect because in being denied membership in the collective, the recognition-seeking state can be represented as "illegitimate" or "second-rate". . . . In response to the insecurity associated with the experience of disrespect, states engage in a struggle for recognition, which can become the motivational impetus for conflict among states.
>
> (135)

In the case of Thailand, its policy-makers became ontologically insecure about their status and identity. Bangkok increasingly felt that Vichy's evasion was an insult to their pride. Although Phibun was apprehensive about the status of his nation, he, however, calmed his people by saying that 'any changes [frontier adjustment – my note] should not be rushed. The government has been looking into the matter' (Publicity Bureau 1940b, 137). The French trickery triggered the psychological anxiety of the Thai elites into thinking that they did not receive proper recognition. This became grounds for Thailand to formulate a proactive foreign policy.

Despite France's evasiveness, in August 1940 the Thai cabinet remained faithful to the pact with France. However, Phibun proposed the idea that, apart from the original border revision blueprint, the Thais should expand demands to France. He suggested that Thailand and France must adopt the Mekong River as a natural frontier between the two nations (TMCM 20/1940, 7-August-1940). Having the Mekong River as an international boundary was for a strategic reason. Technically, the implication was unequivocal: Thailand would gain certain territories from France in order to redraw the Franco-Thai border (Figure 5.1).

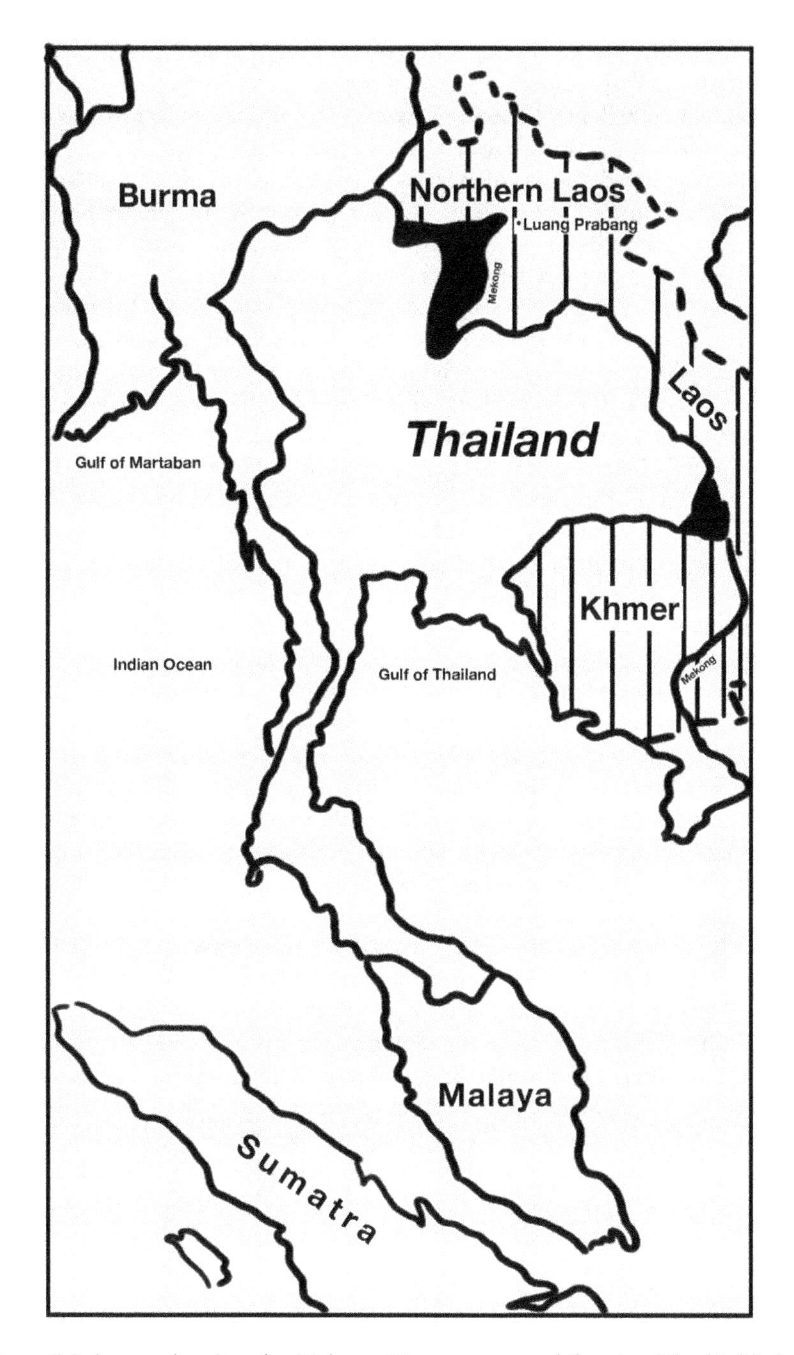

Figure 5.1 A map showing the Mekong River as a natural frontier. The highlighted areas (dark only) are the territories that Thailand would gain.

The extension of Thailand's demands was borne out of indignation towards France's deceitful play, which was seen by the Thai leaders as an affront to their nation's dignity. Phibun's reiteration represented Thailand's resentment as follows: 'Our original request, in fact, was intended . . . so that the historical animosities between the two countries would disappear. But when it becomes like this, our original demands vanish' (NAT-[2]-KoTo-2.4/65).

Phibun predicted that Japan, which was associated with the Berlin-Rome Axis, would soon venture into French Indo-China. In order to achieve his goal, the premier designed a diplomatic strategy in order to negotiate with both the governor of the French and the Japanese cabinet. He was sceptical about the Japanese southern advance. Therefore, he dispatched a goodwill mission to Japan by passing through the French Indo-China route. Because Thailand had committed to strict neutrality, the government did not want to be seen as siding with any war parties. Hence, the Thais similarly appointed other goodwill missions to other European nations such as Italy and Germany, and the Commonwealth of Nations such as British Malaya and India as well (TMCM 20/1940, 7-August-1940). In short, there were three groups of emissaries which would be visiting the world in the name of enhancing friendship. Another motive, however, was to draw international recognition on the Franco-Thai dispute. Nonetheless, the centre of gravity was the mission to Indo-China and Japan.

Colonel Mangkorn Phromyothi was a principal envoy in the mission to Indo-China and Japan. During his voyage to meet with French Indo-China Governor Jean Decoux Phromyodhi's démarches were the border issues and the possibility of the alliance between Thailand and French Indo-China against Japan. According to Flood (1969), the talk 'with Decoux was doomed from the start by the imperious attitude of the Frenchman' (318). An offer from the Thais to form an alliance with Indo-China against the encroachment of Japan was entirely rejected by the stubborn governor (318). Decoux, in conclusion, expressed an insulting attitude towards the Thais (Flood 1967, 278).

On the contrary, Phromyothi's subsequent mission to Tokyo was nobly received. He was rewarded with the Japanese Emperor's Sacred Treasure (NAT-[2]-SoRo-0201.86/17, 83). Prior to the visit, the Thai government was contacted by the Japanese to authorise the envoys with the full power (ibid., 79). Moreover, Japan offered to promote the diplomatic status between the two countries from the ministerial to the ambassadorial level. The rising Asian power similarly proposed other economic and cultural agreements as well (TMCM 22/1940, 21-August-1940). Whether Japan's intent was benign or malign, it was inevitable that Bangkok would maintain a heartfelt perspective towards Tokyo because they acknowledged the stature of the small nation. The comparison of treatments between the two great powers unsurprisingly influenced the perception of the Thai elites on how to react towards France in times of conflict. Although there was no substantial breakthrough from the missions, Phibun voiced a satisfactory tone. Nonetheless, at the end of the day, he never wanted to 'rely on the Japanese, but by himself' (NAT-[2]-SoRo-0201.92.1/6, 5).

As for the Japanese, they had been preoccupied with their campaign on Mainland China since the 1930s. The retreat of France from her grandeur disrupted the balance of power in the region. Asserting influence over Indo-China would increase the strategic advantage of the Imperial Army in surrounding Chiang Kai-Shek. Henceforth, the Japanese played down an offer of military co-operation to Phromyothi's visit (Charivat 1985, 182). For them, partitioning Indo-China should be subject to the disposal of Tokyo, not Bangkok. Thailand's firm presence in Indo-China would complicate the Japanese grand strategy. Exploiting a feeble French Indo-China, on the contrary, was much more preferable than dealing with both Thailand and France altogether. Thus, Japan omitted any possible military commitments with Thailand and decided to manage the Indo-China affairs on their own (Jones 1954, 234).

The political landscape in Southeast Asia had been altered by the Japanese military campaign. On 3 September 1940, Decoux received an ultimatum from Japan to allow the Japanese passage through Indo-China. Subsequently, the French governor acceded to the Japanese request and granted the necessary military facilities to the Imperial Army (NAT-[2]-KoTo-2.4.2/90, 135). The Japanese pledged to respect France's sovereignty and territorial integrity of Indo-China. However, Tonkin would be utilised by the Japanese Army (ibid., 65). The opportunity was ripe for Thailand, a small nation with a revisionist interest, to engulf the desired territories. Decoux became restless to the extent that he pressed for the pact to come into force again without proper ratification. Despite Decoux's overbearing arrogance, Lepissier, the French minister in Bangkok, upheld a different view as regards the case of Thailand. Clearly, there was a division of opinions within the French policy-makers (Flood 1967 306–308). As previously mentioned, he sympathised with the Thais in the matter of the territories, Lepissier even comforted Phibun by suggesting that if the French Indo-China administration could not preserve its sovereignty, the French would retrocede Laos and Cambodia back to Thailand (TMCM 22/1940, 21-August-1940). Phibun therefore announced in the cabinet meeting that 'we should take them back. But we want them for free' (ibid.). By this, he implied that the quest to regain the territories should not affect the policy of neutrality. Strictly speaking, although the condition was accommodating, Phibun did not want to achieve his goals by force, as he told the cabinet that 'we are pursuing a swing policy in order to remain neutral all the time' (TMCM 31/1940, 23-October-1940). Even Wichit, Phibun's aide, who was alleged to be an architect of the foreign policy of aggression, suggested that Thailand *should not* co-operate with Japan because 'the victor is the one who does not enter the war' (TMCM, 2/1940, 17-April-1940).

Pressured by Decoux to neglect diplomatic etiquettes and influenced by Lepissier's propositions, the Thais informed the French that they would promulgate the Franco-Thai Pact without ratification to enhance friendship. However, three conditions were presented to France. Firstly, the Franco-Thai border should be demarcated on the basis of the deep-water channel. Secondly, the border revision should be adjusted by embracing the Mekong River as a natural boundary.

Thirdly, France must relinquish Cambodia and Laos to Thailand in case the sovereignty of France over Indo-China was undermined (NAT-[2]-KoTo-2.7/29; TMCM 25/1940, 11-September-1940).

A rational-materialist explanation might suggest that Phibun's territorial design was to enhance manpower in order to become a great power. It was indisputable that Thailand's capacity would be enlarged from territorial annexation. This, however, was not how the statesman of the time regarded the issue. In accordance with Phibun, he partly wished to acquire those territories because 'the Thais could make use of those lands' (NAT-[2]-SoRo.0201.92.1/6, 6). This bore a resemblance to Hitler's concept of *Lebensraum*. Nonetheless, the cost of incorporating those territories outweighed a fair rate of return. Phibun fully knew the price to pay as he informed the reporters:

> In reality, those territories . . . have nothing. Rice cannot be cultivated and the people have to buy it from us. Apart from that, there is nothing. Economically speaking, if we repossess those areas, it is going to pain us . . . because we have to nourish them heavily. And not only the lands, we will also have to nurture the people culturally.
>
> (ibid., 6–7)

The perception of the policy-makers was obvious: there were foreseeable consequences had the Thais outwitted the French into relinquishing the territories. And during the time of war, administering the new territories would impose a high cost on the state budget.

Moreover, Thailand's claims towards France ran against a strategic perception of itself. One could crudely argue that Thailand's proactive gambits stemmed from the collapse of France. But, as an earlier discussion suggested, the Thais barely exploited the windows of opportunities to invade the French territory. Yes, the French empire was a history in the 1940s' context, but it did not imply that a small nation would risk a military campaign for the territories that would be an economic burden for them. Phibun's son, Ananda (1975b), who was a military man, recounted the views of the Thai elites that the defeat of France in Europe was *not* a rewarding opportunity for Thailand because 'during that time, France maintained the armies throughout her colonies, especially, the troops in Indo-China, which were scarcely affected by the European war' (57). Colonel Luangyuthhasarnprasith, the governor of Nongkhai, the Thai province which was close to Indo-China, similarly thought that the Thais were not well prepared for any war (Rome 2009, 145). According to a Thai diplomat's memoir, Thailand during the time had only six divisions of the military, which were well equipped to wage war (Konthi 1984, 20). Even Phibun admitted later: 'In fact, French Indo-China is stronger than us. For example, their military lieutenants are the level of our professors' (TMCM 10/1941, 26-February-1941). If Phibun desperately wished for war with France for territorial gains, as the standard accounts conventionally propose, how could they explain the periods from the fall of France in June 1940 to December 1940? Yet some might argue that in mid-November 1940, the Thai state formed the Headquarters of the Commander-in-Chief of the Thai Armed Forces as a preparatory measure to wage war against the French. In reality, as the confidential cabinet minutes revealed, the formation of such headquarters was aimed to defend the nation if Japan fought against Britain and France (TMCM 36/1940, 13-November-1940).

Thailand's diplomatic overtures vis-à-vis France could fuel the possibility of war, which would be unpleasant for the nation. From what was described above, the strategic and economic points of view, Thailand was not ready for war. Such material hurdles should have thwarted the Thais from a proactive tendency, but the three bold propositions to France were unmovable. It is important to question Phibun's motive in this case.

Thailand's requests were predicated on the political reality that the French empire was incapacitated in Europe and Asia. Phibun believed that 'our territorial demands would not be successful as we expected' (NAT-[2]-SoRo-0201.92.1/7, 7). The reason, in his words, was because of 'the pride and prestige of the great power that once threatened us. Giving up lands to us would tarnish their reputation' (ibid., 7). If Phibun speculated that his demands would not bring about a satisfying outcome, why would he extend the demands to France? On this question, he explained that

> The three territorial demands we requested from France, if we are to be frank, we might not receive any land. In fact, our demands are not truly a territorial claim. *It is to symbolise that Thailand has lifted our status already* [my emphasis]. It is a combination of international politics.
>
> (NAT-[2]-SoRo.0201.92.1/7, 10)

As a matter of fact, Phibun secretly told the press that since the tide in Europe had turned favourably towards Thailand, the policy of territorial retrocession could enhance his nation's standing:

> I am afraid that the people would demand the territories. . . . It would be too radical and could become inappropriate. . . . Frankly speaking, if we receive those territories, I would be more than happy because we could gain reputation.
>
> (NAT-[2]-SoRo-0201.92.1/4, 9)

Apart from Phibun, Wichit also suggested in one of his speeches which could be summarised as follows: 'the idea of territorial demand was the idea of the nation with the prestige which could not stand other nations bullying us. It is all about preserving our honour' (Supaporn 2003, 66). In other words, the territorial scheme stemmed from the psychological insecurity that the Thai elites encountered. Therefore, the proactive foreign policy move was constructed to test their status and to earn recognition from the great power. In this case, presenting the three territorial propositions would be a litmus test on Thailand's recognition and could bring about a material gain as well.

Thailand's status trepidation could be seen from Phibun's speeches. The Thai prime minister also conveyed a message which confirmed his ontological anxiety:

> We have changed our ways of life so that we can walk shoulder to shoulder with other civilised nations. . . . We have changed enough so that others could not brand us as a barbaric nation. We all should call ourselves "civilised Thailand of Asia".
>
> (Publicity Bureau 1940b, 138)

Although he viewed his cultural programmes as a successful transformative tool to Thailand's way of life, he was constantly insecure about his nation's recognition and acceptance. This was evident in the premier's statement in the cabinet meeting:

> Thailand should have culture, which is on par with other nations, or else there would be no country that wants to get in contact with us, or if they contact us, they would portray their status as more developed than us. This would deprive Thailand of prestige and become inferior. . . . But if our culture is on par with the others, we can preserve our honour, independence, and everything.
>
> (TMCM cited in Saeng 1993, 118)

He later admitted in a closed-door parliamentary session that the reason he was anxious about civilisation was because it 'was the most important element' (TPMP 10/1940, 29-August-1940, 312). The premier emphasised that conforming to the global society would 'garner praises from other developed nations' (ibid.). The relationship between cultural civilisation and foreign policy was significant as he admitted that

> Our territorial demands were just. When we become an adult . . . we befriend other adults, therefore we need to improve ourselves. . . . The Thais need to modernise their ways of lives. This would be an additional element of a country that demands territories. We want them to perceive that we are developed and could maintain a good culture. . . . [If foreigners think we are culturally backward – my note], the Parisians would scornfully remark that the small nation of this stature should not deserve any territories.
>
> (NAT-[2]-SoRo.0201.92.1/7, 12–3)

Recognition and status were the reasons why the Thai elites paid heed to the State Conventions mentioned earlier. In many of the premier's speeches, he stressed the significance of modernising the hearts and minds of the Thais such as dress, duties, and disciplines. According to Phibun, backward culture could be an excuse for the French to mock the Thais that the underdeveloped nation with people who dressed improperly 'is too overconfident to demand the territories. The French colonies are fully developed because of the French' (ibid., 14). In short, the demands from Thailand were originated from the search for psychological validation and the sense of ontological insecurity that the Thai policy-makers acquired.

The Quai d'Orsay, just as Phibun had a premonition, was enraged by the Thai proposals. They abruptly answered with a fierce tone which reflected the sense of superiority of the European master. The core messages of the French memorandum could be summarised as follows. Firstly, France considered that the situation in Indo-China was not unusual. There was no compelling reason for the Thais to be concerned about the issue of sovereignty of the French protectorates. Secondly, the French government was determined to defend against demands and attacks from any directions, which could jeopardise the territorial integrity of Indo-China. Thirdly, the Thai claims on the areas on the right bank of the Mekong were unacceptable, and the renunciation of Laos and Cambodia was unjustified (TMCM 27/1940, 25-September-1940).

The Thai government responded accordingly. Firstly, the fact that Japan stationed their imperial troops in Indo-China could not be read as normal by Thailand. Secondly, for the Thais, those claimed territories were historically and emotionally significant. Although they had been deprived of those lands for many years, they have considered the inhabitants as belonging to the same race. Denying Thailand's rights to reclaim their former lands and branding their requests as unjustified directly damaged the pride and prestige of the Thais. It was outright disrespect of their historical values. According to *Nikorn*, the then newspaper, it was observed that 'We have requested the return of our territories . . . but instead of negotiating France shows us only contempt' (cited in Strate 2009, 54). Recognising the value of equality is, according to Charles Taylor (1995, 250), an acknowledgement of one's worth. On this question, Reinhard Wolf (2011) suggests that,

> Being denied social confirmation of one's rights . . . is seen as an undeserved discrimination vis-à-vis those who are recognized in these respects. . . . As such, this kind of disrespect can threaten an actor's self-esteem in at least two ways: on the one hand, it can amount to a denial of the social value of some specific feature which is of central importance to a group's identity. For instance, playing down some of its historic achievements or denigrating one of its essential cultural values can put the very foundation of the group's self-esteem into question. . . . On the other hand, disrespect can also result from a refusal to acknowledge a group's possession of a feature whose value is commonly accepted. . . . Accordingly, this form of disrespectful behavior arouses an even stronger sense of injustice. It directly attacks an actor's status as an equal, for it denies this actor the recognition that other actors with the same features routinely receive.
>
> (127)

In sum, as Ward (2017) puts: 'When actors speak in terms of the rights and the state is owed on the basis of its position, they are articulating a claim to status'

(63). In other words, France's persistent response neglected Thailand's worthiness. Due to the fact that the question of sovereignty in Indo-China became unanswerable following the Japanese presence in the French colony, the Thais moved to repossess the territories over which France could no longer exercise proper authority. The Thais felt passionate towards the territories in question. Such an idea of Thailand's rights was captured by Phibun's explanation in relation to the territorial retrocession that France 'might atone for their sin' (NAT-[2]-SoRo-0201.92.1/7, 7). Hence, denying Thailand's rights was interpreted as misrecognising the equal status and history of the nation.

A discourteous reply from France only aggravated the Franco-Thai feuds because repudiating Thailand's rights over the problematic areas only ignited a strong sense of injustice. It was predictable that the Thai Foreign Affairs would respond by employing the language of rights to bolster their claims:

> Thailand had lost the vast territories to France. . . . The reason that Thailand gave up the lands on the left bank of the Mekong to France in RorSor 112 (1893) was to settle the disputes. Yet, the lands on the right bank of the Mekong had been recognised by France as belonging to Thailand. . . . The negotiation to adjust the frontiers nowadays. . ., if considering the mutual understanding of international relations proposed by the Thais, is appropriate from every aspect . . . The new border scheme would not cripple France from any massive territories. On the contrary, it would show that the French have been fair and just towards Thailand. . . . The Thai government appeals to France to consider this matter with morality and justice and wishes the French to re-evaluate our friendly understanding and good relationship.
>
> (TMCM 27/1940, 25-September-1940)

The memorandum was indicative of Thailand's intent. In the age of colonisation, Thailand was extorted by force to secede the territories. Now the Thais wanted to project the identity of a proud and equal nation. They expected France and other foreign powers to recognise historical blunders and redeem injustices done in the past. The argument was obvious: their rights were not acknowledged. This was confirmed by the subsequent denunciation, which expressed resentment from the Thais:

> Knowing that Thailand is a small country, we have been silent all the time. . . . When there were any chances to revise any unequal treaties, France had never been the first nation to help Thailand to become fully independent. France is the last nation to finalise any treaties with Thailand. No matter what, Thailand has tried to maintain the relationship all the time. Although recently Thailand has become militarily stronger, the Thais have never shown any sign of enmity towards the French. . . . In 1939, France realised that any wrongdoing the French had committed in the past is still embedded in the memories of the Thai people.
>
> (NAT-[2]-KoTo-2.7/29)

For the Thais, France had frequently been a power that treated Thailand as an inferior nation. Acceding to the Thai demands would reinstate the sense of ontological security to the small but frustrated nation because it meant acknowledging it as an equal by atoning for the sinful misconduct. Henceforth, those territories, which belonged to them in the old days, should be ***rightfully returned*** to the rightful owner, as the Foreign Ministry claimed,

> If the damages inflicted on Thailand in the past concerned the territories, other solutions would definitely not wipe out the vendetta. The only way to make the Thais forget the pain in the past and continue the friendship with France is to revise the frontier according to the principles of natural boundary and justice.
>
> (ibid.)

The statement hinted that the Franco-Thai friendship could only be preserved if the French would respect Thailand's historical trauma by accepting Thailand's demands.

In summary, the Thai government had tirelessly sought grounds to remain neutral. Nevertheless, French evasiveness to discuss the territorial revision triggered the Thai elites to present the three bold propositions to France. The imperious attitudes from the Frenchmen only escalated the hostility between the two nations. As the premier's analysis showed: 'The French accused us of encroaching upon their territory, but they have come to sleep in Vientiane and enslaved us while denying an allegation as an invader. . . . Similarly, since RorSor 112, they claimed that they did not invade us. They said that we bullied them first' (NAT-[2]-SoRo-0201.92.1/8, 6–7). The statement reflected how the inferiority complex and trauma of RorSor 112 played a part in shaping the reactions from the Bangkok elites. France's denial was read as a state of misrecognition of Thailand's standing in the international system.

The Thai public emotion and aggressive request

Thailand's urge to be recognised and France's disrespect did not only catalyse the proactive motions of the Thai elites. These two factors also sparked public outcries from the Thai populace. After Thailand proposed three demands to France, the members of the parliament unanimously offered a compliment to the Phibun government for restoring 'rights and justice' back to the nation (TPMP 14/1940, 19-September-1940). Policy-makers and lawmakers were not the only groups of Thais who were infuriated by the French treatments. The general Thai public passionately followed the news of the Franco-Thai negotiations as well. For the Thais, in terms of their historical consciousness, France and other European powers had been preying upon their nation. The loss of the territories in the nineteenth century bestowed upon them the sense of victimisation and injustice. In this regard, France's diplomatic duplicity prompted the Thais to react and call for recognition and respect from the European nation. Such a behavioural tendency was captured by Subotic and Zarakol (2013): 'If states had collective consciousness as manifest in a national habitus, it would follow that they would also act out various emotions associated with the act of recognition, such as humiliation and loss of self-esteem' (4). This section reveals the vibrancy of the Thai public in relation to France's stance on Indo-China.

During the time when the tension between Thailand and France was at its apex, there was an incident which aggravated the relationship between the two nations. On 26 September 1940, the French Indo-China police killed one of the Thai people in Laos whose name was Nai Chanta (NAT-SoRo-0201.35/6). Nai Chanta was shot by the Indo-China officer for failing to show a passport. The Thai government issued a diplomatic protest immediately after the news and solicited the French to punish any officials involved. Moreover, the Thais demanded that the compensation and indemnity should be provided by France to Nai Chanta's family. Nonetheless, the French denied any allegations and offered an unsatisfactory, sugar-coated reply (TMCM 29/1940, 9-October-1940). They neglected the case completely, which was a slap in the face to Thailand's honour (Publicity Bureau 1941c, 82). The death of Nai Chanta was sacralised by Phibun, who donated a considerable sum of money to organise a proper funeral. The other Thais, viewing the French diplomatic inaction as an insult, carried the corpse around the city of Udonthani province to symbolise the French oppression (ibid., 81, 88). Apparently, France's behaviours and answers riled the Thai counterpart. Hence, the Franco-Thai relationship was on the verge of warfare.

What was even worse was how the French violated Thailand's sovereignty by dispatching the militias to scout within the Thai territory along the Mekong border (ibid., 49). Moreover, they sporadically flew the warplanes across the Thai borders as a tactic to provoke the Thais (ibid., 48). From September to November 1940, there had been 36 provocative flights from Indo-China along the Franco-Thai border (NAT-[2]-KoTo-2.4.1/93). These series of events confirmed the Thai people's biased perception that the French government merely recognised them as a backward nation and unworthy of recognition. Therefore, the infringement on the Thai sovereignty was arbitrarily conducted like how the semi-civilised countries suffered.

The Thais' antagonism towards France had grown steadily. The centre of gravity of the public emotion stemmed from France's supercilious replies, which triggered ferocious responses from the Thai people. For the Thais, the Paknam Crisis, as shortly discussed in Chapter 3, marked and reminded the Thai elites of the nation's inferiority in relation to the West. The incident had collectively traumatised the Thai people's perception towards France. Since 1939, the Thais, however, regarded their nation with pride and prestige. Similar to the Thai elites, the general Thai public would expect decorous treatments from France. The French's mischievous behaviours activated Thailand's traumatic memories. The press, for instance, became indignant towards the French even more. As one media personality wrote: 'We have requested the return of our territories, but instead of negotiating, France shows us only contempt' (Nikorn 13 January 1941 cited in Strate 2009, 54). Another reporter drew on the '1893 Paknam Crisis' and noted that 'France once bullied us with only three warships, they must think we can still be so easily defeated' (Nikorn 11 April 1941 cited in ibid., 55). Drawing from the death of Nai Chanta, some Thais distributed leaflets which reflected the grudge from the nineteenth-century scars:

> Since RorSor 112, the Thai nation was historically ingrained with sorrow. . . . And such scars became indelible. . . . In our time, a similar incident occurs again. The French pads their shoes on our faces . . . and eventually kills our man [Nai chanta – my note], which we see as an affront to our nation beyond any forgiveness. As national fellows, are we prepared? Please be ready, an opportunity has arrived. If you don't want to be a lackey, you need to be in a powerful position.
>
> (NAT-[2]-KoTo-2.4.1/99)

For the Thais, accepting the French misdemeanour was the equivalent of withstanding the nation's unequal status. One vernacular newspaper, such as *Krungtheb Varasab*, which published anecdotes about Thailand's humiliation by France in the nineteenth century, asked whether Thailand's acquiescence would imply an inferior status: 'Shall we become a great power or a slave?' (Lakmuang 4 October 1940 cited in Sarawudhi 2016, 186). 'Thailand', continued a reporter, 'can not be a slave to other nations. . . . The territorial demand is the supremely just demand of Thailand, unlike the injustices that were done to us in the past, which has been bitterly ingrained in our hearts' (ibid., 186). The Thai public intellectuals recalled how the French unjustly coerced their nation in the past and articulated how the Phibun government had never reciprocated France with an intimidating method:

> Since RorSor 112, the Thais endured the pain and sorrow when the Thai government received a request-cum-threat from the French government. . . . [Have we resorted to violence in 1940? – my summary] Not at all. The Thai government tried to negotiate our lost territories in accordance with the manner of the pacifists without threatening or coercing.
>
> (Lakmuang 5 October 1940)

On 8 October 1940, the students from Chulalongkorn University and University of Moral and Political Sciences staged a street demonstration to support the government in reclaiming the territories from France. The scale of the movement was massive. Approximately ten thousand students took to the streets to express their anger. These students were emotionally driven. Their core message, appearing in the movement's leaflets, was intricately linked to how France's disrespect symbolised Thailand's unequal status in international society:

> We invite the Thai brethren to support the government policy in territorial retrocession. The Thais should glorify Thailand's prestige to be recognised throughout the world so that they know we are a passionately robust and

> capable nation. We should all unite to build our nation to the extent that others would worship and respect how civilised we are.
>
> (NAT-SoBo-9-Eak-Weesakul)

Within the movement, there were pamphlets which strongly expressed the desire of the students. The notable phenomena from the demonstration were the messages which pressured the government to take military action in order to fulfil a foreign policy objective. The examples of the messages could be epitomised as follows: 'Thais are willing to die in order to reclaim the lands'; 'We should wage war if they do not return the territories'; 'If words do not work, we should calm them by bullets'; and 'We have asked them peacefully for a long time, shall we use force?' (Supaporn 2003, 72). For the students, the territorial policy was a signifier of Thailand's stature in the international system. Denying Thailand's rights to the territories was seen as an insult. Treating Thailand on an unequal basis also inflated the degree of tension. As such, the advocacy for war became heightened among the people of Thailand. Being impatient towards the government's inertia, a pundit vented out anger:

> The people really wish to know why we are still waiting. . . . We have waited long enough, and we realize that such waiting based on peaceful methods will result in still more waiting without an end.
>
> (Thai Rashdra 11 November 1940 cited in Strate 2009, 53)

In order to prove to the world that Thailand had been on par with others, France should accede to the Thai requests. But since the French had been visibly reluctant, a military means was the remaining option to garner recognition. Strate (2009) captured the situation as follows:

> Finally, a military victory over France would prove to the country and to the world how far their country had advanced in the past decades. In the past, Thailand had been defeated due to lack of armaments, but it was no longer the same country as in 1893.
>
> (56)

The tide of the Thais was turning in favour of war to resolve the conflict and to reassert a proper identity of Thailand. More citizens, apart from the students, became actively involved in activities, which propelled the government to take serious action against the French. The people throughout the nation began to donate their money in support of the government's military campaign. One of the notable donors was former Prime Minister Phahol, who, despite claiming to be senile, offered moral and financial support for the military crusade (Publicity Bureau 1941c, 45).

Elsewhere, there were mass demonstrations and donations to pressure the government to take action. For example, in Yala province, the Christians and Muslims in Thailand marched on the street and chanted 'Thailand's victory'.

They also donated money to support the government's policy. Civil servants also willingly sliced off 10 per cent of their remuneration to this quest (NAT-SoTo-0701.28/29; NAT-SoRo-0201.35/8). The amount of money was substantial as the Ministry of Defence tallied after the war that it was 677,784.49 ticals (Anand 1975a, 148). Some gave up their personal cars for the military purpose. Islamic preachers and Buddhist monks stepped out of the religious sphere and pledged to go to the frontline if the government requested their services (NAT-MoTo-0201.2.1.14/3). Phibun himself was astonished by the public awareness, remarking that 'In some places, all the monks volunteer to fight in the frontline. . . . I feel startled' (NAT-[2]-SoRo-0201.92.1/7, 9). The scale of the mass demonstration was unprecedented.

The rage of the Thais became overwhelmingly unstoppable. The people had reproduced maps of the lost territories and distributed them freely throughout the nation in order to arouse Thailand's traumatic memories inflicted by France. Additionally, these people had also printed out the maps of Thailand, showing how the British similarly engulfed certain territories from the Siamese in the nineteenth century. The government thus became concerned about the maps and their relationship with Britain. Due to the fact that Britain respected Thailand much more than France and the latter should be the target of the verbal assault rather than the former, the government decided to order the suspension of the maps which indicated how Britain had acquired the lands from Siam in the past. This was evident in the secret and urgent document: 'the process of map-printing to show the lost territories should be focused only the areas seceded to France. It is forbidden to print out the territories lost to other powers. We hope you will co-operate with the government' (NAT-MoTo-0201.2.1.14/1).

In part, the government's prohibition of the British-related materials could be because of a concern that the nation could be hemmed in by the two-front enemies. At the end of the day, Phibun and his cabinet felt it was in their nation's strategic interest to curb and control the people's fanaticism. Henceforth, he ordered a speechwriter to prepare words to express gratitude to the people's activism and to cease excessive emotional demonstrations. The premier hardly forgot to request his speechwriter to stress the importance of the civilised ways of life. The reason given was because 'in the future, we will be great. If we receive the territories, we should act honourably, not wearing Sarong [local attire – my note]' (TMCM 30/1940, 16-October-1940). Receiving territories was inadequate, but the Western approbation of the nation's standing was equally vital to Thai foreign policy of the period.

In summary, apart from the elites, the Thai public became inimical towards France. The central concerns were how the French reacted towards the Thais with disgrace. Such a condition forced the government to bring about substance in order to quench the people's demand and accommodate their sense of existential insecurity. Eventually, Phibun admitted that if the French remained stubborn, he would have to 'listen to the people. Since there is no quid pro quo, the Non-aggression pact should be renounced. They may invade us or vice versa' (NAT-[2]-SoRo-0201.92.1/6, 11). By committing to the military methods, Thailand would have to turn its terms against the earlier obligation. Firstly, it meant Thailand would have to violate its principle of neutrality, which was domestically decreed and promulgated as law. Secondly, an act of aggression could be seen as detrimental to the sanctity of the contractual agreement. Although the status of the pact was not yet ratified, a policy of retaliation by arms could ruin the nation's credibility. Phibun's words could be interpreted as Thailand aspiring to risk its physical security for its ontological security.

Phibun's strategic offensive

The Thai state was strongly determined to reclaim the lost territories from France. However, the direct armed clashes were the last option on the list. This section examines how the Thais sidelined France and interacted with the Cambodians and Laotians. It also shows how the idea of status parity and civilisation was utilised to justify Thailand's strategies. Moreover, it stretches out how the status concern and inferiority complex played their parts in the war and settlement processes.

Indirect tactics: we are civilised

As Phibun hinted, the government's inaction could erode the authority of the regime. As such, the government was impelled to initiate hard-line responses. Despite Thailand's strong urge to reclaim the territories, Phibun was uncertain whether an overt campaign of war could bring success to the nation's stature and objective. Although his hands were tied to the public opinion, he later admitted in a closed-door meeting that he did not want to wage war: 'In fact, the territorial demand was not war-prone. This war contradicted my intention . . . but the people do not know my agenda. I have told them to be calm all the time. This war was not intentional. Luckily we win' (TMCM 8/1941, 12-February-1941). Originally the Thai cabinet proposed that the French return the territories if France lost her control in the region. However, the situation was escalated by the Thai public movements. For a leader of Thailand, inaction would project the national status as inferior to domestic audiences, whereas internationally it would mean accommodating the demands of a greater power. In this regard, the government designed indirect strategies to cope with the situation without defying the French overtly.

Firstly, Phibun realised that the demands of the people of Thailand would expedite the tendency of the Franco-Thai skirmish. Instead of gambling with the nadir of the French empire by launching a whole-scale military crusade, Thailand's premier initially pursued a strategy to internationalise the issue and victimise his nation. The government ordered the Publicity Bureau to publish a book about the Franco-Thai historical conflicts in different languages. The book, which was titled *How Thailand Lost Territories to France*, were distributed to the Thai embassies and consuls throughout the world (NAT-[2]-KoTo-2.4.1/82). The details of the book explained how, since the nineteenth century, Thailand was intimidated by France to give up a large body of territories. The publication of the books was to draw international attention and to construct a justification to pressure France to accede to Thailand's bold requests. What was the core message of the books?

The disseminated books, apart from the discussion of the historical blemishes, which traumatised the Thais collectively, represented how Thailand reached a respectful level as a nation and should be accorded properly. They expected the world to realise that Thailand was not an aggressively revisionist power but obtained a reasonable ground to launch their demands. As previously discussed, the Thai elites were obsessed with how others perceived them after 1939; it was not startling to find a glimpse of such sentiments in this case. Wichit (2003), Phibun's Joseph Goebbels pointed out the historical narrative as follows:

> We accepted the lost territories because we could not fight against France in the past. But there is no intermittent force that can compel us to accept such a fate. When we reach the status parity to the extent that we can make a plea for justice, we request it. As I have said earlier, we did not demand the territories when France was defeated. The question of territories was discussed even prior to the war.
>
> (469)

At least Wichit's reflection of foreign policy indicated an upsetting feeling to protect the identity and status of Thailand.

Secondly, the Thai government pursued a tactic to *Thailandise* the people of Laos and Cambodia who resided under the protectorates of France. The objective of the move was to form a Pan-Thai movement and to incite a revolt from within Indo-China. They began an initial step by issuing the decree to exempt immigration fees for the Laotians and Cambodians in order to encourage immigration from the French colonies. Immigrants from Luang Prabang, Vientiane, Champasak, and Cambodia should be exempted from any relevant fee and procedure (TMCM 24/1940, 4-September-1940). The reason given for this decision, according to Thawee Bunyaket, the then Secretary of the cabinet, was because these people were racially Thais who had been scattering all over Mainland Southeast Asia. But, for political reasons, they had been wretchedly placed under foreign jurisdictions (ibid.).

The following measure taken by the Thai elites was to promulgate an order throughout the nation to enforce the Thais to call the Laotians and Cambodians the 'Thai people in Laos and Thai people in Cambodia' (TMCM 35/1940, 6-November-1940). The Publicity Bureau also transmitted a message to persuade the Laos and Cambodians to live under the umbra of Thailand: 'Please Come. The Thai brethren will have Laos and Cambodia altogether to build our nation to progress as a great power' (NAT-SoRo-0201.37.6/18). And in order to attract more immigration from the neighbouring countries, the Thai state encouraged the Thai people and civil servants to donate ten per cent of their incomes to support those Laotians and Cambodians who fled from the French authorities (TMCM 33/1940, 30-October-1940). Apart from the humanitarian reason, the donation scheme was primarily aimed to express an identity of a civilised country as the cabinet resolution concluded that aiding the immigrants would 'express the national culture as well' (ibid; NAT-SoRo-0201.35/8). This was to show that Thailand was on an equal footing with other nations and was a favourable destination.

To ensure that moving to Thailand would be honourable, if not preferable to living under the French, the Thai state formulated a measure to portray the exquisiteness of residing in Thailand as opposed to France. The level of Thailand's enthusiasm on this matter could be proven by its formation of the Indo-China Department under the command of the Ministry of Interior in order to collect information about the people from Indo-China (TMCM 38/1940, 27-November-1940). The government also ordered the co-ordination of different governmental departments and ministries for the purpose of pursuing the Indo-China policy by peaceful means (NAT-SoRo-0201.35/11). Each department and ministry was responsible for studying the ways of living of the Laotians and Cambodian people under France. Such an order should be considered an additional assignment of any civil servants. The core task was to investigate how the French authorities had maltreated the locals. The collected information would be utilised to propagate the different living conditions between Thailand and France. The propagation duty, according to the government, should be executed throughout the nation. In Bangkok, the Publicity Bureau was assigned to broadcast such a story, whereas in other provinces the governors should concentrate their efforts on narrating the bliss of Thailand (ibid.).

On the one hand, the implication of such a strategy was to transmit a message that Thailand entered a new phase as a civilised nation. On the other hand, the strategy of Thailandisation was practised to arouse the Laotians and Cambodians to revolt from within and later unite with Thailand rather than spearheading the project of independence among themselves (Murashima 2005, 342). The ultimate goals were to incorporate a larger group of populations from Laos and Cambodia and to regain former territories without confronting a European power directly. The rationale for executing the strategy of Thailandisation to recover the lands was intricately tied to the sense of honour, as Wichit (2003) explained:

> The idea of territorial retrocession is not a thought of a thief stealing resources, not a notion to enslave the people, and not an impression to excavate resourceful properties of others to benefit us, but it is the thinking of the nation with honour. Every honourable nation cannot stand their fellow patriots being subjected to the abuse of others. We are Thai [free – my note] and we want our brethren to be Thai [free – my note]. The important issue of the lands is about race. The lost territories are not the colonies and not aliens. They have Thai blood. . . . That is why we need them back.
>
> (468)

As the statement suggested, by Thailandising the ethnic Laotians and Cambodians, France's obstinacy to cling onto Laos and Cambodia could be interpreted as denying Thailand's international status because a sovereign nation was rightfully entitled to manage its own citizens. Therefore, Thailand's indifference to the brethren in Laos and Cambodia was not an option.

The third strategy of Thailand in relation to its Indo-China policy was to abet the independence movements within Laos and Cambodia. According to Murashima (2005), the Thai ruling elites initiated contacts with the leaders of the independent movements in Laos and Cambodian in order to rise against the French if necessary. In the case of Laos, it was evident that the governor of Nongkhai recommended to the Thai government, Prince Phetsarath of Laos, who was the descendant of Luang Prabang and was appointed by France as inspector general, could be a great support to Thailand's subversive designs in the region (NAT-[2]-KoTo-2.4.1/83). Dignified by his royal title, Phetsarath, however, would not commit to Thailand's plan unless Thailand guaranteed the independent status of Laos and regarded the people from Laos as Laotians as opposed to Thais (Murashima 2005, 350). On the contrary, Oun Sananikone, one of the founders of the Free Laos Movement saw it necessary to co-operate with Thailand in evicting the French overlords from the region (ibid., 357). Working closely with the Publicity Bureau, Oun courted assistance from the Laotians by broadcasting his opinion as to how Thailand was a haven:

> When I crossed into the land full of freedom [Thailand – my note], I was warmly welcomed by the Thais from all ranks . . . and was greatly supported by merchants. . . . I would like to tell the Laotian brethren that such welcoming is unprecedented in my life. . . . This is the first time that I am becoming a human with liberty and freedom as in the case of the citizens of the civilised countries.
>
> (Publicity Bureau 1941a, 288)

As regards the Cambodian asset, the Thais collaborated with Phrapisetphanit, a Cambodian aristocratic heir who organised the Cambodian independent movement (Murashima 2005, 363). As a rebellious figure who was exiled and was warmly received to Thailand, Phrapisetphanit looked up to Thailand's rapid transformation and commented that: 'since its constitutional revolution, Thailand has been striving to develop as a nation. Like the countries of Europe, the Thai nation has been striving to progress on its own' (ibid., 364). For the likes of Phrapisetphanit, Thailand was a paradise. The core difference between the two states was 'Thailand is an independent country and Cambodia is a French colony. . . . The Thai government is resolutely determined to support the Khmers in Thailand and in Cambodia so they can free themselves from French suppression. . . . I also want to help the Thai government in its effort to expel the French from Indochina' (ibid., 365).

The three strategies, which the government operationalised, were predicated on a caution that the war with France might actually occur and affect the nation. But for the government inaction could be seen as inferior by France, the international community, and the Thai people. Therefore, it initiated the campaign by addressing the global audiences of Thailand's just cause to request territories from France. The Thai state's sponsors of the independent movement of Laos and Cambodia corresponded to the strategy of Thailandisation and the support of immigration. Such tactics exemplified the image of Thailand as a civilised patron. Whether the world saw Thailand's reaction as aggressive, whether the Laotians and Cambodians wished to migrate to Thailand, or whether Thailand's sponsorship of the independent movements affected the stability of France's authority, it was undeniable that the Thai elites were agitated by the notion of its national honour. Deeply perturbed by how others would view their status, they resorted to informing others, including the Laotians and Cambodians, that their nation had ascended a respectable level and should be regarded as such.

War, settlements, and prestige

If Phibun prodded the French with the indirect strategies to call for France's attention, when was the outbreak of the Franco-Thai direct confrontations? The premier did not want any war with France. But all of the conditions articulated earlier had contributed to the war between the two nations. Although Phibun had calmed his fellow patriots as regards the issues of Indo-China, public emotions trumped rational considerations. As head of the government, France's intransigence and provocative behaviours could not be easily tolerated. Since the melodramatic conflicts between the two states, French aircraft flew over the Thai borders several times. On 28 November 1940, the French flew over to bombard Nakorn Phranom province. The provocation cost six deaths of Thai civilians. Phibun issued a statement of condemnation as follows:

> I have learnt the news with the melancholy feeling because the French are not being a gentleman. They spread the rumours to exploit others and superciliously think that they are superior to others, which is amoral and is not the practice of the civilised people. For the Thai Armed Forces, we never wickedly allege others. . . . We pride ourselves as a nation with morality. . . . When I see the situation, I think that since the French have invaded Indo-China for so long, we should retaliate so that we can live in peace.
>
> (Publicity Bureau 1940a, 2085)

The Thais, according to the condemnation, interpreted the French aggression as an affront, not only to Thai sovereignty but to national dignity as well. For the Thai elites, a nation with equal status would not have acted towards others on such grounds. The statement echoed how the Thais perceived that France barely recognised them as an equal partner. By dint of the fact that Thailand regarded itself as a civilised nation, inaction would implicate inferiority. Hence, Phibun responded by commanding the Thai air forces to blast Indo-China. Hostilities between the two states became official from this triggering event.

Following the armed conflict on 28 November 1940, there had been a sporadic exchange of shells between the two countries. However, the Thai Northern Division started crossing into the border of French Indo-China in early

January 1941 (Publicity Bureau 1941a, 121). The fact that Thailand could cross into the opponents' lands meant that Thailand had gained strategic advantages over France in ground operations. They were able to capture Champasak and some parts of Luang Prabang as well. However, Thailand's Royal Navy was vanquished by the French fleets in the Gulf of Thailand. One Thai Royal Fleet was sunk. The damage from the naval battle was humiliating to the extent that Somsak Jiamteeraskul, a Thai historian, questioned whether the Thai military actually won the war (Charnvit et al. 2001, 114).

Casting the issue of victory aside, the reality that Thailand gained the upper hand in the ground battle was in itself a pride of the nation. Not only had they seized strategic lands, but the Thai army also captured approximately 200 French prisoners of war (Supaporn 2003, 86). What was noteworthy about the French prisoners of war was how the Thai government treated them. Since the nineteenth century, the consciousness of being inferior to the West had been collectively embedded in the hearts and minds of Thai people. Despite the claims by the Thai officials that the prisoners of war had been treated fairly well in accordance with Thailand's 'civilised ethos' (Publicity Bureau 1941a, 339), the reality did not reflect such claims. As such, in order to display parity, if not superiority, over the French nationals, the Thai government exhibited the prisoners of war at the Amporn Garden, which was then the centre of Bangkok (ibid.). Similarly, the weapons seized from France were showcased at the same location. The government also invited the Thai people to witness the awful French prisoners humiliated by the mighty Thais. Interestingly, the exhibition opened for keen viewers at 'any time' (ibid., 372).

Thailand's treatments of the French prisoners had been viewed as its hardening attitudes towards the Occidentals (NAT-[2]-KoTo-2.1.6/10). Such behaviours would not make sense out of the context of how Thailand had been concerned about its standing vis-à-vis the West. Hiromichi Yahara, a former assistant attaché of the Japanese Imperial Army in Thailand, attested to his notable observation in a comparative manner:

> The Thai government brought the young French prisoners of war and caged them so that the Thais could sightsee them in order to eradicate the inferiority complex of the Thais. . . . In the Russo-Japanese War, Japan did something similar to this, hence, we [Japanese] should not insult this method because it is a general feeling of Asians to avenge against the white people, who act aggressively towards the Asians and think of themselves as more progressive and more intelligent.
>
> (Murashima & Sorasak 1986, 85)

More important than ever, despite the disgrace from the naval annihilation, the Thai elites prided themselves on how not a single one of their soldiers was captured by France. Hence, the government publicly broadcasted that any agreement with France should not involve an exchange of the prisoners of war (Publicity Bureau 1941a, 337).

On 21 January 1941, the Vichy government sent a telegram to Direk, who was then responsible for managing routines of foreign relations. According to Direk's disclosure, the French enquired as to whether Thailand wished a ceasefire provided that the status quo ante agreement on border adjustment could be achieved between the two countries. However, he replied to France that this could not be agreed. Despite the naval disaster and Phibun's anxiety of Thailand's strength from the on-going campaign as he admitted that he 'no longer wants to fight' (TMCM 6/1941, 3-February-1941), France's ceasefire offer was brushed off the table. The reason for the dismissal of the French proposition was pertinent to the recognition of Thailand's status: 'Our side has invested so much. If we suddenly agree to a ceasefire without any clear objective, the military faction and the people would dissent it' (TMCM 3/1941, 22-January-1941). The genuine intent according to Direk was for the 'French to show us that they are amicable'. And to prove such points, it should 'agree to give us two pieces of lands [see Figure 5.2 – my note] and the islets in the Mekong without any conditions so that we can restart negotiating again' (ibid.). In a simpler term, for the Thais, without acknowledgement of Thailand's historical claims, a ceasefire would signify inferiority and weakness. It would project an image that Thailand was bent easily. They, however, anticipated the French to show more respect to the Thai past.

A few days after France's deadlock in the ceasefire proposal, the Vichy government solicited Japan to mediate the conflict on behalf of the two countries (TMCM 4/1941 25-January-1941). For Thailand, the Japanese extension of an invitation to mediate the conflict was 'an honour of the nation' (TMCM 6/1941, 3-February-1941). However, the consent to allow the Japanese mediation was not the equivalent of adhering to the ceasefire agreement. Concerned with the Thai obstinacy to accept the ceasefire, the Japanese Thai Room diplomat lobbied the Thai ruling elites to agree to a halt. The Thai elites would comply only if the Japanese and French truly respected the Thais as Thawan Thamrongnawasawat, the Minister of Justice, explained in the cabinet meeting:

> There is a suspicion that Japan would not help Thailand genuinely. I tell them [Japanese – my note] that this is about the hearts and minds of the people. We cannot proceed without Japanese making us feel the way we should because Thailand has a highly regarded culture and we are grateful to helpers.
>
> (TMCM 5/1941, 29-January-1941)

For the Thai decision-makers, misrecognition of Thailand's stature could be construed as disrespect and would result in reneging on the agreement. What the Thais expected the French and Japanese to recognise was the territories lost to France, as Prince Wan advised that,

> The agreed principle for the negotiation is that we need to inform the Japanese of the territories which we had in the past and how the French tricked

> us into seceding them. . . . For the sake of peace, France should return them to us. In terms of discussion, we claim the RorSor 112 and all the rights we had over the left bank of the Mekong should be returned to us.
>
> (ibid.)

Although Tua Palanukrom, the Minister without portfolio, voiced his concern as to whether the international community would recognise their demands, Prince Wan, wistful to redeem the traumatic scar in the past, was adamant in his stance, as he believed that 'we should stand on RorSor 112 because we shall take revenge on them' (ibid.). The implication of this stance was that the French would have to be removed from Mainland Southeast Asia, which would be impossible in practice.

In the tripartite conference, the Japanese pleaded to Thailand to retreat ten kilometres from Ban Chanka and to announce a ceasefire between the two nations in order to further the negotiating process. The Thai counterpart had refused to comply with the Japanese demand, which infuriated the Japanese representatives along the process (NAT-SoRo-0201.35/26). Thailand's intransigence, despite the naval defeat and the third-party request, indicated that it would neither bow to Japan nor France. For the Thais, risking the continuation of war with France and military intervention from other countries would be preferable to being seen as a small country without rights and privileges. Although the Thais yielded to the Japanese request, it later issued a secret war plan in case the terms of the negotiations could not be reached among the three nations (NAT-BoKoSungsut-1.16/3). The reason Thailand agreed to the ceasefire was not because of the Japanese. It was, however, because the Thai premier felt it necessary to accept the ceasefire lest the Americans or other great powers could intervene to complicate the matter (TMCM 8/1941, 12-February-1941, 29).

As a mediator, Tokyo realised the difficulty of constructing equilibrium between Thailand and France. Hence, Japan secretly promised Thailand that she would return the regions of Laos and Cambodia to Thailand in the future conditional upon compliance from the Thai counterpart (TMCM 10/1941, 26-February-1941). Such a promise was confirmed by Germany as well (TMCM13/1941, 12-March-1941). Japan invented a proposition that Thailand would repossess the provinces on the right bank of the Mekong and would obtain a province on the opposite side of Luang Prabang. In sum, the Thais should be rewarded with the four provinces, namely, Sayabouri, Champasak, Sieamreap, and Battambang. This proposition differed from what Prince Wan had originally outlined and the Thai military would be more than animated to continue their campaign to deracinate the remnant of the French empire.

The government encountered a dilemma. On the one hand, as mentioned earlier, Phibun himself viewed the eruption of this war as deviating from his inchoate plan. As such, terminating this war would benefit the nation. For him, the victor was the one who does not wage war (ibid., 9). On the other hand, by acceding to the Japanese terms, Thailand could be viewed as a satellite state of Japan and

Germany. The Japanese understood this reason fully well as its representative remarked to Phibun that,

> Japan know[s] that if Thailand accept[s] the demand, Thailand could appear weak. But the younger faction in Japan accuses the Japanese government of being weak. . . . If we use force against Indo-China, there would be no guarantee that the younger faction in Japan would not want them to use force against Thailand later. . . . Thailand will be in the same status as Manchuria. (ibid., 7)

The policy of the present Japanese government, however, was not to colonise Thailand. As a result, the Japanese prime minister and foreign minister extended an appeal to the Thai government to accept the terms for the time being (ibid., 7).

At face value, the Japanese warning could be perceived as a threat. Nevertheless, the appeal from the leaders of the Japanese government was a national honour and a sign that a great power in the region, such as Japan, acknowledged the historical trauma of Thailand by offering more territories than the Thais had claimed prior to the outbreak of war (see Figure 5.2 and compare with Figure 5.1). Apart from the territorial deal, the Mekong border would be demarcated by the deep-water channel, whereas the islets would be governed by the Franco-Thai authorities (TMCM 14/1941, 17-March-1941).

In order to settle the issues with France, the Thai government would have to compensate the French four-million ticals. This issue raised some unrest over the dignity of the nation because the Thais felt they were victimised by France, and, therefore, paying them in exchange for the territories would not redeem the sin that the French had committed (TPMP 1/1941, 9-June-1941). Overall, the interests from the Japanese deal did not tarnish the reputation of the Phibun government. On the contrary, the deal would enhance the glory of the nation and Phibun himself. Although Phibun partially blamed himself in the cabinet meeting for the outbreak of war, some minister worshipped the deal as an honourary success: 'I think how the war materialises must be considered on the basis of emotion. But what we have done this time is the honour of the nation' (TMCM 10/1941, 26-February-1941). At the end of the day, Thailand accepted the Japanese terms without any difficulty.

The quest to regain the lost territories from France brought about eminent fame for Phibun and his administration. It had been the first time since the exposure to the Western international system that Thailand could dictate its own terms over a European power such as France. Although some members of the parliament questioned the material utility of the returned territories, Phibun realised that such scenarios were pertinent to symbolic gestures, as Wichit noted: 'The land we've asked for might be a little more than jungle, but it's our jungle and we want it back' (cited in Strate 2009, 64).

The war and its settlements mirrored Thailand's inferiority complex vis-à-vis the West. The nation emerged with prestige similar to Japan's when she could stand over Russia in 1904. The clear evidence was the government's approval of a budget to construct the so-called Victory Monument in central Bangkok

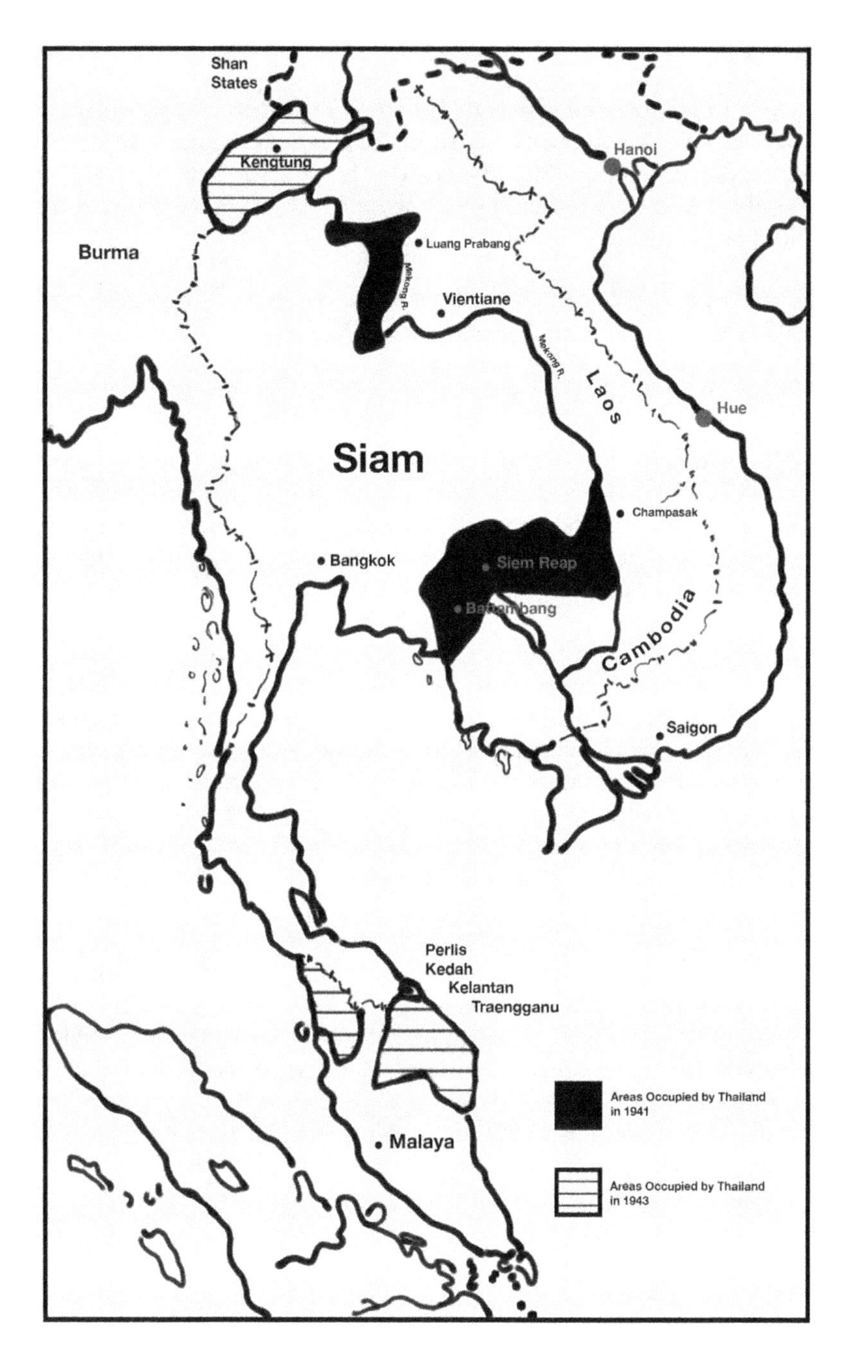

Figure 5.2 A map showing territories "returned" to Thailand in 1941 and 1943

to symbolise how the nation stood on par with the Europeans with whom they had been catching up for decades. The war signified the standing of the nation. Phibun's scriptwriter wrote:

> One of the significant results of this war is to pride the Thais with honour in order to develop themselves so that they can be on par with the Western civilised countries. After the Franco-Thai conflict, Field Marshal Phibun becomes a leader who transforms any outdated culture to conform to the world's modernity.
>
> (Sang 1944, 146)

The Thais became sentimental because they had a strong conviction that this war would restructure how the international community should perceive their image, as one local newspaper observed:

> This success has not only drawn the map of Thailand, it has redrawn the map of our hearts and minds. That is to say, it has made us realize that our beloved nation of Thailand has increased in honor, and caused the world to recognise that we are not the same country as forty years ago. Quite the opposite, other nations are now praising us.
>
> (Nikorn 2 April 1941, cited in Strate 2009, 65)

The Thai government also published a photo book about the triumph of Thailand and disseminated English copies throughout the world to show its post-war civilised image (Publicity Bureau 1941b). The book exaggeratedly illustrated the military strength and valour of the Thai Army. It also described how the veterans had received accolades from the premier. But most importantly, it contained an article titled, 'Thailand is no[t] inferior to Foreigners' (ibid., 52). After the settlements, the feeling of reaching equal status was incrementally boosted. This was revealed in one article:

> Now, we are fully becoming adults, which means we are arriving at the civilised stage. We should know that we are not inferior to Farangs [Westerners – my note]. This consciousness shall bring benefits to the nation. From this war, from the fight to retrocede the territories, and from foreign policy formulation, the Thai people . . . we could see that the foreigners are not special or higher than us. They are humans like us. . . . Therefore, the Thais should not adore Farangs as if they are our masters. We should befriend them on an equal basis. We should not worship their mystical culture as a tool to demote our status.
>
> (ibid., 52–23)

Similarly, even Seni, who personally disliked Phibun's foreign policy, could not but think that the war success 'makes the Thais proud of their country, especially, the Thais who live in the US. Because, wherever they go or get into any meetings, they can keep their heads up. They can be on par with the foreigners because the historical blemish and humiliation have been redeemed' (NAT-KoTo-73.2.4.1/17)

In other words, it was the making of war which increased the international stature of Thailand and its people's sense of equality.

Conclusion

The Franco-Thai clashes began from the negotiations of the frontier adjustment and the negotiation of the Non-aggression Pact between the two governments. Thailand in the context of the Second World War was a small nation with a revisionist interest. It was a jackal state with an opportunistic tendency and likely to follow on the trails of a bigger revisionist power. Nonetheless, this chapter showed that given various windows of opportunities, from the French and British preoccupation in the European continent, physical insecurity along the Thai borders, and the downfall of the French empire, the Thai government did not resort to exploiting its opportunities in ways mainstream theories would predict.

In order to make sense of the Thai foreign policy behaviours in this period, it is necessary to take into account the factor of status concerns and historical contingencies. A renowned Thai historian, Nakarin Mektrairat, comments that the Franco-Thai war could only be understood if scholars ponder upon 'the question of the Revolutionary Party, particularly the Phibun branch that organised a festival to celebrate the complete independence day in 1939. I think that is the beginning of the new Thai nation and not the old one' (printed in Thamrongsak 1990, 94–95). Similarly, as Chalong Suntravanich suggests, 'emotion is also an important key to make sense of the movement [Anti-French – my note]' (printed in ibid., 95). Without ruminating on the expansion of the Western powers to Southeast Asia in the nineteenth century and without any consideration of the status anxiety and ontological security, the outcomes of the Franco-Thai cataclysm would have been unintelligible.

As this chapter has expounded, from 1939 onwards, the Thais prided themselves as a new nation with a purportedly clear direction of neutral policy. However, international recognition, prestige, and national honour determined Thailand's courses of action vis-à-vis the French, which finally drove them into the war. France's sleight of hands was interpreted as an affront, not only to the Thai ruling elites but also to the Thai public. Its avoidance to ratify the treaty according to international law was seen as treating Thailand as a second-rate nation. The Thais therefore pushed for a higher demand accordingly, and the Franco-Thai crisis was escalated when the Thai public emotionally petitioned the Thai government to avenge the historical trauma to redeem injustices of the nineteenth century. Finally, the war between the two nations erupted and the settlements were fulfilled in favour of the Thais. For them, the war and the victory reproduced not only the material gains but also the symbolic values. Overcoming France was the equivalent of overcoming the inferiority complex Thailand had acquired since the nineteenth century.

Note

1 Phibun was notorious for his anti-Chinese attitude. See the British report on Chinese discrimination (TNA-FO371/23586-F19040/43/40).

6 Alliance anxiety

Thailand's search for recognition from Japan

In late 1941, according to the official historiography, Thailand became an ally of the Japanese Imperial Army. The conventional accounts on this subject generally explain that Thailand pursued the flexible foreign policy vis-à-vis Japan from 1941 until the end of the war. The Thai behaviours were predicated on the ebb and flow of the war situations. Thailand, as the common narratives normally portray, joined with Japan to avert threats to its survival and turned against them when opportunities were presented. Such an explanation is partly correct. Nevertheless, relying on the assumption that Thailand merely prioritised its existential survival is inadequate to explain why Thailand, materially inferior to Japan in terms of capabilities, opted to deviate from the Japanese directions even before the Imperial Army became strategically disadvantageous during the war. In other words, Thailand became proactive vis-à-vis Japan from 1941 to 1944. This chapter examines Thai foreign policy from the aforementioned period. It describes how Thailand's concern for status shaped foreign policy reactions towards Japan, which brought about uneasiness and tension in Tokyo-Bangkok ties.

Structural opportunities and the choices of Thailand

Following the Franco-Thai conflicts, Thailand perceived itself as a notable entity. From the outset, it had overcome the French and retroceded certain territories back. Yet the sovereignty over the whole regions of Laos and Cambodia remained under the French protectorate. Apparently, the settled conditions deviated from the great expectations of the Thai elites. Having received some parts of the lands, Thailand's aspiration to build the greater Thai empire was no hidden agenda. It is convincing to view Thailand from 1941 to 1944 as a small state with a limited revisionist objective. Territorial expansion and the great power conquest were central to Phibun's cabinet. This section discusses Thai foreign policy in 1941 and describes how, given opportunities before the Japanese invasion in December 1941, Thailand played a card of neutral policy.

Continuation of neutrality

The Japanese responsibility in mediating conflicts in East Asia offered spectators a variety of perspectives. Although the Thais were obliged to compensate the

French with money to settle the disputes, the yielding result, which appeared to the world, was how Japan supported Thailand in its territorial demands. US Secretary of State Cordell Hull, for example, believed that Thailand was 'at present in the clutches of Japan and that no one can tell when there may be a separation of these special relations' (FRUS-1941-Vol.5-Document136). France and Britain, suspicious of Japan's desire to dominate Asia, were undoubtedly agitated by the possible Japanese-Thai co-operation against the white race as Crosby (1945) observed that there was a prevalent idea that Thailand's recent bellicosity was instigated by Japan (120). As such, Thailand received the intelligence report that the British troops in Malaya stepped close to the Thai borders and would be more than ready to break the Japanese-Thai coalition (MPH-Vol.1-Document413, A-217; NAT-SoRo-0201.33/53).

On the European front, the tide turned against the Allied powers. The British Expeditionary Force was humiliated in Dunkirk, whereas France capitulated to Germany in 1940. London was heavily bombarded. Bulgaria joined with the Axis, and at the same time, the German-Italy partnership seemingly dominated the Mediterranean. On the surface, the Axis was on the rise in Europe. The conditions were ripe for Thailand to re-design Mainland Southeast Asia by bandwagoning with greater revisionist powers such as Germany, Italy, and Japan to overhaul the international order. Or, the Thais could launch a swift attack on British Malaya in collaboration with the Japanese on the grounds of self-defence. But, for the Thai elites, despite a revisionist interest, the true victor is the one who does not wage war.

Contrary to what usual theoretical predictions would lead us to expect, Thailand continued its policy of absolute neutrality. Prince Wan ensured Huge G. Grant, the American minister to Bangkok, that Thailand pledged neither political nor military commitment to Japan during the mediating process (FRUS-1941-Vol.5-Document191). Wan's assurance statement could be dismissed as pretentious. However, the cabinet members similarly adhered to the same principle of neutrality and non-commitment to any powers. Phibun, for example, commented that 'we wish to be neutral forever. . . . But being neutral should be economically profitable' (TMCM 26/1941, 14-May-1941, 16). In his view, 'our country is completely under the influence of England, but they do not support us, whereas Japan has no influence over us, but seek[s] to support us every way' (ibid., 21). Although, by influence, the Thais meant selling oil to Thailand, it was clearly indicative of Thailand's continuation of a neutral policy.

Even Japan could not but reckon that Thailand would hardly depart from its neutral stance (FRUS-1941-Vol.5-Document239; MPH-Appendix-Vol.3-Document1122, A-569). Some Japanese newspapers, such as *Yomiuri*, the *Osaka Mainichi*, and the *Tokyo Nichi Nichi*, criticised the Thai government for its softening attitudes toward the West (NAT-[2]-KoTo-2.1.6/10). Thailand, unmovable in its neutral policy, ordered Phraya Srisena, the Thai minister to Japan, to protest on the grounds that these news agencies sought to draw Thailand from its neutrality. On the bright side, Phibun, Direk, and Srisena were of the opinion that such news was great because it informed the world that Thailand was neither pro-Japanese nor pro-West (ibid.). The news illustrated the image of a neutral country striving to strike a balance.

In order to demonstrate the commitment to neutrality, the Thai premier openly appealed to the world community to terminate the European war for the sake of humanity (NAT-SoRo-0201.44/45). The Thai policy-makers fully realised that the war between Britain and Japan would be inevitable and Thailand would be trapped in the middle of the great power conflict. Joining either side was not an option. The core objectives of Thai foreign policy were to remain independent and to be respected in the world. Affiliating with any camp was a zero-sum game because the country could incur economic losses and receive condemnations.

The government even enacted a law which stipulated the wartime duties of the Thai people. In principle, this law outlined how the Thai citizens were obliged to fight against any invading armies (NAT-[2]-SoRo-0201.98/2). The underlying reason for legislating this law mainly involved ontological security. In reality, had either Japan or Britain violated the Thai neutrality, the Thai Army of no more than 40,000 men, not to mention the inexperienced citizens, would not be able to organise resistance. Even the Japanese military factions were wholly confident on the prospect of the superiority of the British and Japanese forces marching on Thai soil (MPH-Appendix-Vol.4-Document1137, A-515). However, the Thai law was promulgated in order to preserve the national honour and status. Phibun was aware that winning or losing the fight against invasion could affect the status and dignity:

> We should adhere to the policy of self-defence. There can be two results: winning and losing. If we lose, we still preserve honour. Although we might lose the sovereignty, our name will appear to the world. But, if we win, we will have independence and greater standing. If we avoid fighting as in the case of Denmark and Indo-China, we will lose our dignity and independence.
> (TMCM 47/1941, 23-August-1941)

Phibun even considered the possibility of legislating another law to permit killing the citizens who would not fight off encroachers (ibid.). For him and others, being a slavish nation was worse than being slaughtered in battles (ibid.). Ultimately, he confessed that this law would be a mechanism to tell the world that Thailand would be solemn in resisting foreign intruders (ibid., 6). As Supreme Commander, Phibun secretly instructed the military on 2 December 1941 to fight to the death in case any foreign powers violated the nation's neutrality (Kobkua 1989, 25). The government also issued an order to plan the defensive lines in the country in preparation for any worst-case scenarios (TMCM 52/1941, 10-September-1941).

Apart from the affairs of national security and foreign relations, the government became increasingly concerned with the ways of living of the Thais. The Thai policy-makers were constantly alarmed by how their people dressed indecorously. Anxious by how other powers might misperceive Thailand's status, which could affect the neutral policy, the government attempted to modernise the traditional ways of living of the Thais by enacting laws to enforce prototypical conducts for the citizens (see Chapter 4 on 'Dresses and Duties'). Because the Thai ways of living bore a resemblance to backward countries, Phibun commented that: 'now we have nothing great . . . we are this backward, how can we be civilised? . . . If the nation is this bad, how can the nation survive?' (TMCM 49/1941, 30-August-1941). Ontological security is interrelated to physical security. For the ruling elites, if foreign powers recognised their nation as backward, they could potentially intervene in Thai domestic affairs on the grounds of civilising the underdeveloped nation. As a country of strategic importance, Thailand's policy of neutrality was a precarious enterprise amidst the conflict of the two great powers. Thailand could be engulfed by Japan as part of the Greater East Asia Co-Prosperity Sphere or could be occupied by Britain due to its strategic interest against Japan's southward expansion. In this light, the government's social-engineering programmes could, on the one hand, fulfil the ruling elites' sense of ontological insecurity and could be an instrument to guarantee the status as a developed nation.

In sum, after the Franco-Thai confrontation, there were available windows of opportunities for Thailand's revisionism. Thailand could explicitly align with the Axis powers or form a coalition with Japan to eradicate the Western influence from Asia so they could reclaim all of the lost territories. Instead of pursuing such belligerent policies, the Thai policy-makers stood firmly on a neutral path. Its assertiveness in the case of French Indochina in late 1940 to early 1941 was due to the French stigmatisation of Thailand's status. As such, when the conflict was settled, the Thais reverted back to absolute neutrality.

Befriending Japan: preserving and enhancing honour

In November 1941, the Japanese clearly outlined the Japanese war plan and marked Thailand as one of the key areas to execute their grand designs (Ike 1967, 242). The Japanese invasion on Thai soil was not unforeseeable because the Thai cabinet members were discreetly informed by the British intelligence a few days after Japan's November decision (MPH-Appendix-Vol.4-Document1150, A-520). Ultimately, as the common historiography suggests, the Thais aligned with the Japanese until the end of the war. The explanation that Thailand was a jackal state which pursued an opportunistic route along with other greater revisionist powers could not fully grasp Thailand's foreign policy decisions towards Japan.

Considering Japan's strategy in Asia, the Imperial government's plan towards Thailand could be categorised as less violent than any other places. This was due to the fact that the Japanese campaign against Britain required the bases, supplies, and aids in Thailand more than ever in order to defend against the British troops in Malaya and Burma. As such, Thailand's partial or reluctant compliance would thwart the Japanese operations and could result in a war of attrition. Occupying the nation by force would render the war tasks difficult as the telegram to Tokyo indicated as follows:

> No matter how weak a country she is, if we were to make an enemy of Siam, it would create great difficulties for our Burma operations for which we

> need transit through Siamese territory, and also for our use of the Southern Siam RR lines for our Army operating in Malaya. In addition, it would cause untold difficulties from the point of view of establishment of our ultimate goal . . . the best idea is to prepare a plan of operations so that southern Siam be sacrificed if unavoidable but that the neutrality of the greater part of Siam be preserved.
>
> (MPH-Appendix-Vol.4-Document1105, A-504)

It could be inferred from the message that antagonising Thailand would be the least desirable option for Japan to execute its grand strategy.

Fundamentally, Japan sought the rights of its army's passage with essential aids from the Thai government. In the document that outlined the Japanese plans, it was specified that a mutual defence pact could be concluded between the two nations if Thailand strongly craved it (Ike 1967, 242). Nonetheless, the original intention of the Japanese was neither about any agreement on Thailand's military participation in the Imperial Army's campaigns in Burma nor Thailand's declarations of war against the Allied powers.

The central purpose of the Imperial government was to utilise Thailand as a stationary hub and to avoid trampling on Thailand's dignity. Teiji Tsubokami, the Japanese ambassador[1] to Thailand, recommended that if the Burma and Malaya operations had been completed, it would be necessary that 'the independence of Thai would be respected even more than at present while Thai is maintaining neutrality' (MPH-Appendix-Vol.4-Document1175, A-529). He continued his emphasis that the vision of the East Asia Co-Prosperity Sphere should consider the reality that,

> Thailand's sovereignty must not be impaired beyond the minimum limits of necessity, and that her standing as an independent nation must be maintained to the very last.
>
> (ibid.)

Similarly, Hiroshi Tamura, the Japanese military attaché to Thailand, cautioned against undermining Thailand's sense of dignity, as he notified the Japanese Southern Area Army (SAA) by quoting Phibun that he expected the Japanese forces to avoid marching on central parts of the nation 'because this would have its impact on Thailand's honour and dignity' (Swan 1987, 277). Tamura asserted again on 4 December 1941 that,

> By our respecting the dignity of the Thai Government, there will be no interference with Japanese army invasions of Prachuab and southwards. Moreover he [Phibun – Swan's note] is determined to get the whole nation to cooperate in a positive way
>
> (ibid., 278)

The comments of the Japanese diplomats were indicative of how Thailand's status concerns mattered greatly to their foreign policy decisions. As their analyses had shown, defying the Thais' standing could trigger resistance and non-cooperation. Hence, maintaining a friendly relationship without dishonouring them by offering a mutual defence agreement could be an effective tool to appease the Thais. Asada Shunsuke, the Japanese consul-general to Thailand, wrote in his memoir that any mutual pacts with the Thai government should be agreed to permit the Japanese passage. However, such pacts were nothing more than a symbol:

> [O]ur purpose was to secure friendly relations between the two countries in spite of military exigencies. So the contents of the draft treaties didn't have much substance. Expressions like "Mutual cooperation", "joint defence", or "military alliance" didn't indicate clearly our intentions or plan. Therefore, I could go so far as to say that they had no meaning in a political sense.
> (Batson & Hajime 1990, 62)

The Japanese 15th Army, under the command of the SAA, launched an attack on the Thai nation through the six parts of the Southern provinces of Thailand on 7 December 1941. Fifteen Japanese ships had blockaded the Gulf of Thailand, which meant the Thais were isolated from other powers. As a result of Phibun's secret order, there had been military and civilian opposition which deprived the Japanese and Thais of 141 and 183 men respectively. From the night of 7 December to the morning of 8 December 1941, the Japanese requested their rights of passage through Thailand's territories. For the Thai policy-makers, the threat was imminent. Yet the only concern of the government revolved around how the Thais could be subjugated to an inferior position. Adun Adundescharas, the chief of the Police Department and Deputy Minister of Interior, suggested that: 'if we fight, it would not last a year. This defeat is the equivalent of being a slave, which means we would be a colony for certainty' (TMCM-Special-Cabinet-Meeting, 7–8-December-1941[2]). His recommendation was that the Thais should solely grant the Japanese the rights to march through the country without declaring war on the US and Britain. From this move, the Allies would sympathise with Thailand's judgment call because the rights of passage, according to Adun, was 'a compromise but it does not amount to co-operation. . . . Yes, our level of independence may be diminished, but it would be better than becoming a colony' (ibid.). Phibun, late for the historic cabinet meeting, asked whether to fight to the death. He personally expected to negotiate a ceasefire first and if the cabinet members decided to ward off the intruders, he would get along with any propositions (ibid.). The policy-makers, especially Phibun, a military man, thoroughly knew the power differential between the two nations. Yet, on the verge of crisis, they did not rule out the option to fight. The rationale behind the immediate confrontation with the Japanese troops and the continuation to fight was related to the elites' concern about how the British and Americans might perceive Thailand as a Japanese stooge. This was evident in Phibun's statement in response to how the Thais lost their lives: 'the British could not blame us' (ibid.). Thawan Thamrongnawasawat, the Minister of Justice, reiterated that 'the reality has surfaced that we have fought. They [the Allied powers – my note] should understand us' (ibid.).

As planned beforehand, the Japanese proposed four types of agreement for the Thais to consider. The first agreement was the conclusion of the military alliance between the two nations. The second agreement was the proposition for Thailand to co-operate by joining the Axis. The third agreement was a treaty stipulating that Thailand would endorse the Japanese passage and provide necessary aids to the Imperial Army. The fourth agreement was pertinent to the language of common defence. Despite differences in the gist of each agreement, the four drafts shared the same clause on how the Japanese would guarantee Thailand's sovereignty and respect the nation's dignity. This provision was specifically crafted to avoid riling Thailand's sense of honour. And to incentivise the Thais further, each agreement, with the exception of the third version, suggested that Japan would eventually return the lost territories to Thailand.

There were two major decisions facing the Thai elites: fighting or negotiating the terms of the proposed treaties. As a revisionist nation with limited aspirations, the first, second, and fourth agreements were captivating. Bandwagoning with Japan would be a rational option. On the contrary, the cabinet members were debating the issues of honour and how the world would view Thailand's status under the Japanese orbit. As for the premier, he was open to either fight or not fight. Wichit, for example, renounced the fourth agreement on common defence because, it would make Thailand appear 'in the same status as Indo-China [under Japanese dictate – my note] and Thailand's honour would be eroded' (ibid.). Direk advocated a non-fighting alternative which was predicated on status and recognition:

> I think we cannot put up a fight. . . . In fact, they [Japanese] said that they respected us, we should permit their passage, but forcing us to join with them cannot be acceptable. We only want them to honour our nation's prestige if we still love one another.
>
> (ibid.)

Pora Samarharn, the minister without portfolio, summarised the interest of Thailand in a well-rounded manner: 'In this case, I heartily believe that the Japanese returning the lost territories is not important. I think we should show the world that we do it because it is necessary' (ibid.). In conclusion, Pridi recommended that the government should simply grant the rights of passage to the Japanese troops without any consideration of the lost territories, and, ultimately, the cabinet members consented to this resolution. Anxious about how this decision could tarnish the nation's prestige, Pridi felt it imperative to announce to the Thais that 'we have fought already . . . but later the Japanese had solicited a negotiation with us' (ibid.). Stating how Japan was the one proposing a negotiation, according to Pridi, would not damage the government's image and the nation's dignity.

Thailand's decision on the morning of 8 December 1941 was what the Japanese desired in the first place: the rights of passage without Thailand's involvements in Japan's military affairs. The British and Americans were initially sympathetic to Thailand's fate to the extent that the Thai nation was treated as an enemy-occupied area (FRUS-1941-Vol.5-Document411, Document429). However, on 11 December 1941, a few days after the conclusion of the treaties, Thailand secretly became a formal military ally of Japan (FRUS-1941-Vol.5-Document416). The clauses of the military agreement included how Japan would bolster Thailand's recovery of the lost territories.

Why had Thailand swiftly turned towards a close association with Japan after a firm commitment to limited co-operation? There had been various historical explanations offered to shed light on the puzzle. Nonetheless, the circumstantial evidence generally presented to interpret Thailand's precipitation of the alliance was Japan's immediate success in attacking Pearl Harbor and the sinking of the renowned British warships *Prince of Wales* and *Repulse* (Charivat 1985, 230; Kobkua 1989, 51). Such events were drawn to make sense of Thailand's bandwagon policy which conformed to the traditional framework of flexible foreign policy. That is, Thailand's Japan policy was implemented to bend with the prevailing wind. At face value, the factor of the international situation was persuasive. However, the reason par excellence could be branded as either *cum hoc ergo propter hoc* or *post hoc ergo propter hoc*. In other words, the Japanese seemingly advantageous situation might not influence how the policy-makers decided their nation's fate. In their perceptions, the successes were indecisive, as Thawan suggested that he heard that both the American and Japanese fleets were equally damaged (TMCM-Special-Cabinet-Meeting, 8-December-1941). Similarly, Pora warned the cabinet members to assess the pros and cons of Japan's possibility of winning and losing (TMCM-Special-Cabinet-Meeting, 10-December-1941). Thus, for the Thais, Japan's immediate successes would not ensure a future victory. In order to explain Thailand's complete reinvigoration of foreign policy, it is imperative to describe the development in the aftermath of the unofficial military alignment in a chronological fashion.

For the Japanese, the military agreement with Thailand would amount to nothing more than a mere symbol to undergird 'friendly wartime relations' (Batson & Hajime 1990, 62) Nevertheless, several Japanese officials disputed the ideas of the alliance as Asada wrote,

> When I returned home the following February, I was asked a strange question by one of the highest executive officials in the Ministry of Foreign Affairs. He wanted to know why we went to the extent of concluding the alliance treaty, when the Ministry of Foreign Affairs regarded the agreement on troop passage as sufficient. . . . I was very perplexed by the fact that many others held a totally opposite view.
>
> (ibid., 62–63)

It could imply that some factions in Tokyo strongly opposed the formation of the alliance even for symbolic reasons because they felt disturbed due to the possibility that the agreement could ignite Thailand's spirits to entangle with Japan's grand strategy in Asia. In spite of differences within Japan, the goal was identical: maintaining Thailand's role in the war as a passive rather than a proactive actor.

After the conclusion of the passage treaty, the Thais were content that their sovereignty was preserved, as evident in how the members of parliament applauded Phahol's praise on how 'independence is not going anywhere' (Ananda 1975b, 282) The swift reinvigoration of the policy was due to the concern for recognition from Japan. In the cabinet meeting on 11 December 1941, Adun reported to the session that the Japanese troops arbitrarily disarmed the Thai authorities in different places on Thai soil (TMCM-Special-Cabinet-Meeting, 11-December-1941). Such insolent behaviours were defiant to Thailand's status as an equal, sovereign nation. As for Phibun, he was fearful of his country becoming another Manchukuo under the Japanese thumb (ibid.). All being said, Ministry of Defence Mangkorn Phromyodhi was the first to suggest that the government 'militarily align with Japan to preserve the independence' (TMCM-Special-Cabinet-Meeting, 7–8-December-1941). Henceforth, regarding Thai foreign policy thinking, befriending the Japanese through the alliance channel could elevate the status of the nation from a supposedly enemy-occupied country to a partner-based country. This strand of thinking was reflected in the premier's announcement of the Japanese-Thai pact:

> The government wishes to announce that our agreement with the Japanese government is carefully considered, and is seen as the best for the country. . . . Therefore, please keep in mind that Japan is the friend of Thailand in order to enhance honour altogether.
>
> (Publicity Bureau 1941a, 2735)

Phibun's public broadcast could be viewed as a mere façade. The revisionist interest of the Thai elites could be a vital factor to influence Thailand's military bandwagoning for profit. The evidence was the secret understanding between Thailand and Japan in the agreement signed on 21 December 1941, which stated how Japan would bolster Thailand to realise its territorial ambition. Accepting such an assumption without questioning its validity could not wholly capture how, given opportunities before the Japanese invasion until the night Japan requested the troop passage, the Thais firmly adhered to neutrality. It would also not be able to account for the behaviours, which are to be discussed in the following sections.

The war for recognition

After formalising military ties with Japan, Thailand became increasingly proactive towards Japan. The interpretation of this case would not be completed without considering Thailand's anxiety to be recognised by Japan. The fear of survival and territorial greed might dictate Thailand's bandwagoning policy. These factors, however, might not characterise how Thailand disobeyed Japan and acted on its own accord. This section demonstrates how Thailand's sense of ontological insecurity propelled the Thais to pursue policies independent of Japan. They wanted to express an identity of being a partner rather than a satellite country.

Seeking an equal partnership in an inescapable war

For Japan, the inking of the military pact was nothing more than a talk shop. Hence, the Japanese, in the entire years of alliance, would seek to limit Thailand's participation to the minimum level. This guideline certainly included the secret memorandum on recovering the lost territories with Thailand, as the Japanese document revealed the command from the Imperial Guard Headquarters (IGH):

> [On the secret agreement – my note]. . . . However, we want you to avoid at this time any positive expression about allowing the recovery of lost territory, the extent of territory to be recovered or when recovery might take place.
> (cited in Murashima 2006, 1068)

The instruction was for the SAA to avoid arousing Thailand to entangle with Japan's war plan in Burma (ibid., 1068). Given an ulterior intention of Japan to hamper any of Thailand's aspirations to participate in the campaign and given the fact that Japan was materially superior to Thailand, the Thai leaders should be discouraged to pursue any policies independent or insubordinate to Japan. On the contrary, the Thais deviated from the textbook expectations.

In reality, the Thais could passively deal with the Japanese to avoid major condemnation from the Allied powers or to avoid frictions with the presence of the SAA. Since Japan was reluctant to involve Thailand in any military campaigns, the optimal path for the Thais would be to limit their participation to only facilitating necessary aids to the SAA and to negotiating the return of the territories, leaving Tokyo with her vigorous operations. This strategy could kill two birds with one stone. On the one hand, if the Allies achieved victory, Thailand could claim that it was an enemy-occupied country. On the other hand, if the Axis thrived, Thailand could also claim a share of the spoils from the conquerors. In this light, the behaviours of Thailand according to this optimal choice could be described as bandwagoning for profit.

Although the formal ceremony to sign the Japanese-Thai alliance took place on 21 December 1941, the content of the military agreement had been discussed since 14 December 1941. The Thais, without material leverage in the relationship, determined to improve themselves to the status of Japan. The language of the agreement, which was composed by the Japanese, was erased and corrected on several occasions (NAT-BokoSungsut-1.12/45). This was to ensure that the language would not implicate Thailand's inferior relations with Japan. Any words and phrases which insinuated that Japan commanded or ordered Thailand were crossed out and edited to signify an equal-footing co-operation. Certain problematic clauses could be drawn to present as follows:

- **Original Clause 2**: 'In a necessary case, Thailand *must* build stronger naval bases to defend the west and east coasts of Thailand's Kra Isthmus'.
  - **Amended Clause 2**: 'Japan *wishes* Thailand to build and enhance naval bases for patrolling . . . in the west and east coasts of Thailand in the

country's southern areas. The purpose is to defend Thailand's coastal areas when and where it is necessary'.

- **Original Clause 3**: 'Thailand will *yield* to the Japanese troops to use bases and facilities along the coastal areas whenever Japan *wants*'.
    - **Amended Clause 3**: 'Thailand will *facilitate* the Japanese troops for patrolling . . . when Japan deems it necessary'.
- **Original Clause 4**: 'In defending Thailand's water, the Thai government *must* consult with the Japanese navy first'.
    - **Amended Clause 4**: 'In defending Thailand's water, Japan *asks* Thailand to proceed by consulting and agreeing with the Japanese navy'.
- **Original Clause 7**: 'The Thai railway, which the Japanese Division would utilise for military transportation, *must* be prioritised over others'.
    - **Amended Clause 7**: 'Regarding, the Japanese military transportation by the Thai railway, the Japanese *asks* for priority . . . with the exception of when there is a joint operation, both armies could utilise the railway altogether'.[3]

Although the matter of wording could be viewed as unimportant, it did matter to the Thais because the treaty would institutionalise the foundations of the relationship between the two countries, and the Thai government preferred proper standing in the alliance. But for Japan, the agreement, as previously mentioned, was to satisfy Thailand's search for honour.

For the Thais, equal status in a relationship mattered to their physical and ontological security. Although the Thais became a Japanese ally on 11 December 1941 through a secret agreement, both nations ceremoniously sanctified the treaty on 21 December 1941 in Thailand's Wat Phra Kaew. Regarding Thailand's best interest, silencing the issue of the secret pact on 11 December 1941 could be employed as a justification of Japan's coercion if the tide turned against Japan later. Holding a ceremony on 21 December 1941 was vainglorious and unnecessary because it amounted to formally declaring Thailand's connivance with Japan. Wichit, a newly appointed foreign minister, testified about this to the parliament:

> The form of the treaty signed on 11 December was the method Japan did to Manchukuo. Hence, Japan wants us to adopt another type of agreement, which was the platform Japan does to Germany. Since an offer was put forth, which could be our honour, we agreed.
>
> (TPMP 4/1941, 23-December-1941)

It was clear that the transition from 11 December to 21 December 1941 was predicated on the anxiety of an unequal relationship and Japan's approbation. The elites were troubled by how Japan might transform its nation into another Manchukuo. In this regard, Thailand's ritualisation of the bilateral agreement was significant because it explicitly exhibited how Thailand differed from other Japanese satellites.

The majority of the members of parliament unanimously voted in confidence for the Thai-Japanese alliance. Their only concern was the status of Thailand in Japan's vision of regional order and alliance, as Chamlong Daoruang, Phibun's political critic, raised a motion: 'What would happen with Thailand's honour? And, regarding the treaty we signed with Japan, do we have a chance to stand on a shoulder-to-shoulder basis with them?' (ibid.).

The foreign policy thinking in the early period of the Thai-Japanese alliance revolved around the concern of its nation's status with Japan. Phibun's right-hand man, Chai Prathipasen, voiced his concern as follows:

> We should go along with Japan's military operations and give the Japanese army the things it demands. But at the same time we should not forget that there is not loss to us. Our helping Japan does not make us Japan's servants or slaves.
> (cited in Murashima 2002, 197–198)

Since 1939 and since Thailand's prestige reached the apex after the Franco-Thai war, the policy-makers viewed their country as one of the equal countries in the world. Phibun's reflection on Thailand's mastery of agriculture exemplified such a tendency:

> I think that Japan wants to study agriculture and other ideas from Thailand. . . . So if we completely achieve our works [showing them Thailand's qualities – my note], it would be the way for them to respect our independence and sovereignty. . . . We can concentrate to become the leader of the school of all Asians at a great pace.
> (NAT-[2]-SoRo-0201.98/9)

For the Thais, highlighting their own qualities and educating the Japanese on agricultural dimensions was meaningful to the policy-makers in relation to status concern. They maintained a strong conviction that the Japanese approbation and recognition of their competence in agriculture could symbolise an equal-footing relationship, which would earn respect from the imperial government. The prudence in its own civilised ways of life could be captured by Thailand's Premier private comment:

> [Regarding Japan's construction of railway] I think it is problematic to attack India, but if they build them, it would be great. We can spread our culture following the Japanese troops. This is how an ally helps one another.
> (NAT-BokoSungsut-2.4.1.2/1)

Only a nation that considered itself as reaching a civilised stage would propose to spread its culture. In summary, the Thai elites approached the alliance from a perspective which involved status and recognition.

Instead of pursuing a pragmatic policy, the Thais proactively moved against Japan's scheme by asserting themselves to participate more as a partner. In order to achieve such goals, the first step was to show to the world that it was not Japan's satellite country. In order to express an identity of partnership with Japan, Thailand conformed to Japan's ideal of liberating Asia from the Western influence by pleading with Chiang Kai-Shek to terminate the Sino-Japanese war in order to unify the Asians to build 'culture and civilisation' (NAT-[2]-KoTo-1.1/17). Phibun also stressed the importance of the Asian co-operation: 'I invite you all to help recover Asian honour together. I honestly wish you to create a mutual understanding with Japan' (ibid.). In his speech, he initially emphasised that his announcement was not forced upon him by any parties.

In fact, the Thais had a choice to avoid the broadcast, which could turn against them later. They initially sought to transmit the message to Chiang via a private channel. However, the means of communication to Chungking was severed. As Prince Wan noted, 'The reason we have to broadcast was that we could not send a telegram to them. . . . But it only meant to be a message to Field Marshal Chiang Kai-Shek only' (ibid., 13). Delivering such a speech unnecessarily portrayed an image of Thailand's commitment towards Japanese ambitions. The message to the Chinese leaders was published throughout the world. The implication was simply how the Thais wished to be seen as a partner to construct the Asian order as opposed to a colony under Japan's thumb.

Another daring move undertaken by the Thais was the declaration of war against the British and Americans. Following the formalisation of the alliance on 21 December 1941, Thailand declared war on the Allied powers on 25 January 1942 without the consent of Japan. Since the Japanese invasion of Thailand, the country had been acknowledged as an enemy-occupied territory. Strategically speaking, such perceptions were advantageous to the Japanese because the Allied powers could be reluctant to bombard Thailand. The declaration of war, according to Direk, would unnecessarily illustrate Thailand's deep commitment to Japan. In other words, the state of war could be a burden on the Thais later (Direk & Keyes 1978, 76). Prince Wan even admitted later that the state of war technically began after Thailand's signature of the alliance. Henceforth, the declaration of war was nothing but 'a matter of formality' (Reynolds 1994, 264).

For the Thai elites, as an ally in a large-scale war, inaction could be interpreted as dependent on Japan. On 22 January 1942, the Thai elites became furious by how the Swiss press published the story and depicted Thailand as Japan's lackey. The telegram was sent from Switzerland, the country where the king of Thailand resided during wartime, to the government. The discontent of the Thais could be captured by the message of the king's assistant:

> Swiss press always publish news either we are occupied or controlled by Japanese troops. Since war broken in Pacific yesterday was the first time that the radio saying Thai troops now started openly to attack Burma but the Swiss press published they are under the command of Japanese officers.
>
> (NAT-[2]-SoRo-0201.92/13)

A Swiss map-making company similarly reproduced a map which showed how Thailand had been under Japanese control along with Indo-China, Java, Malaya, and Burma. Hence, the Thai elites became hectic to correct its image to show to the world (NAT-[2]-SoRo-0201.21.3/5). Branding Thailand as a nation under the Japanese dictate hurt the prestige of the nation and introduced the recognition question to the surface. It was beyond toleration to the extent that the government issued a statement of protest as follows:

> [Regarding the story that Thailand was under the command of Japan – my note] The news is without foundation. You all know that our relationship with Japan has rooted in the Alliance pact signed in Bangkok, and each contracting party respects independence and sovereignty of one another. . . . There is no single Japanese military personnel appointed to supervise our activities. . . . It would be much appreciated if you can inform the Swiss government about this.
>
> (NAT-[2]-SoRo-0201.92/13)

For the world, Thailand's status was comparable to Manchukuo. The message to the Swiss was notable because it implied how Thailand anticipated the world to acknowledge itself as an equal partner of Japan rather than a colony. In order to correct such an image, its declaration of war against the Allies without Japan was crucial.

The quest to declare war was not in Thailand's best interest. Firstly, as Wichit admitted to the parliament: 'Japan does not encourage us to declare war' (TMPM 4/1941, 23-December-1941). The Japanese evidence similarly noted the intent of Japan:

> Why should we trust such a country [Thailand – my note]? . . . There is no benefit to us in Thailand declaring war. There is only some propaganda value. Recovering the lost territories is a problem that complicates our operations in Burma.
>
> (Murashima 2006, 1069)

Despite Japan's reluctance, Thailand proactively sought to formalise the state of war between its nation and the Allied powers. In fact, the declaration of war on 25 January 1941 was undertaken without any official notice to the Japanese (ibid., 1072). Lieutenant Colonel Okikatsu Arao, the senior military personnel of the SAA, fervently expressed his emotion as follows: 'We heard that Thailand had declared war on Britain and the United States at 12:00. It is regrettable that they did not notify us in advance' (cited in ibid., 1072).

The conspicuous event of Thailand's pronouncing its state of war with the Allied powers without Japanese approval was to seek recognition as an equal partner. As a historian observes: 'By declaring war on its own initiative, the Thai leaders certainly wanted to demonstrate that Thailand was not a country subordinate to Japan' (ibid., 1072). Thamsook Numnonda (1978), a historian on

Thailand and the Second World War, offers a similar analysis: 'The government of Field Marshal Phibunsongkhram may want to show that his government could act independently without any permission' (14). Phibun reaffirmed this point in the cabinet that,

> We should not let them [Japanese] build Asia alone. . . . It is better than allowing Tokyo to build everything. They will appreciate us. There may not be any harm in declaring war.
>
> (the cabinet minutes on 25 January 1942 cited in Vinita 1975, 224)[4]

The comment indicated that the declaration of war was tied to the struggle for recognition. The Germans, responsible for the European theatre, congratulated the Thais for participating in the war. Content for receiving recognition from the major European power, Wichit, appointed as a foreign minister after the Japanese-Thai alliance, replied to the German minister that,

> The declaration of war has received a consensus from the Thai brethren, and the Thais feel honoured to be able to stand along with the chivalrous nation such as Germany.
>
> (NAT-[2]-KoTo-1.1.5/9)

Clearly, the questions of standing and recognition from other war partners were prevalent concerns among the Thai elites. Bandwagoning for profit without any action was inadequate to explain such behaviours. Apart from reaping a share of spoils from the greater power, the Thais craved to become another architect and gatekeeper of the regional order. Strictly speaking, Thailand avoided subjecting itself to the tutelage of Japan's East Asian scheme. As a military ally with equal status, Thailand's passive foreign policy could be misconstrued as a state under the Japanese federation in which foreign affairs should be hinged on the central government.

To further demonstrate that the Thai nation was not subservient to Japan, Thailand independently sought to become a formal member of the Axis powers. The rationale of Thailand to join the Axis was to exemplify that it was a partner in the war. One concerning citizen petitioned the government to enhance equality with the Axis countries so that anyone could not look down on Thailand (NAT-SoRo-0201.8/99). The policy elites also shared common ground on this approach. For instance, the secret order from Phibun was sent from Bangkok to the Thai embassy in Tokyo to sound out the Japanese opinions regarding Thailand's chance to be admitted as a member of the Axis powers (NAT-[2]-KoTo-1.1/23). Such a bold move, however, was not welcomed by Japan. Japanese Prime Minister Hideki Tojo and Foreign Minister Shigenori Togo opposed the idea of Thailand's potential status as part of the Axis powers because Thailand's Axis membership would jeopardise the Japanese leadership in Asia (Reynolds 1988, 353) and it would undesirably enhance the ties between Thailand and Germany, which would provide more manoeuvring options for Thailand in the region (Murashima 2006, 1070).

The intention of joining the Axis enterprise was genuine as Phibun emphasised that if the secret instruction had been compromised, he would execute any person involved (Konthi 1984, 106). In the quest for recognition, Phibun confessed that: 'the question of the Tripartite Pact, if we succeed, it would be our masterpiece. We should try' (NAT-[2]-KoTo-1.1.5/9). The reason was a concern for status. Akira Muto, chief of the Japanese Army Ministry, read between the lines and concluded that 'Thailand is eager to join [the Axis – my note], and they need it to save face as an independent country' (Murashima 2006, 1070). As Wichit stated in his diplomatic cable that without being recognised as a partner in this war, Thailand might be 'treated as a small country without any rights or influence' (Direk & Keyes 1978, 76). The Thai leaders, undistinguished from the case of the First World War, craved for their place in the peace talks after the war (ibid.). Such an incentive was evident in their secret order to collect pertinent information for the post-war settlement in case Thailand could demand reparations as a victor (NAT-BokoSungsut-1/103). Being present at a post-war peace talk would greatly enhance the status of the nation as in the case of Siam after the First World War.

In order to achieve such ends, the Thais circumvented the Japanese by boosting more interactions with the Germans and Italians by organising dining events (NAT-[2]-KoTo-8.1.1/27). The strategy was to weave Germany and Italy into the process of recognising Thailand as a war partner in Asia. For instance, the Thai government sponsored the German cultural institute and the Thai-German Association. The ultimate goal of Thailand's supportive stance towards Germany was to 'uplift the status of the Thai-German Association to be equal to the Japanese-Thai Association' (NAT-[2]-KoTo-1.1.5/9). The Thai leaders also resorted to providing the German Minister in Bangkok with classical music to win hearts and minds of the Germans. Regarding the relationship with Italy, Phibun expressed his opinion as follows:

> We should expand our affairs into Italy to become a European mediator. This will be proper. I feel like Germany greatly appeased Japan. In relation to supporting us, the Germans would have wanted to help, but they are worried about Japan.
>
> (ibid.)

All in all, the Thai leaders played the Axis powers against one another in order to obtain admission into the alliance without the Japanese endorsement. As a central broker of the Axis, the Germans were indecisive to intervene in Asian affairs. The Reich realised from the inchoate inception of the Axis that Japan was the natural leader of the region (NAT-[2]-SoRo-0201.86/129). Prayoon, Phibun's close aide, was informed that because 'Thailand is located in the area where Japan is a leader, admission [into the Axis – my note] would be successful only when Japan holds nothing against it' (ibid.). As such, the German Minister informed Wichit that he knew 'Japan desires to hamper Thailand's entry into the Tripartite Pact. However, the German government believes that they cannot obstruct this tendency forever' (NAT-[2]-KoTo-1.1.5/9). The German Minister therefore assured Wichit that 'it would not be too long before Thailand's admittance' (ibid.).

Eventually, Direk, a newly appointed ambassador to Tokyo, adhered to the premier's instruction to sound out the Japanese government with regard to Thailand's Axis membership. As expected by the Thais, Togo personally informed Direk that the co-operation between Thailand and Japan had been satisfactory; hence, it would be unnecessary to depend on others for help (Konthi 1984, 106). Despite the failed bid for its place among the equals, the effort to seek recognition was genuine. In fact, joining the Axis could be an irrational move. Firstly, the Thais had signed the military pact with Japan at the early stage of the war. Both nations were, according to the principle of *pacta sunt servanda*, obliged to defend and aid each other. As a small nation, the military agreement should be a sufficient stronghold to reap benefits without deep imbroglios. Secondly, in consideration of the viewpoint of the small state, the crystallisation of its status in the Axis could bring about harsh treatments to itself if the Axis had suffered defeat. In summary, Thailand's Axis card appeared unwise to play. A simple explanation which highlights a material factor and interest would not be able to cope with Thailand's deviant behaviour.

Because the Thai leaders were disturbed by its position as a junior nation within the Japanese order, they became assertively insistent in seeking recognition from the great powers through the Axis membership. The intent of the move was unpretentious to the extent that even though the Japanese barred them from the Axis club, the Thai elites circumvented Tokyo by negotiating with Rome and Berlin through a back channel. It is important to note that even before Phibun came to power, the Thais aspired to emerge as another great power. Hence, given the fact that Thailand and Japan coalesced to construct Asia for the Asians, the Thai leaders would equally wish to acquire the status of mastery in the region as well.

Wilful deployment: Thailand's operations in Burma

The failed attempt to bid for the Axis membership did not break Thailand's ambition to elevate its status in the alliance. On the contrary, the Thais were ignited to devise a plan to obtain recognition from Japan and the global community. In order to demonstrate that Thailand was not subjected to Japanese directives, it unbendingly decided to collaborate with Japan's military operations by offering to deploy the Thai troops into Burma.

Since the beginning of the Pacific War, Japan had been reluctant to permit Thailand's involvements in any of her war plans. Although the possibility of the advancement of Thailand's army into British Burma could begin in January 1942, when the terms of the military co-operation between the two nations were finalised, the Thai Army only received clearance from the Imperial Army to deploy its troops into Burma in May 1942 (TNA-HW-1/571). The period when the Thai Army crossed into Burma coincided with the rainy season, which would be a hurdle for any military expeditions. The scenario of how Thailand dispatched its troops into Burma riddled IR scholars with two puzzles. Firstly, why would Thailand futilely squander its wartime resources to the extent of deploying its men into Burma? As an ally, it was already duty-bound to support Japan in finances and supplies. The military campaign on foreign soil would impose extra fiscal burdens on the Thai state and it would intricately tie Bangkok to Tokyo in the long run. Secondly, despite Japan's reluctance, how was it possible for Thailand to assert itself in a proactive manner to deviate from Japan's original plans? The Imperial Army was materially superior to the Thai Army in terms of capabilities. Yet the Thai leaders defied Japan's domineering attitudes by claiming for its part in the Burmese campaign. Regardless of such conditions, a counterargument could be raised to explain the Thai policy. For example, Thailand's proactive policies could stem from its interest in annexing Burma. However, the explanation that Thailand coveted Burma's Shan states was far from satisfaction because it inadequately accounted for why the small-sized Thai Army would explore its ways into Burma even though Japan was obliged to return the territories to them later.

The SAA had been thwarting Thailand's military aspirations in Burma from the beginning of their military relationship. As the Japanese evidence suggested,

> The defense of the Tenassarim region at the outset should be the responsibility of the Japanese army. . . . And the Thai army will not be requested to participate.
>
> (Murashima 2006, 1067)

Likewise, Okikatsu Arao, SAA's senior military lieutenant, objected to Thailand's initiative because it could hinder Japan's policy: 'To effectively implementing central command's policies, the Thais should not be allowed to go [into Burma – Musrahima's note]' (ibid., 1078). Not only did Japan intentionally disapprove of Thailand's military proposition, but the guidelines of the military conduct, which prevented Thailand from playing a greater role in the war, were also institutionalised in the Nippon-Thai military deal. According to the military agreement signed earlier between the two nations, Thailand's central duty was purely defensive:

> [Regarding the military agreement between Thailand and Japan – my note], the mission of the Thai army for the present is the defense of Thailand. For this purpose, it should waste no time in strongly fortifying the northwest border so that it can independently repel any serious enemy attacks.
>
> (ibid., 1077)

In other words, regardless of Japan's unwillingness, the Thais were legally prevented from undertaking their military expedition.

The defensive responsibility, which was assigned to Thailand by Japan, singled out the Thais from the Japanese empire's order. The Thai leaders became frustrated with how Japan precluded them from participating in military affairs.

For instance, when the Imperial Army successfully occupied Singapore and Rangoon, the Thai press enquired into the role of Thailand in Japan's triumph. Teiji Tsubokami, the Japanese ambassador, ambiguously replied that,

> Speaking in military terms, Japan and Thailand have co-operated in this war, that is, we have strategically co-operated in a unifying manner. The subjugation of Singapore and Rangoon was a product of consistent war practice between Japan and Thailand, which means the Thais have pursued a policy according to the alliance treaty.
>
> (NAT-[2]-SoRo-0201.98.1/6)

The statement, in other words, produced no substance regarding Thailand's actual role in the war success.

Japan's hindrance of her war ally to participate in any campaign and Thailand's desire to exert its activism could be shown from the conflict between the SAA and Thailand's Chief of Publicity Bureau Pairote Jayanam. As chief of the Thai propaganda machine, Pairote, as any other Thai elites, realised that Thailand was placed in a less assertive position. Thus, Pairote volunteered to dispatch his men to cover the news of the operations in Burma. He even assured Japan that the Thai government would be financially responsible for the relevant budget regarding the trip. His agenda was obvious: the Thais should be recognised as an equal partner in the war (NAT-[2]-SoRo-0201.98/19). Pairote's insistence was, however, dismissed by the Japanese. The reason for a blunt dismissal was abstruse: 'If the Thais wanted to follow to the frontline [Burma – my note], it would amount to hardship because the Japanese troops travel day and night, which would exhaust the Thai entourage' (ibid.). Additionally, as a measure of discouragement, Japan strictly requested Thailand to halt any reports on the Burmese front. Japan, in other words, was mildly reluctant to permit Thailand to become part of any active campaigns. As a potential partner, such inclination signified Thailand's inferior position in the alliance, which became a source of Thailand's status frustration.

In order to ensure Thailand's existential security, the Thais became visibly desperate to send their troops into the Shan states. For example, following Japan's novel successes, Phibun initiated a plan to court Japan to endorse Thailand's operations by sending a military mission to congratulate the SAA in Saigon. The Japanese document recorded the intention of Phibun's mission as an attempt to 'facilitate the liaison of joint operations' (Murashima 2006, 1077). Nonetheless, Japan shrugged off Thailand's courtesy on the grounds of being preoccupied with other affairs and it would be an inconvenience to receive any mission (ibid., 1078).

As a measure to pressure Japan and to exhibit Thailand as a desirable place to reside, the Thai state independently enacted the law to exempt immigration fees for the people who migrated from the Shan states. Moreover, the government insisted on giving citizenship to any Burmese who had resided in Thailand prior to the promulgation of the law. The reason given by the Thai officials was that the Burmese belonged to the same race but were dispersed throughout Mainland

Southeast Asia due to political reasons (NAT-[2]-SoRo-0201.82/20). Eiji Murashima (2002, 202) observes how Thailand's legal technique bore a resemblance to its proactive strategy implemented towards the Laotians and Cambodians when the Thai leaders were in conflict with France in 1940. In principle, the Thais enticed the Burmese to move into the country in order to convey a message to the Japanese. On the one hand, the message to Japan was visibly plain: the people in the Shan states were racially Thais and therefore the Thai government would be rightfully obligated to liberate their subjects from a plight. On the other hand, Thailand's strategy implicitly indicated how the Thais stratified their nation as more developed than other neighbouring countries.

Tokyo, however, was heedless of Thailand's intent. Japan's cold shoulder compelled Phibun to concoct a story to draw Japanese attention. As such, the Thai premier informed his Japanese compatriots that any hurdles to the Thai Army's expeditions could undermine his own legitimacy and authority as a leader, which would eventually take its toll on Japanese presence in Thailand (Murashima 2006, 1079). Thailand therefore requested Japan's authorisation to deploy troops without any material support from its ally (ibid., 1079). The instability of the government would be the least desirable option for the Japanese troops in Thailand. Amidst the uncertainty, the IGH ordered the SAA to sanction Thailand's Burma campaigns immediately because, according to the Japanese records, 'there is the need to consider the country's political situation, especially the position of Prime Minister Phibun' (ibid., 1080). Despite Tokyo's green light, the IGH expressed one reservation: the Thai representatives should offer a formal statement of apology to the Japanese government for killing several Japanese men on the date when the Japanese troops landed on Thai soil (ibid., 1081).

On the one hand, Thailand obtained permission to march into the Shan states as it originally wished. On the other hand, a demand for an official apology would be shameful to Thailand's position as a partner. The deaths of the Japanese soldiers were a result of Thailand's exercising its rights of self-defence. A formal apology would damage Thailand's status as a sovereign nation. Nonetheless, if Thailand failed to accede to the Japanese demand, it could not proceed with the campaign, which was designed to express its identity of equal partnership. Candidly speaking, the Thai elites encountered a crucial dilemma: the Thai participation would improve its partnership status, whereas the demand for an apology would amount to Thailand's dishonour.

Since the Shan campaign could become a pivotal moment which could alter Thailand's status, the Thais drafted a letter of apology in preparation for the public announcement. However, such a letter was crossed out and was never presented to Japan (NAT-BokoSungsut-1.12/141). The existence of the letter partly indicated the significance of the campaign in question. Eventually, to resolve such an issue, the Thais commenced a military mission to Saigon and offered an oral and private apology to Hisaichi Terauchi, the chief of the SAA (Murashima 2006, 1084). This strategy would avoid losing face to the world and would allow the Thais to negotiate the terms of the agreement regarding the Shan operations. Colonel Arao of the Japanese troops, holding dubious views towards Tokyo's leniency, felt that an oral apology from Thailand and Japan's forgiveness amounted to nothing but a matter of political convenience (ibid., 1083).

At any rate, since Thailand's apology was accepted, the remaining agenda between the two countries prior to the execution of the military deployment was the negotiation of the additional agreement regarding Thailand's role abroad. The terms of the agreement, which was signed on 5 May 1942, would be unfavourable to Thailand's policy options in the long run. The first clause stipulated that: 'the Thai Army will operate in both offence and defence in the Shan states' (ibid., 1082; NAT-BokoSungsut-1.12/45, 41). Despite the appealing tone of the first clause, the fourth and fifth clauses of the agreement would have dispirited Thailand from reaching a consensus with Japan. The fourth clause, for instance, stated that: 'The issue of incorporating the territories where Thailand operated as suggested in the first clause is not embraced in this agreement' (ibid., 41). Similarly, the fifth clause obligated Thailand to maintain its operations in defending the Burmese frontiers without retreating unless approved by the SAA (ibid., 41).

These two latter clauses subjected Thailand's Shan campaign to a disadvantageous position. Firstly, in accordance with the terms and conditions, the Thais, in spite of lavishing tremendous resources on the campaign, would not be guaranteed the repossession of the Shan states. From a rationalist point of view, participating in the Shan campaign would not only be a costly enterprise because the Thais did not request any material assistance from Japan, but it would also risk the lives of the Thai men in vain because there was no assurance of any substantial reward from the campaign. Secondly, the withdrawal of the Thai troops from Burma would be impossible without the SAA's endorsement. Given the fact that Thailand's military deployment began in a rainy season, which could be detrimental to the morale of the troops due to malaria and travelling hardships, the fifth clause would unnecessarily constrain Thailand's strategic options. Notwithstanding the unfavourable terms, the Thai leaders were adamantly determined to seal the agreement with Japan and dispatch their men to occupy the Shan states.

After the aspired campaign had been endorsed, the Thai Army marched into the Shan states and seized Kengtung without any difficulties. For the Thai government, the successful capture of the Shan region signified the nation's prestige and partnership in this war. They could, for the first time since December 1941, claim that they had become an involving partner in the war to liberate Asia from the Western powers. The significance of the campaign was the improvement of Thailand's status and global recognition. Phibun explained such a point as follows:

> The battle becomes a great success again in nation's history, that is, in a short period of time, we could capture the Shan states. . . . Now the world appreciates the capabilities of our national troops on this occasion. The witness is Japan, our ally, who congratulates us sincerely. Moreover, other countries,

> which sympathise with us [Germany and Italy – my note], have similarly praised us.
>
> (Publicity Bureau 1942, 807)

From the statement, it was hinted that garnering recognition and approbation from Japan and other great powers were of paramount importance for the Thai leaders in this campaign. The Shan deployment was a modus operandi to demonstrate Thailand's identity as an equal partner in this war.

As evidence of Thailand's status concern, the successful episode was earmarked for a symbol of status parity. In celebrating the war success, some Thai people took to the street to express their jubilation to the government. As an emblem of support, they donated money to boost the morale of the Thai Army (NAT-BokoSungsut-1.16/71). Boonwasth, prince of Kengtung, delivered a public statement in welcoming the presence of the Thai Army in Kengtung and wished that the Thai government would bring peace and prosperity to his motherland. To demonstrate Thailand's status accomplishment, Phibun ordered the government to propagate the news (NAT-BokoSungsut-1/157). Furthermore, the three members of the Royal Council of Regency, one of them, Pridi, who had opposed Phibun's foreign policy since day one of the Japanese invasion, even issued a private statement complimenting the triumph: 'The Council of Regency . . . extolls the intrepidity of the infantrymen and lieutenants of the Thai Army for glorifying the prestige of Thailand's troops on the battlefield' (NAT-BokoSungsut-1/155).

In the Japanese-Thai crusade, any decision from the Thai counterpart had to receive Japan's rubber stamp prior to execution. Nevertheless, following their victory, the Thais saw their nation in a different light. They now had the inclination to pursue policies independent of Japan. Such tendencies represented the Thais' perception that their nation was not inferior to Japan. There had been instances when the Thais clashed with the Japanese over divergent directions of policy. Thailand's daring moves exemplified its hubris and vanity in the alliance. One of the contended issues between the two nations was related to Thailand's unilateral behaviours in war affairs.

For instance, according to the common protocols, any public statements on war development should be mutually consulted between the two parties (NAT-[2]-SoRo-0201.98/19, 58). Since the occupation of Kengtung, Thailand's impetus to act on its own accord became more strenuous than ever. The Publicity Bureau, headed by Pairote, a nationalist figure, ventured to declare the nation's successful conquest without informing Japan. As chief of Asia's New Deal, Japan was infuriated by Thailand's indifference and carelessness in dishonouring alliance arrangements. The Japanese military attaché therefore protested against Thailand's independent announcement of the war trumpet. For the Thais, a unilateral proclamation of victory was nothing more than a will to manifest their status prowess. However, the Japanese uproar could not be entirely snubbed. Phibun's hands were tied. He had to punish Pairote by reducing 20 per cent of his remuneration (Reynolds 1994, 116).

Thailand's continuation of independent moves ensued despite Japan's exasperation. According to the joint military contract signed in May 1942, the Thais were only responsible for defending the Shan areas from the Chinese and British men. They were neither entitled to claim jurisdiction nor permitted to incorporate any territories in question. By defending the Shan region, Thailand was tasked to administer the occupied territories with martial law (NAT-[2]-SoRo-0201.98.2/1). Any potential projects by Thailand to claim ownership of the territories would definitely be shunted aside by the agreement with Japan in the first place.

Due to its sense of pride and superiority over the conquered region, the Thai government declared that the Shan people belong to the Thai race and therefore have been liberated by the Thai Army. The Thai infantrymen were strictly instructed to treat the locals as Thai compatriots, without any mental and physical abuse (ibid.). What was noteworthy was how the government circulated a document to notify the civil servants that the Shan territories were 'under our occupation and could be treated as part of our kingdom' (NAT-[2]-SoTo-15.3/42). To further show that Thailand was one of the equals in the war, Thailand impudently changed the name of the Shan states in the Thai language from 'Greater United States of the Thai Territories' to 'Unified Former Thai Territories' (NAT-[2]-SoRo-0201.98.3/3). The official reason for changing the name of the state was to symbolise that the Shan areas were integral to Thailand's historic missions and the people in the region were racially Thai. This name-changing enterprise was also undertaken without any prior notice to Japan. Although the question of Thailand's ownership of the occupied territories remained uncertain, the Thai policies towards the Shan states were motivated by the desire to avoid being subservient to Japan. To put it bluntly, Thailand posed a direct challenge to Japan's imperious attitudes. Such tendencies reflected how Thailand's status concerns drove a materially inferior nation to pursue an arguably reckless policy which could deteriorate the nearly fragile relationship between the two countries.

The accomplishment of Thailand's campaign did not halt its exhaustive aspirations. On the contrary, the Thai leaders were fuelled by the will to become more assertive in the construction of the new Asian order. As mentioned earlier, a rainy season would factor into the Thai Army's suffering from disease and hardship. Additionally, the Thai state was obliged to defend the Shan region, and the potential troop withdrawal should be sanctioned by the SAA. In spite of the restraining conditions, the Thai government, instead of terminating any military operations, sought to be more active in other military affairs. Since the main forces of the Thai Army were concentrated in Burma, a full-scale retreat of the troops would be dismissed by Tokyo (Murashima 2006, 1088). The optimal choice of Thailand at this stage would be to administer the occupied territories in a passive manner and to retain the already frail battalions.

Contrary to avoiding exhausting human and financial resources, the Thai Army strived to become involved in another campaign to annex the entire French Indo-China. Thailand's intelligence unit had received the rumour that the French government in Indo-China had mobilised the people in Vientiane in preparation to invade Thailand. According to the secret discussion between Moriya and the Thai Armed Forces, the rumour was unfounded (NAT-[2]-SoRo-0201.21.3/5). In response to the rumour, Thailand's Secretary of the Ministry of Defence Genereal Projon Mahadilok proposed that he expected the government to 'come up with a tricky plan to turn the rumour into the true event so that Thailand and Japan could ***instantaneously annex the territories and share between the two countries*** [My emphasis]' (ibid.).

The Japanese were alarmed, not only by the troop mobilisation in Indo-China but also by how Thailand's military prospects would upset the imperial strategy in Mainland Southeast Asia. For Japan, if Thailand's territorial ambition in Indo-China was rekindled, it would imply that the Thai men would be relocated to Indo-China, leaving the Shan states vulnerable to the British and Chinese troops. Henceforth, Moriya was compelled to issue a letter to prevent any of the attempts to move the Thai forces from Burma to Indo-China (NAT-BokoSungsut-1.12/201). Japan, according to the letter, explicitly accused Thailand of designing a devious plan to transfer its men to a battle in Indo-China (NAT-BokoSungsut-1.12/203).

Although Thailand's plan to fabricate this rumour did not materialise, the intent of the Thai leaders was obvious: Thailand would not cease its military campaign despite shortcomings in resources. It, however, would be more than willing to partake in any battles which could help position itself on an equal basis with Japan. Phibun's response to Moriya exemplified such a motive:

> I pledge that since both nations have signed a mutual agreement, the policy of our government . . . has an utmost intention to fight shoulder to shoulder with your nation with our greatest ability.
>
> (NAT-BokoSungsut-1.12/201)

The archival document revealed Phibun's private plans about reassuring Japan, which he scribbled down as follows: 'We have no tricks. We only hope to build our nation. We don't need anyone's territories' (NAT-BokoSungsut-1.12/203, 2). His opinion indicated that Thailand's actions were predicated on Thailand's standing in the alliance.

Later, after Thailand administered the Shan states for some time, the Japanese requested the Thai government to readjust the boundary of the military operation by replacing the Salween River, which was a natural frontier, with the demarcation line that Japan suggested (NAT-BokoSungsut-1.12/45, 29). According to the Thai military strategists, the new boundary in the Shan states proposed by Tokyo would be much less beneficial in any strategic sense. Accepting Japan's border proposal would further complicate the military operations as opposed to maintaining the existing natural frontier because it would be a burden on the Thai Army to position each military division in various locations (ibid., 27). The Thais were fully aware that Japan's proposition had a political agenda. Partly, it could be because the Japanese expected the Thais to interact more with the Burmese government (ibid., 29). Nonetheless, according to the military's assessment, the only advantage that Thailand would receive from accepting Japan's proposal was, as the Thai documents suggested, Japan's 'respect towards Thailand's sovereignty in political terms only. But, such an advantage would not facilitate any military affairs' (ibid., 27).

From a rationalist account, a reasonable policy selection for the Thai policymakers would be to discard Japan's demarcation line in favour of the existing natural frontier. Firstly, the Japanese option would unnecessarily squander Thailand's human and financial resources. Scattering several military divisions throughout the new demarcation line could render the defensive line vulnerable in comparison to the concentration of the armed forces behind the Salween River, which was the then standing natural boundary. Secondly, the only advantage of accepting Japan's proposition was overtly intangible: respect from the ally. On the surface, the Thai elites would not hesitate to denounce Japan's scheme. As it turned out, the Thai establishments decided to readjust the frontier of the Shan states according to the Japanese recommendation (ibid., 33). Such a decision was strategically unwise due to the expensive price Thailand was obliged to pay. Nevertheless, Thailand's decision was noteworthy because it ran counter to what the others would generally expect. The reason for the Thai government to prioritise the Japanese option, as shown in the Thai archival records, was the desire to gain respect and recognition from its war partner. This was due to Thailand's constant sense of ontological insecurity as an equal partner in this war. Hence, in order to reinstate the appreciation of existential security, the Thai elites opted for the choice which they presupposed would obtain esteem from Japan.

In summary, since the formation of the alliance, Japan had relentlessly disenfranchised Thailand from any participating rights in military operations. Considering it from a cost-benefit perspective, Japan's sole responsibility of her imperial affairs at the expense of Thailand should be in the Thai interest. However, the Thai elites were overwrought by their nation's status in the alliance and how the international community would perceive Thailand as a Japanese lackey. In this regard, Thailand's sense of existential anxiety was a source which drove the small nation's proactive foreign policies. And, in the case of Thailand's seeking status parity with Japan, military assertiveness could prove that it was on par with Japan's duty to reshape the Asian order. The evidence was obvious: the Thai government remained staunch to the military deployment in spite of the new military agreement which did not guarantee Thailand any territorial entitlement. Additionally, the Thais' proactive policies could potentially rile the Japanese, which would be perilous to Thailand's sovereignty. As such, the ontological security framework could be able to explain Thailand's irrational and reckless moves towards Japan. It helps make sense as to why Thailand challenged its ally which was far more superior in terms of material capabilities.

Inferiority complex: a gradual turn against Japan

In the conventional historiography of the Japanese-Thai relations during the Second World War, historians often depict how Thailand turned against its ally due to Japan's detrimental situations in the Pacific Theater in late 1943. The dictating reason for Thailand to switch sides, according to the common historical account, was due to its versatile nature as a small nation that struggled to master the art of bending with any prevailing wind (Charivat 1985, 233–237; Kobkua 1989; Nakamura 1991, 86; Flood 1967; Reynolds 1994). On paper, the flexible approach of foreign policy is persuasive. This section, however, provides a counterargument against such a dominant view. It argues that Thailand's status dissatisfaction in the alliance, not the Japanese nadir in the war, was a source of Thailand's resistance towards Japan. The frustration of the status difference in the Thai perception also resulted in various measures implemented by the Thai government in order to maintain equal status and reinstate the sense of ontological security.

As the preceding sections described, the Thai government found its passage to become the Japanese partner in the war. It was historically undeniable that the Thai-Japanese relations worsened when the war neared its end. A series of controversial, yet fundamental, questions to ask in this place was as follows: When did the relationship between the two Asian allies become hostile?; What were the determining factors that contributed to the deterioration of the relationship?; and How did the Thai government respond to the situation? Speaking through a rationalist approach, Thailand's failing to preserve a cosy relationship with Japan and subsequently turning against them pique an interest for IR students to question the Thai leaders' motive. As a small nation, accommodating the great power demands and awaiting spoils of war should be preferable alternatives. On the contrary, Thailand stepped up challenges against Japan with the realisation that the Imperial Army could formally destroy the entire Thai Army. This scenario introduced a puzzle in analysing Thailand policy-making.

Status distress: Thailand as a junior

Regarding the issue of the soured relationship between Japan and Thailand, the reason for the meltdown of the ties in the alliance was not Japan's encounter with the late-1942 offensive of the Allied forces in the Battles of Midway and Guadalcanal, which were marked as a critical turning point in the Pacific War. As Murashima (2002, 193) points out, the defining cause of an uneasy relationship between the two nations was the Japanese behaviours towards the Thais rather than the changing war climate. Such an observation could be complemented by the weekly reports and analyses on the war situations of the Ministry of Foreign Affairs, which barely professed disadvantageous situations of Japan in the Pacific rim from 1941 to 1943 (NAT-[2]-KoTo-1.1.1.1/1–7). In fact, the first time that the Thais were perceptibly aware of Japan's full-scale losses was actually in February 1944 when one of the Thai documents addressed how Japan admitted her war shortcomings for the first time (NAT-[2]-SoRo-0201.86/133). By this logic, Thailand's strategic turn against Japan should begin in 1944, when the Thais could bend towards the possible victors. Nonetheless, the conflicts in the Japanese-Thai relationship suggest how a concern for standing was a causal feature drove the ebb and flow of the bilateral relations since the inchoate stage of the alliance.

Essentially, a source of the relationship embitterment stemmed from how the Japanese military divisions in Thailand treated the Thai people as if they were under the empire's colonial administration. The Japanese soldiers frequently employed brutal and terrifying methods in dealing with the local Thai people, which often resulted in animosity the Thais held towards Japan. The boiling point of the Japanese-Thai relations was reaffirmed by the August 1942 report from the Japanese embassy in Thailand, which analysed how the Japanese Army's disrespect of Thai laws and Thai people and how they treated and perceived Thailand as a colony worsened the relationship between the two countries (ibid., 203).

To raise a crucial example, one of the disturbing incidents which nearly brought about the war between the two nations was the so-called Banpong Incident in 1942. The origin of the conflict began with how a Japanese private slapped a Thai monk on his face for giving a cigarette to one of the British prisoners of war. The scene, which occurred along the Thai-Burmese border, sparked uproars among the locals because monks are highly revered in Thailand. In response to the Japanese indecent practice, the Thai locals violently clashed with the Japanese soldiers, which cost the lives of eight Japanese men. An uprising was interpreted by Japan as resistance from the occupied country. Hence, it was rumoured that the Japanese Embassy secretly recommended that Tokyo 'take over the Western provinces of Thailand to be under the Japanese control' (NAT-BokoSungsut-1.12/212, 2). The Thai military factions perceived Japan's malign intent; hence, the army divisions in Bangkok fortified the city in preparation for the Japanese attack (ibid., 2).

Although the crisis was resolved through top-level negotiations, such as when Phibun intervened to prevent an escalation, the incident marked one of many instances in which the Japanese viewed Thailand as an inferior nation. Foreign troops generally had no rights to mistreat the locals. To the Thais, an act of slapping one's face was an affront to their honour and dignity. Phibun himself voiced his concern in the cabinet meeting:

> The misdemeanours of Japanese low-ranking officers violate law and morality . . . one Thai governor . . . was slapped on his face. . . . This will create a rift. . . . For instance, if they slap our military generals, the military factions would not tolerate it.
>
> (TMCM 16/1942, 18-March-1942)

To further demonstrate how the Thai elites were concerned about any face-slapping incidents, the Thai premier ordered his subordinates to record every instance in which the Japanese soldiers intimidated the Thais. It was widely observed by the Thai government that all of the conflicts had generally been triggered by the Japanese slapping Thai people's faces (NAT-[2]-KoTo-7.1/6).

The attempt to create an understanding with the Japanese was shown by how Phibun's cabinet decided to appoint a special mission led by Phahol, Thailand's former premier, to pay a state visit to Japan in order to create a shared understanding as regards the status of Thailand in the alliance (TMCM 16/1942, 18-March-1942). One of the complaints from Phahol to Tojo was how the Japanese infantrymen in Thailand were disrespectful towards the locals. In response to the goodwill mission from Thailand, Tojo promised to harshly discipline the Japanese divisions (Reynolds 1994, 199).

For the Thais, the political reality that they had been part of the Asian order architecture enhanced their senses of equality with Japan and superiority over other Southeast Asian nations. Regarding the sense of parity with Tokyo, Phibun's vision to establish the Ministry of Industry was indicative of Thailand's status perception:

> The reason I have the Ministry of Industry established is due to a political reason, that is, in Asia, there are Japan and us, which are the only two independent countries. . . . Japan thinks that the Southeast Asian locals don't trust them. . . . Because of this, I feel that the Asians cherish Thailand more than ever. In Tavoy [Burma – my note], the locals want us to govern them. . . . The neighbours admire our prestige and wish we could govern them. In the future, our two nations cannot be separated. . . . We need to accelerate our nation-building projects and position ourselves so that the neighbours look up to us. We *de facto* are leading other Asians, we should make ourselves a true leader. . . . In joining Japan's Co-Prosperity Sphere, the Japanese are the leaders. But we should have our own Co-Prosperity Sphere as well. It could be a small Sphere in Southeast Asia.
>
> (TMCM 15/1942, 29-April-1942)

Despite the Thai government's participation in the war and its self-image as Japan's partner, Phibun's statement insinuated that the Thais had been constantly concerned about its standing vis-à-vis Japan. Apart from assisting Japan in its quest for building a sphere, the Thais aspired to construct their own sphere of influence to alleviate their status. Because the Thais felt that they had been on par with their war ally, Japan's overbearing attitudes and practices became the stimuli for the relationship breakdown. For instance, in response to how the Japanese Army mistreated the Thais, Pairote, chief of Thai public relations, expressed his irritation towards the Japanese as follows:

> Some Japanese factions do not understand. They thought that they have taken over Thailand already, which often result in misunderstandings and killings. Please educate the Japanese to realise that Thailand is a high-status nation. We are more advanced thought than Burmese, Malays, Vietnamese, Javanese, and the Filipinos. . . . To simply put, those people have been under the Western colonisation. When the Westerners are gone, they have been replaced by Japan. Hence, they would not feel strange [to be under the Japanese control – my note]. . . . Nevertheless, the Thais here have never been a stooge to the West.
>
> (NAT-[2]-SoRo-0201.98/19)

What Pairote remarked was noteworthy. The Thais generally assumed that their nation's position was higher than other nations which had been under Western control. Henceforth, Japan's colonial treatments of Thailand damaged the pride and dignity of its leaders.

Although Thailand's part in the war could redecorate its status, Japan's mis-recognition of the Thais' standing damaged their self-esteem. Recognition and status are interrelated. Recognising someone as an unequal cohort could be an emblem of disrespect. Axel Honneth (2014) captures this phenomenon as follows:

> On the most basic level, we demand attention from an audience. We want to be recognised in the sense of being noticed. But our stories also ask for respect. That is, we insist that our audiences treat us as equal to others and endowed with the same rights as everyone else.
>
> (7)

Similarly, Thailand was demeaned by Japan's domineering practices. Its leaders felt that, as a nation of the same rank, their rights and respect were not properly recognised. Dissatisfaction due to status misrecognition accounted for the spiral relationship between the two countries. One private letter to Phibun's daughter could fully grasp Thailand's status grievance:

> Come to think of it, if Japan wins, what would we get? We could receive some trivial rewards as a stooge. . . . This is the same as being a slave working for an overlord, who rewards a loyal subordinate for achieving some tasks. This is not a partnership. We are not what we know as a partner. . . . How can we be ecstatic? We would be like Korea or Manchukuo. And every day, we must turn our faces towards Japan and salute their emperor, just like the nations under the Japanese control before us. . . . If Japan wishes us well . . . they would not treat us like a servant. Why hadn't the Axis taken us as a member when we applied for membership? Why were we crossed out?. . . . We are proud of being an independent country and our efforts in this war are equally as significant as other allies. We are accidentally drawn into the middle of this war. We hope that the Axis would have won so that we can alleviate our status further and greater. . . . If Japan is honest with us, why don't they count us as an equal? Why don't they count us as a partner? Why?[5]

The excerpt from the letter markedly represented how the Thai policy-makers were distraught by Japan's imperialist tendency.

The honeymoon period between Japan and Thailand was in fact short-lived. The reason, as mentioned on several occasions, was how Thailand's status was not accorded with proper treatments. Even though Thailand was committed to the Japanese grand strategy by dispatching their troops into Burma in May 1942, the feeling of inferiority in relation to Japan prompted the Thais to start to mildly turn against Japan as early as in mid-1942.

For the Thai policy-makers, the Japanese question could no longer be confined to the Foreign Ministry. The problems of status-seeking policy and domestic affairs could not be considered separately. In order to prevent any of the Japanese exploitations, Thailand's premier ordered each ministry to form the 'Foreign Relations Committee' (FRC). The objective of the FRC was to convene a weekly meeting on any issues relating to foreign affairs and submit reports directly to the prime minister. The formation of the FRC was to prevent any interference from foreign powers, notably Japan in this case (NAT-[2]-SoRo-0201.21.3/1). The weekly meetings, according to the government's decree, should not be neglected because 'any results from the meetings would make the nation lead other countries without following them nowadays' (ibid.). The statement reflected the spirit of the Thais to build their national status. Regarding the relationship with Japan, the FRC guideline suggested that each ministry should be wary of 'preserving independence and sovereignty of Thailand' (ibid.). Every department should also be watchful of any Japanese movements as well (ibid.). In a nutshell, Thailand sought to countermeasure any attempts by Japan to treat the Thais as an inferior unit. Phibun wrote his thought down as follows: 'The foreign affairs problems which should be considered are abnormal. We cannot let foreigners abuse us and we must think of solutions' (ibid.).

Due to Thailand's status dissatisfaction, the trust between the two nations was further eroded. In July 1942, a month after Thailand conquered the Shan states, the Army Division received a document from Japan which encouraged the Thai government to tread further into Yunnan (Luang Saranuchit 1979). In the Thai archival records, the Japanese from time to time half seriously expected the Thai troops to break into China (NAT-BokoSungsut-1.12/45, 27). Since, Japan ranked Thailand as an inferior nation, the Thai premier, unwilling to co-operate with Japan, obstinately disobeyed any directions which could picture Thailand as a colony. Such independent thinking appeared in Phibun's notes in July 1942:

> I think Japan tries to destroy our troops by having us battle against the Chinese. If our troops remain in a great condition, they would be a thorn in East Asia for Japan. Moreover, there is a rumour that Japan instigates Indo-China to mobilise and to threaten us in our north-eastern borders. . . . So, in working this time, we must be careful not to let it be according to Japan's objectives. . . . Try to preserve our troops to our best.
>
> (Luang Saranuchit 1979[6])

In the same month, Phibun discussed the Japanese question in the cabinet. The anti-Japanese tone could be captured from the records of the cabinet meeting:

> In principle, we should support Japan to be a great power, but we cannot wholeheartedly do that because they are petty and selfish. Additionally, their

> military treated us badly. If Japan is genuinely honest with us by respecting our independence and sovereignty, and don't treat us like Manchukuo, being with Japan would be splendid.
>
> (TMCM 36/1942, 22-July-1942)

For the Thais, being classified as a colony was intolerable. The level of independence and sovereignty was a benchmark for Thailand's status evaluation. They were particularly sensitive to their national status and recognition from Japan to the extent that one high-ranking Japanese diplomat questioned why the Thais regularly emphasised any issues pertinent to sovereignty and independence. The central response from the Thais, however, was the complaints about Japanese imperial maltreatments towards the locals (ibid.).

In October 1942, the Thai premier covertly issued an order to collect and record evidence with regard to how 'Thailand did not truly support Japan' (NAT-BokoSungsut-1.12/192; Murashima 2006, 1090). The list of the instances consisted of 19 events which exemplified how Thailand assisted Japan out of necessity. According to Murashima (2002), this document was composed to present to the Chiang Kai-Shek government in order to garner sympathy from China. In January 1943, the Thais could eventually establish contact with the Chinese 93 Army Division at the border of the Shan states (Chira 1979, 62; Murashima 2006, 1091). The significance of the document was how Thailand bravely and carefully crafted a scheme under Japan's watch. Thailand's attempts to turn towards China began even before the fate of Japan's shortcoming was sealed in the war.

The Japanese-Thai relations became increasingly tumultuous after Japan's Asian imperialist policy had been visibly developed. Apart from the overbearing practices in Thailand, another triggering issue which directly injured the status of Thailand was how Tokyo established the 'Greater East Asia Ministry' in late 1942. The central aim of the new Japanese ministry was to handle political and economic affairs of the countries in the Southern region, namely, Manchukuo, Thailand, and Indo-China (Togo 1975, 84). After the creation of the new ministry, the countries in East Asia should contact Japan through the Greater East Asia Ministry instead of the Japanese Foreign Ministry. As a sovereign nation, foreign matters should only be contacted through the foreign ministry. The creation of the new ministry relegated the standing of Thailand to be a country under the Japanese occupation because the Thais would have no foreign policy independence.

For Japan, this ministry was a stepping-stone effort to realise her policy of Greater East Asia Co-Prosperity Sphere. In short, the new ministry was the equivalent of the colonial ministry. The then Japanese Foreign Minister Shigenori Togo opposed the creation of the ministry because its existence could send a false signal to the countries in question. They could perceive that Japan endeavoured to disrespect their sovereignty and independence (ibid., 85). Classifying Thailand on the same level as Manchukuo and other Indo-China countries was indicative of how the Japanese treated the Thais as inferior. As Togo predicted, the Thai elites, especially Phibun, were infuriated by the formation of the new colonial ministry (TMCM 50/1942, 14-October-1942). Direk recorded that there was a rumour among the Thai diplomats that the new ministry was a colonial organisation (NAT-[2]-KoTo-3.6.3/1, 2). He understood that the incorporation of Thailand along with Manchukuo was not a good sign for Thailand's status (NAT-SoRo-0201.37.2/18). His concern was observant:

> Regarding external relations, I think that Thailand should contact the Foreign Ministry as usual and on the basis of equality as other independent countries in Europe or South America. However, it seems certain that the Thai Foreign Ministry should communicate with the new Ministry in relation to any matters relevant to Thailand.
>
> (ibid.)

Clearly, Thailand was sceptical of Japan's project. Phibun's trepidation was straightforward:

> [For Japan], The Foreign Ministry is to communicate with the white people. It means that the Greater East Asia Ministry controls all countries in Asia. It would become impossible for us to contact other countries without prior permission from Japan.
>
> (TMCM 50/1942, 14-October-1942)

In theory, the formation of the ministry was seen as the equivalent of annexing Thailand and other Asian nations into part of the Japanese confederation, which would relegate Thailand's standing to an inferior rank.

Although Tojo justified the duty of the new ministry by assuring Direk that the Thai-Japanese relations would be conducted on a brotherly basis, it did not change how the Thais were dismayed by Japan's imperious practices because, for Direk, it gave him a concern 'in the eyes of others', because 'the situation would look somewhat odd' (Direk & Keyes 1978, 87–88). In other words, the Thai leaders were concerned by how the international community would view Thailand as a Japanese colony because their nation was clustered around former Western colonies (Reynolds 1994, 134).

To Thailand, Japan's Co-Prosperity Sphere and its propaganda to respect independence and sovereignty were nothing more than diplomatic flummeries. The Italian diplomatic corps circulated an observation regarding this issue as follows:

> The creation of the Ministry of Greater East Asia has been received with apprehension by certain political circles in Thailand who have for some time deplored the submission of the Thai government to Japanese authorities. Japan might have the intention of exercising a greater interference in the internal policy of Asiatic countries.
>
> (NAT-[2]-KoTo-8.1.1/29)

One policy report from the Thais referred to Japan's definition of Co-Prosperity Sphere in the sense that every country within the sphere should abandon any former understanding of independence and sovereignty. Essentially, the new definitions of independence and sovereignty suggested how countries within the sphere should rely on each other in politics, economy, and culture. According to the report, the country which was subjected to the new definitions of independence and sovereignty was Manchukuo (NAT-[2]-SoRo-0201.86/129, 118). Bluntly speaking, countries within the sphere were nothing more than second-rate colonies under the administration of Japan.

Tojo was completely aware that his grand vision of Co-Prosperity Sphere could undermine the already fragile relationship with Thailand. In order to restore a cosy tie of the alliance, he established the 'Military Headquarters' in Thailand in January 1943 and appointed General Aketo Nakamura as a commander-in-chief. The central task of Nakamura (1991), as written in his memoir, was to heal the wounds and to lessen the distance in the Japanese-Thai relations (3). The Thais similarly speculated that the formation of the garrison command in Thailand was to discipline bad behaviours of the Japanese military in Thailand (NAT-[2]-SoRo-98.1/13)

The presence of Nakamura and his well-intentioned purposes were not a panacea to the broken relationship and Thailand's sense of inferiority. On the contrary, Tojo's move further offended the Thais. Although Tokyo informed Bangkok that the existence of the Military Headquarters would not interfere in Thailand's domestic affairs and that the Japanese government would respect Thailand's independence and sovereignty (ibid.), it did not alter the negative perception that the Thais held towards the Japanese. The Thai leaders interpreted the formation of the Military Headquarters as a disrespectful measure towards their national standing. Wichit noted his concern as follows:

> The set up of the Military Headquarters has a downside in the sense that Bangkok will become one of Japan's military garrisons, which, if it is fully established, we will never know when they will close it down. . . . Japan might take a further step by appointing this commander-in-chief as an ambassador. This is the worst-case scenario.
>
> (NAT-BokoSungsut-2/67, 32)

The creation of the Military Headquarters only reinforced the feeling among the Thais that Japan designated Thailand as one of her satellite nations in the Japanese orbit.

For the Thai policy-makers, the only countermeasure to Japan's domineering policy was to alleviate its own status without yielding to Japan's exploitation. In order to reinstate the sense of ontological security, Phibun established a foreign relations organisation to show to Japan and the world that Thailand was an ally, not an enemy-occupied territory. Firstly, he replaced the 'Thai-Japanese Coordination Committee Office', which was formed immediately after both nations entered into an alliance to co-operate over general issues, with 'the Liaison Office of Alliance' (LOA). The function of both organisations was not indistinguishable (ibid.). The reason for renaming the organisation, as explained by Phibun, was because the former's name 'sounds as if Japan will stay here forever . . . it should be the Liaison Office of Alliance' (ibid., 65). An interesting point of observation on the enterprise to rebrand the LOA was how Phibun stressed the importance of the word 'Alliance' in every official document relating to the establishment of the LOA (ibid.). He, for example, included the word 'Alliance' right after any sentences which were pertinent to Japan. This indicated how the Thais sought to seek the status equality while the Japanese tried to position herself as a superior nation.

The concern about status was the core reason for Thailand's LOA project. In fact, the LOA was formed to model after Japan's 'Greater East Asia Ministry' (ibid., 56). The blueprint of the structural organisation of the Greater East Asia Ministry was attached as a leading template for the Thais to replicate. The objective of the LOA became clearer as stated in the organisational guidelines:

> The new form of missions, according to the supreme commander, who wishes to expand foreign affairs just like the Greater East Asia Ministry, is to be consistent with the principle of assisting an ally and to be consistent with Japanese affairs.
>
> (ibid., 58)

As such, instead of contacting with Japan through the Greater East Asia Ministry, which would make Thailand appear as a colonial unit, the LOA would be responsible for dealing with Japan directly (ibid., 66). In sum, Thailand rectified the LOA to strengthen its standing vis-à-vis Japan. It was a policy response to assert itself as being on par with Japan. To confirm such a concern, Phibun jotted his thoughts in his private notebook that if Japan wished to contact Thailand over any affairs, she should either communicate through the Foreign Ministry or the LOA (MCN, 20-January-1943-to-4-May-1943, 347).

By 1943, Thailand's animosity towards Japan was even palpable to the Japanese leaders. Apart from the formation of the Military Headquarters in Thailand, which only inflamed Thailand's frustration, Tokyo decided to dispatch Kasuo Aoki, the Minister of Greater East Asia, to pay a state visit to Thailand to cement ties between the two countries. For the Thais, the visit of the Minister of Greater East Asia was seen as the equivalent to how the colonial governor trod on a colony. Aoki's Thailand tour did not yield a satisfactory result despite both nations issuing a symbolic joint declaration of commitment and co-operation (NAT-[2]-KoTo-1.1.5/11,). At the same time, messages were conveyed from Thailand's embassy in Tokyo that some Japanese newspapers remarked that Thailand could not preserve its independence and sovereignty if it did not co-operate with Japan in a serious manner (NAT-[2]-SoRo-0201.86/129, 114). Japan's contradictory behaviours only reinforced Thailand's conviction that its status was not on par with its ally. The representation of such a perception could be seen in Phibun's handwritten comments following Aoki's visit:

> The news that we do not support our people to co-operate with Japan is definite. . . . Because Japan does not truly show us that they would not position

> us as a stooge. Japan intimidates our people. They slap our people in the face and sometimes it amounts to killing. . . . The good way is that Japan should be mature. They should show us that they have a great wish for Thailand so that we are confident in our sovereignty and independence.
>
> (ibid.)

The message implied that the only way to break the frosty relationship was for Tokyo to recognise Thailand's status as an equal partner by words and deeds.

Strongly convinced that other methods did not work to boost the war spirits of the Thais, Tojo seduced the Thai leaders by announcing his state visit in July 1943. The visit of the Japanese premier to Thailand was a symbolic gesture of recognising Thailand's status. To demonstrate Japan's commitment to upholding Thailand's partnership status, the Japanese prime minister surprised the Thai elites by announcing that Tokyo would acknowledge Thailand's ownership and sovereignty over the Shan states and the four Malay states, namely, Perlis, Kedah, Kelantan, and Trengganu.

As a revisionist state with a limited interest, receiving these lands should fulfil its objective as a jackal state, and hence, according to this theoretical logic, the Thais should be gratified. Contrary to such expectations, the Thais, apart from a public façade, perceived Japan's intent with a negative impression. For example, the moment when Tojo surprisingly made an announcement regarding the return of the territories, it was observed by Nakamura (1991) that Phibun barely smiled at the news (75). He even mentioned in the cabinet meeting that, 'in fact, we do not want these states. But they give them to us. . . . If they really want Kengtung [part of the Shan states – my note], we can return it to them' (TMCM, x/1943, 8-September-1943).[7] The unpleasant feeling was tied to how Japan had disrespected Thailand's status from the beginning of the war. As Phibun wrote,

> There will be hassles following the return of the territories. . . . the territorial retrocession was propaganda in itself. Because every other nation, namely, Burma, the Philippines, Java, China, and Manchukuo, were promised something in return. But Thailand has not received any. The assistance to Japan, which nearly bankrupts us, was responded by imperfect respect of our sovereignty.
>
> (NAT-[2]-KoTo-1.1.5/11)

Generally speaking, a material interest such as territorial retrocession should improve how a small state reacts to a great power. But in the case of Thailand, Japan's continuous disregard for Thailand's status as a sovereign, equal partner defined its genuine sentiment towards Japan's seemingly altruistic policy. Instead of viewing Japan's return of territories as a war share, the Thais viewed it as Japanese propaganda to promote the Co-Prosperity Sphere.

The Thai government's defiance of Japan became more obvious when Tojo's government desired to demonstrate the prowess of Japan's Co-Prosperity Sphere and to strengthen Asian solidarity by holding the Greater East Asia Conference in November 1943. With respect to the conference, Japan invited every national leader under her sphere to attend the meeting in Tokyo (NAT-SoRo-0201.24/46). Although the meeting was nothing more than a diplomatic talk shop, it signified Japanese influence in Asia. Every highest-ranking leader of each nation, namely, head of the state or head of the government, would be invited to be present at the conference.

As a head of the Thai government, Phibun would be obliged to attend the grandiose meeting in person. In addition, given the fact that Tojo himself paid a state visit in July 1943, it would be a matter of courtesy for Phibun to reciprocate Japan's friendliness. As a matter of fact, when Aoki was on tour in Thailand, he sounded out the possibility of Phibun travelling to Japan as part of the alliance consolidation project (NAT-[2]-SoRo-0201.86/129, 206). Phibun avoided such an invitation and informed Wichit that he would rather resign from the post than travel to Tokyo (NAT-[2]-KoTo-1.1.5/11). Nakamura was also instructed by Tokyo to try to encourage Phibun to attend the conference. However, the Thai premier explicitly refused to affirm his decision, citing his health issues, aviophobia, seasickness, and being afraid of staying at hotels. Nakamura (1991) recounted his plea as follows: 'If Field Marshal does not like an aeroplane; we shall have a warship to transport you. If you are fearful of danger from getting on a ship, we shall have submarines to follow your ship' (87). Phibun, however, remained adamant in his resolution and turned down Nakamura's request.

The reason was straightforward. The Thai policy-makers regarded the conference as Japan's efforts to showcase her leadership and superiority over other Asians in the region. As a partner and ally in this war, if the prime minister participated in the meeting, it would signify that Thailand was drawn into the Japanese orbit and was no different from Manchukuo, India, Burma, and China, whose leaders were pressured to attend. As Aoki noticed, 'Phibun wished to avoid going to Japan because he objected to the Japanese dealing with Thailand on the same level as the puppet regimes in Manchukuo and China' (Reynolds 1994, 163). As such, the Thai government resolved this problem by sending Prince Wan, who was a counsellor to Phibun and held no ministerial post in the cabinet, to join the conference (NAT-SoRo-0201.24/46, 136).

Thailand's response was an affront to Japan as one Japanese official commented that, 'Thailand, which could be said to be a senior nation because it has co-operated with Japan since the beginning, should be a leading nation of the family to get through obstacles. If its leaders are negligent, other newly independent countries would be unenthusiastic' (NAT-[2]-SoRo-0201.98.1/6). Such an opinion was a direct criticism to Phibun for non-compliance. The presence of Prince Wan was a political symbol. Firstly, the absence of the Thai prime minister implied that Thailand was not part of the Japanese colonies; hence, the premier was not obliged to attend the imperial gala. Secondly, designating Prince Wan, who held no political post, as a delegate symbolised that the Thais played down the significance of the event.

As such, any declarations and speeches at the conference would not amount to any political influence on Thailand. For instance, the Thai premier personally ordered the public relations department to propagate how Thailand was not a colony of Japan. In Phibun's words, he personally wrote that instead of proclaiming that Thailand was dependent on Japan, core messages should be that Thailand and the others were 'mutually dependent on one another and would respect independence and sovereignty of each other in Asia. These messages should be conveyed to our people in order to verify our status' (NAT-SoRo-0201.24/46). Such a statement was indicative of how the Thais were concerned about their status issue with Japan and how they were anxious about the perceptions of the international community.

All in all, the fallout between the two allies became visibly apparent in 1943. Japan's imperious attitudes had been an impetus to distance Thailand from the Japanese hub-and-spoke circuit. Apart from the Thai proactive behaviours in response to Japan's exercises of imperial superiority, the Thai elites surreptitiously organised underground resistance against the Japanese. One of the notable attempts in history was Phibun's project to relocate the nation's capital from Bangkok to Phetchabun. In a published memoir, Netr Khemayothin (1967), Phibun's subordinate, explained how the government's relocation scheme to Phetchabun was to fight against the Japanese troops which were stationed throughout Bangkok. The new capital, which was a mountainous region, would provide the government with a geopolitical advantage to defend against the Japanese encroachment and bombardment (5–7). Netr also believed that Phetchabun could be an important location to preserve the armed forces in order to ward off any threats to independence (NAT-BokoSungsut-1.8/6, 113). As regards the relocation plan, Phibun had initiated this project in June 1943. He personally wrote in his handwriting that, 'this preparation should be kept mostly secretive' (NAT-BokoSungsut-1.9/1, 110). Such a preparation, Wichit warned, would render the Japanese suspicious of Thailand's ulterior motives. Henceforth, the measures, as Wichit advised, should be undertaken gradually and unhurriedly (NAT-BokoSungsut-1.8/6).

A sign of a rift in the Japanese-Thai alliance became clearer in December 1943 when the Allies bombarded Bangkok heavily, which resulted in physical and moral damages to the Thais (Nakamura 1991, 92). Nakamura, assigned to cement the ties between the two nations, recommended that the SAA and Tokyo issue a statement to console the Thai people for losses. However, the Japanese counterpart dismissed such a request on the grounds that it would show that Thailand was too important. Besides, for Tokyo, Phibun's absence from the Greater East Asia Conference was seen as an insult to the big brother. Thus, Japan was firm to be silent on the losses of her ally (ibid., 94).

The anger of the Thai elites further blossomed, as indicated by Thailand's inaction in December 1943. Earlier in December 1942, the Thai government held a celebratory event to commemorate a one-year anniversary of the Thai-Japanese alliance. Whether the event was organised as a public veneer, it signified the level of the relationship maintenance. Nonetheless, in December 1943, the Thais decided to play down the event. The anniversary festival was confined to only a dining session on 21 December 1943. To further express Thailand's distance from Japan, the premier did not attend the dinner (Murashima 2002, 211). Such a daring move sent a sharp signal to Tokyo that the feud between the two countries had reached a non-reconcilable point.

Seeking status through cultural measures

Since mid-1942, Thailand became ontologically insecure vis-à-vis Japan. The fundamental source of such existential insecurity was how the Tokyo policy elites and military generals treated Thailand as a colony. In response to such misperceptions, the Thai leaders initiated plans to improve Thailand's cultural values in order to show the international community, and Japan in particular, that they were one of the respectable powers on the global stage. By demonstrating that Thailand had reputably high culture, it would also imply that Thailand was on par with its war partner. It would also guard against any attempts of Japan to colonise Thailand after the Western powers vacated the region.

The relationship between Japan and Thailand had been rough and uneven since 1942. In theory, Japan regarded Thailand as an independent nation. However, the Japanese sought to integrate Thailand as a part of the Greater East Asian order by guiding the Thais in economic and financial realms (Reynolds 1991, 99). As regards the cultural aspect, Japan expected to build the so-called 'new East Asian culture' in order to enhance the image of Japan as a creator and protector of Asia. At best, it was an attempt to Japanise the regional order with the Japanese culture (ibid., 99). One of the pioneering projects of Japan's aspiration towards Thailand was how Tokyo sent Gen Yanagisawa to Thailand to discuss the possibility of forming Japan's Cultural Institution in Thailand (NAT-[3]-SoRo-0201.55/21). Although the sugar-coated justification of Japan's cultural attempt was to strengthen the bilateral relationship, it was more than obvious that the Japanese effort was to spread her culture throughout Asia. In other words, Japan engaged in what contemporary IR scholars would call a 'soft-power policy'.

As previously mentioned, for the Thai leaders, culture was an important tool to manifest the national status. Backward culture in the eyes of the others would be a symbol of inferiority and would not be accorded with proper recognition and treatment. Phibun, for example, jotted in his notebook that, 'culture is highly important to show that man is different from animals and is more civilised. If any nation neglects culture or lacks culture, it could not stand as a nation' (CICN, 1-June-1944-to-13-August-1944; see also CUCN, 6-March-1943-to-25-July-1944). As a nation in constant restlessness, Thailand equated Japan's cultural policy as cultural imperialism. Additionally, Japan's imperious behaviours towards Thailand reaffirmed its anxiety that Tokyo viewed Bangkok as an unequal partner.

In order to counter against Japan's imposition of superiority, Thailand exercised a status-seeking activity through cultural modification programmes. Wichit echoed his thoughts on the relationship between status and culture in the following words: 'What will happen with our status is hinged on us. . . . Regarding culture, if we make it superior, they [Japan – my note] cannot do anything. . . . It depends. If we can make ourselves respectable for Japan' (TMCM 1/1943, 2-January-1943). The Thais, in a nutshell, equated the cultural improvements with status-building and recognition.

Japan's initial launch of her cultural policy was to educate the Asians with the Japanese language by dispatching language teachers throughout Asia. Adopting the Japanese language would portray Thailand as inferior in terms of status. This was the case with how the Japanese language became compulsory in Manchukuo, Taiwan, Korean, and Indo-China (TMCM 27/1942, 13-May-1942). The Thai cabinet was troubled by the Japanese cultural invasion, as Phibun voiced his concern and solution:

> In sum, the Thai language is not well because we always mingle with foreign words. Hence, we should boost the literacy of our language. . . . If we are late, the Japanese language would take over. As such, we should choose between Thai and Japanese. Regarding our tertiary education, we should translate all materials into Thai.
>
> (ibid.)

Hence, the premier decreed an order that all textbooks should be based on the Thai language. Furthermore, he also commanded all the governmental and bureaucratic organs to remove all foreign-language elements and search for ways to transliterate them into Thai words (TMCM 28/1942, 20-May-1942). The government went further to simplify the Thai language. Any spellings and alphabets which were linguistically redundant had been obliterated from the official Thai language. The language re-officialisation project was formulated to defend against Japan and to enhance the national status. The reason of language modification was given as follows:

> The most important thing about the improvement this time is tied to the progress of the nation in the future. Any nation without their own language would lose their status as a nation. For Thailand, we have our own language. We need to modify our language in a succinct and accessible manner. At this stage, the Thai language is difficult to learn because there are several spellings and marks. Moreover, we have to adopt words from other languages, which is indecent for Thailand as an independent and high-cultured nation.
>
> (Thamsook 1978, 55)

The objective of the Thais was not to deter the expansion of foreign culture because they were cognisant of the unlikelihood of preventing such tendencies (NAT-[3]-SoRo.0201.55/16, 17). For them, the solution was to spread the Thai culture to other places including Japan (ibid., 17). A policy guideline on 'Cultural Enhancement and Expansion' documented the plan as follows:

> We must find a solution to build our culture to be higher than others. We allow the Thai people to recognise how foreign culture is like, but we cannot

> allow them to admire it. . . . We must find ways to convince them that our culture is higher than others.
>
> (ibid., 39)

To be able to achieve such a goal, Thailand's strategy was to spread the Thai culture to two areas. The first areas included Japan, China, Europe, and America, whereas the second areas were Thailand's surrounding neighbours. The basic plan was to utilise embassies and consuls in each place to promote the Thai culture (ibid., 40). All in all, the Thais aspired to establish Thailand as a 'central hub of culture in Southern Asia' (ibid., 40; NAT-[3]-SoRo.0201.55/21, 10).

The attempts to picture the Thai culture as an anchor in South Asia and to disseminate it throughout Mainland Indo-China reflected Thailand's interest to seek equal status with Japan and other civilised nations. By portraying its culture as exquisite and central in South Asia, the Thais implied that they were more superior to those countries that were colonised in the age of imperialism. Wichit averred such positions in a statement when Japan and Thailand concluded the cultural agreement:

> Both Japan and Thailand share their own stable cultures. Thailand, apart from having high culture since the ancient days, still preserves and becomes a central hub of culture in South Asia while other countries in South Asia fell under the influence of foreigners for a long time. . . . Thailand, which has been independent until now, is a guardian of neighbours' culture.
>
> (NAT-[2]-KoTo-1.1/20)

The emphases of the statement were placed on the parity between Thailand and Japan and how the Thai culture was the oasis of South Asia. The temerity to exaggerate the supreme qualities of the Thai culture indicated how Thailand perceived that it was on par with other developed nations and not as backward as its neighbours. Culture did matter to status and recognition for the Thai elites, as Phibun remarked: 'in order to communicate with other countries we must be equal to them culturally, so as to preserve our national honor' (Reynolds 1991, 107).

The Thai government felt compelled to improve the national culture and correct cultural blemishes of its people in order to avoid being stigmatised as an inferior country. To realise such aims, Thailand formed the 'National Council of Culture' (NCC) to modify, invent, and establish policy cultural practices of the Thai people. This organisation would also be responsible for spreading the Thai culture to the neighbouring nations and to advise the government on any matters concerning the cultural modifications (NAT-[3]-SoRo-0201.55/19, 24). The gravity of Thailand's solemnity about this programme could be proven by how its government fully authorised the NCC to wield more power over any other bureaucratic organisations with the exception of the government itself (NAT-[3]-SoRo-0201.55/47).

In fact, the cultural modification programmes that had been implemented by the NCC were indistinguishable from what Phibun had imposed on the Thais before the arrival of the Japanese in 1941. The primary reform spearheaded by the government was the enforcement of the Thai people to wear 'proper attire' in public spaces. With respect to the proper attire, the point of reference was the Western-style dresses such as shirts, trousers, coats, leather shoes, skirts, and gloves (See Chapter 4.2.3). Any traditional clothes for both men and women were strictly forbidden in public. Wearing hats became mandatory for the Thai people. The slogan, which best represented the foreign policy thinking of the cultural reforms in the Phibun era, was: 'hats would lead Thailand to be a great power' (Thamsook 1978, 51). Thailand's traditional *modus vivendi* could bring about shame to the nation. This bore a striking resemblance to the case of Turkey where Kemal Ataturk understood that wearing hats would not 'separate the Turkish nation from civilized nations' (Zarakol 2007, 117). For the Thai elites, wearing hats was a measure of civilised status and would gain approbation from others. Expecting to embellish Thailand's civilised outlook, foreign residents such as Indians, Chinese, and Italians, were also required to dress appropriately in public (NAT-[3]-SoRo-0201.55/45).

Apart from the dress reforms, the Phibun government also launched other cultural modifications which were pertinent to the Thai people's customary ways of living. For example, tremendous efforts and resources were directed to discourage the people from chewing betel nut, which could be seen as backward by foreign spectators (Thamsook 1978, 54). The government went another step to dictate the overall aspects of the Thai people's lives. European manners and etiquettes were reintroduced to Thai people to be followed. A cultural guideline booklet was published and distributed to the people to practise throughout the nation (NAT-[3]-SoRo-0201.55/44). As Thamsook (1977) summarises, the cultural enforcements incorporated the following elements:

> rules of etiquette governing the cremation ceremony, the marriage ceremony, the use of visiting cards, the bus-riding system, etc. Detailed advice was published in the press as to what dress the bride and groom should wear on the wedding day, what the proper size of visiting cards should be, how to use the cards, how to behave when waiting for a bus, how to lower one's head gracefully when greeting important people.
>
> (35)

These cultural adaptation policies were not intrinsic to domestic affairs. They were purposely executed to convey messages to the international community that Thailand was one of the equals. As one governmental circulation signed by Phibun stated:

> I think that this time, it is important for Thailand to try to enhance our culture to be on par with our allies and other civilised nations. The fact that the population of the nation maintains a civilised culture would help preserve the Thainess of the nation. Hence, I personally request you all to improve the Thai culture to be better in a unified manner in order to fulfil objectives.
>
> (NAT-SoTo-0701.29/1)

Despite all of the confidential plans to spread the Thai culture to other places, the centre of gravity during the period was Japan. Henceforth, the major tribulations revolved around the issues of counteracting Japan's cultural aggression. Aside from domestic cultural alterations, the Thais pursued proactive cultural policies towards Japan in order to exhibit the status parity of the Thai culture. As early as mid-1942, the Thai Foreign Ministry suggested that,

> It is known that there is Japan's intention to establish an organisation to spread their culture in Bangkok, which could persuade the Thais to admire Japan excessively. It would be appropriate to form an organisation to promote the Thai culture in Japan as well.
>
> (NAT-[2]-KoTo-7.1/10)

Such a policy recommendation mirrored Thailand's ontological insecurity in terms of how Japan would acknowledge Thailand's status and identity as a partner. The Thai leaders held a belief that Thailand's offensive cultural policy would generate shared cultural understandings among the Japanese with respect to Thailand's status. This could be confirmed by Phibun's private thoughts prior to the conclusion of the cultural treaty: 'It would be proper for the Thai embassy in Tokyo to be responsible to spread Thailand's culture so that they know we are more developed than other nations' (NAT-[3]-SoRo-0201.55/24, 2).

The Japanese-Thai cultural agreement was signed on 21 December 1942. The pact, though institutionalising Japan's cultural quests, was not a one-way cultural scheme in which Japan would be entitled to promote its culture in Thailand. Nonetheless, the agreement allowed Thailand to spread its culture in Japan as well. Thawan, the justice minister, articulated the spirit of the pact as follows:

> The cultural pact that we have agreed with Japan refers to an exchange of cultural knowledge of each other. But it does not mean that Japan must adopt the Thai culture or Thailand must embrace the Japanese culture. On the contrary, the major principle in the preamble states that each party shall respect the uniqueness of each other's culture.
>
> (Nipaporn 2002, 105)

The outcome of the finalised agreement was churned out from Thailand's anxieties over Japan's cultural intrusion. As previously mentioned, the Thais were aware that a complete blockade of foreign culture was an impossible task. The solutions, however, were to renovate the culture and to expand it to other regions. As in the case of the negotiation of the cultural agreement, the Thai cabinet compared the cultural agreements that Japan had signed with Italy, Germany, and Hungary, and replicated the clauses that would permit both parties to set up a cultural institute in one another's territory (TMCM 47/1942, 25-September-1942; NAT-[3]-SoRo-0201.55/21, 10). Therefore, the matter of cultural proselytisation became reciprocal, which meant that the Thais could formally spread their culture in Japan as well.

As regards Thailand's proactive measures towards Japan, the underlying strategy was to begin the cultural pursuit from the Thai embassy in Tokyo by dispatching cultural specialists to Tokyo and to set up a store to sell Thailand's cultural products such as arts and handicraft products in Japan's capital city (NAT-SoTo-0701.9.5.1/13). The long-term plan was to establish Thailand's cultural institute in Japan as a mecca of the Thai culture on foreign soil.

Direk, who was moved to position as an ambassador in Tokyo, collaborated with the government's policy by delivering lectures relating to the Thai culture in various Japanese institutions. To be able to prepare for lectures effectively, he sent a telegram to the government to ship all books pertaining to the Thai studies to Tokyo (NAT-[2]-KoTo-7.1/11). As the telegram to Bangkok showed,

> With regard to steps to be taken by this Embassy in order to make Thai Culture better known among the Japanese as instructed by His Excellency (the) Premier, I beg to report that even before the conclusion of the Cultural Agreement my staff and most of them have been trying our best to propagate our Culture through speeches, and lectures, and books containing my lectures in Japan are being printed.
>
> (NAT-[2]-KoTo-3.6.3/1)

The purpose of those lectures, as Direk wrote, was to 'show them our real culture for it leads to mutual understanding between the two countries and respect for our country' (NAT-[2]-KoTo-7.1/11). In order to disseminate more about the Thai culture in Japan, it was recommended that the government should invest time and resources to teach the Thai language in Japan, to introduce Thai plays at theatre, to display Thai produce, to present Thai songs, and to publish pamphlets and books on Thai politics, economy, society, and culture (NAT-[3]-SoRo-0201.55/24, 17–18; TMCM x/1943, 29-September-1943.). Wichit further advised the cabinet to dispatch eight cultural specialists to Tokyo for the sake of expanding the government's cultural programmes. Those specialists included two female dancers, two female singers, one female musician, one male musician, one male painter, and one literary scholar (TMCM x/1943, 29-September-1943). A budget for the cultural scheme in Tokyo was also prepared for those cultural experts (ibid.).

For the Thai elites, Thailand's projects to establish the cultural centre in Tokyo had certain implications. Firstly, if the cultural institute could be successfully formed, it implied that Thailand's culture and status were accepted as worthy of recognition. It would render the Thais satisfactory of the fact that their status as an equal partner was accepted. This was because Germany, Italy, and Hungary could similarly finalise the cultural agreement with Japan. The spread of the European culture in Japan, in a nutshell, was a benchmark for Thailand's cultural aspirations in Asia.

Japan captured Thailand's enthusiastic move in culture as Tsubokami noted that Thailand's recalibration of its cultural policies was a reaction to 'stimulus for the advance of Japanese culture' (Reynolds 1991, 108). Nevertheless, Japan's inaction towards Thailand's cultural counterattack in mid-1943 was due to the empire's preoccupation with the Pacific situation. Although Thailand's cultural institute in Tokyo had never been formed due to the war situation and the downfall of Phibun in 1944, the genuine intent and interest of the Thai leaders in elevating the cultural affairs as a measure to enhance Thailand's status could be seen through the relevant documents revealed throughout this section. The concern for status and Japanese misrecognition of Thailand's partnership had been the foreign policy determinants which drove the Thais to intensify their cultural projects.

Conclusion

Before Phibun stepped down from power in July 1944, his campaign against Japan had become more apparent than the period from 1942 to 1943. This could be interpreted from how he arrested Wanit Pananonda, who was the minister without portfolio and was entrusted to communicate with the Japanese, for treason (NAT-[3]-SoRo-0201.2.7/49). The purpose was to depict the picture of Thailand's disobedience to Japan when the war was drawing to an end (Interview with Ananda Pananonda on 10 April 2016). Despite Phibun's bellicosity towards Japan in 1944, the interpretations that this chapter offered could be summarised as follows.

The governing dynamic of Thailand's foreign policy behaviours towards Japan revolved around Thailand's concerns about status and recognition. Following the victory over France, Thailand's sense of pride and reputation reached its apex. Clearly, the Thais had a limited, revisionist interest to regain the lost territories from the European powers. Given an opportunity to achieve its objectives by launching a pre-emptive strike while the French and British were preoccupied with the war on the European front, the Thai government continued a policy of strict neutrality instead of secretly negotiating with Japan to conquer its former lands.

Japan's alteration of her war policy in attacking the Pearl Harbor invited the war-prone situations to Thailand. The Japanese demand was nothing more than a request to place Thailand as a stationary hub for the empire's military operations in Asia. The Thai government, as this chapter traced the decision-making from the cabinet minutes, acceded to the Japanese demands because of its status anxiety. The Thais did not want to be placed as a colony under imperial Japan. Thailand's choice to adhere to Japan's grand strategy was to preserve independence and honour. Although this explanation could fit the interpretations of the flexible foreign policy approach and Schweller's category of a jackal state, they could not wholly explain why Thailand remained resolved to the policy of absolute neutrality even the night before the Japanese invasion.

On the surface, the two explanations could offer satisfactory interpretations regarding Thailand's sudden alignment with Japan. The flexible foreign policy approach, for instance, would explain that Thailand simply bent towards the prevailing wind, whereas Schweller's theory would view Thailand's foreign policy overhaul as a result of its revisionist interest. Neither of the two accounts could fully grasp an understanding of Thailand's proactive behaviours. Speaking from the material and rationalist perspectives, it would be reasonable for Thailand to remain inactive and passive after the Japanese invasion because the war situation in early 1942 was unpredictable, and if the imperial troops were vanquished, the Thais could undoubtedly draw international sympathies and preserve dignity.

On the contrary, Thailand, in pursuit of status and recognition, wished to reaffirm its existence and identity as a partner by venturing to declare war on the Allies, trying to join the Axis, and seeking to become involved in the military campaigns. The Thai counterpart could play an optimal card by restraining itself from an active engagement with the Japanese and only responding to necessarily unavoidable demands. Thailand, however, practised proactive foreign policies towards Japan in order to be on an equal footing with its war ally. The concerns about status and recognition drove the Thai foreign relations towards Japan.

Moreover, Thailand's turn against Japan was not due to the war retreat. The main factor for the deterioration of the Japanese-Thai relations was how Japan treated Thailand as a colony. As a nation which prided itself as independent, the Japanese imperious attitude was an affront to Thailand's prestige. Henceforth, Thailand resorted to policies in defence of its status as an equal, sovereign country. Phibun's antagonistic persistence against Japan could be highlighted even when Japan prized Thailand with the lost territories. Japan's reward of the territories to Thailand did not remedy the brittle relationship between the two countries. Moreover, in order to display the nation's civilised status, the Thai government initiated plans to adjust and modify the Thai culture. Its aspiration also reached the extent to which the Thai leaders secretly designed a grand strategy to spread the culture to its neighbours and in Japan. From the analyses of the leaders' private thinking, Thailand's cultural responses towards Japan stemmed from its status anxiety and Japan's high-handed exercises.

Notes

1 The Japanese-Thai diplomatic relations were elevated to an ambassadorial rank in August 1941.
2 It is noteworthy to remark in this place that the original copies of the cabinet minutes from December 1941 to February 1942 mysteriously disappeared from the Office of the Secretariat of the Cabinet. However, the copies of the historic cabinet minutes on 7–8 December 1941 and 10–12 December 1941 have been published in the memoirs of Phibun's son. And, these copies are the most recognised cabinet minutes.
3 The entire text of the agreement is only archived in Thailand, where photocopying is strictly forbidden.
4 The original copy of the cabinet minutes on 25 January 1942 disappeared from the Office of the Secretariat of the Cabinet. Vinita Kririksh's sources were perhaps available by the time she first conducted her research several years ago.
5 The original copy of this document is held by Dr. Puli Fuwongcharoen (puli.fu@gmail.com). In 2016, a group of Thai historians gathered to interview Phibun's daughter, Chirawats Panyarachun, and to retrieve private documents. I am allowed

to take notes of some of the useful documents from this group project. This is the letter sent to Chirawats from one of her friends under the pen name 'Su'. Some part of this document has been published in Nakarin et al. (2018).

6 In Luang Saranuchit's funerary volume, the official documents were inserted at the end of his book for some reason.

7 Some of the original copies of the cabinet minutes in 1943 were damaged from bombardment. Therefore, it is impossible to determine the number of meetings. 'X' is a substitute for the missing number.

7 Conclusion

Overall summary

This book begins with a simple question: Why did Thailand pursue proactive foreign policies during the Second World War? The dominant approach to explain Thai foreign policy behaviours suggests that Thailand is less prone to be proactive in international affairs. Henceforth, the events of the Franco-Thai War (1940–41) and Japanese-Thai relations (1941–44) pose an interesting puzzle for IR scholars to invent appropriate approaches to explain such phenomena. This book builds on Zarakol's theoretical framework (2007, 2011) to interpret these cases by highlighting the importance of stigmatisation, status concern, and recognition as central components in an empirical analysis.

The book began by tracing Thailand's historical account in the nineteenth century in order to see the development of how the Thai state was confronted with the advent of the European powers in Asia and experienced the imported European modes of living. It was found that the Siamese elites had gradually internalised the Western values from encounters with the Western counterparts and realised that their customary ways of living were not appreciated within European international society. The Siamese leaders, in other words, were stigmatised from the club of civilisation and, hence, were treated as an inferior entity. Shameful of their existence, the Siamese effortlessly transformed and adjusted their *modus vivendi* for the purpose of gaining approbation from the Western nations. As such, a number of modernising measures had been widely imposed upon the local Siamese in order to exemplify Siamese civilised status in the international arena. The Siamese kings, namely Mongkut, Chulalongkorn, and Vajiravudh, generally sought to position Siam as one of the equals to the European powers.

Such experiences and concerns about status and recognition in the nineteenth century formed a basic guideline of how subsequent leaders had conducted foreign policy. It would be insurmountable and unimaginable for the Siamese/Thais to formulate any foreign policy independent of the status concerns and the consideration of the international community. After the exposure to Western international society, any foreign policies generated came to be seen as more or less based on references to the Western counterparts. These legacies were institutionalised and embedded in the foreign practices of the Thai leaders even after the end of absolute monarchy in 1932. These legacies, in other words, had defined Thailand's national interests in terms of status and recognition. As Chapter 4 argued, the Thai elites after 1932 could not but unremittingly worry about their nation's standing in relation to other countries. Thailand's stable, continuous sense of self should be derived from recognition as an equal, sovereign nation by the then great powers.

The flexible foreign policy approach, which has widely been employed as a framework to explain Thai foreign affairs, does not offer a satisfactory account to understand the two minor cases on which this book focuses. As in the case of the Franco-Thai dispute, how would the flexible foreign policy approach explain Thailand's proactive foreign policy vis-à-vis France even before the French regime surrendered to Nazi Germany? In a similar vein, how could Schweller's neo-classical realist model explain the jackal state as in the case of Thailand during the marked period? Thailand could be dubbed as a small state with a limited, revisionist interest. France's preoccupation with the war in Europe was a ripe opportunity for Thailand to undertake a military operation to annex the lost territories. Contrary to what traditional theories would predict, Thailand, as Chapter 5 has demonstrated, was content with a policy of strict neutrality.

While France defended against the German encroachment in Europe, she was desperate to seal the Non-aggression Pact with the Thai government in order to preclude the possibility of Thailand's engulfing French Indo-China. Thailand thus gained the upper hand in the situation. It was in a position to pose greater demands from France or reject the French proposition entirely. As opposed to demanding that all of the territories secede to France in the nineteenth century, the Thai leaders requested the border revision with French Indo-China. The Thais viewed France's attempt to conclude the Non-aggression Pact as a symbol of how one of the major European powers acknowledged the status of Thailand as a sovereign and independent nation. Even in June 1940, when France conceded to Germany and the Italians joined the war, Thailand was entitled to dismiss the pact, to bid for a better deal, or to negotiate with Japan and incorporate the territories amidst the chaos within France. As it turned out, the Thai government faithfully committed to the pact as agreed prior to the transformation of the international situation.

Nonetheless, Thailand's proactive gambit vis-à-vis France stemmed from its sense of existential insecurity. The French intentionally delayed the border adjustment with Thailand as originally agreed; yet she urged the Thais to ratify the Non-aggression Pact in order to safeguard her colonial affairs in Asia. To the Thai people, France's move was seen as disrespectful to their nation's status. France treated Thailand as if it were a second-rate nation. Correspondingly, the Thai policy-makers translated the French maltreatments as a sign that the European power did not acknowledge Thailand's worth on the international stage.

Henceforth, in order to garner recognition from France, the Thai elites offered a diplomatic quid pro quo. France agreed to ratify the pact provided that the Quai d'Orsay consented to undertake the original border delimitation deal to adjust the Franco-Thai border by marking the Mekong River a natural frontier and to pledge to return the lost territories to Thailand if the French sovereignty in Indo-China became insolvent. These conditions, if France acceded to them, would amount to an acknowledgement of Thailand's status. Or at least this was the perception of the Thai leaders. Such conditions, as Phibun was fully aware, would hurt the honour and prestige of the French empire. France's response to these conditions would mean Thailand's prestige at the expense of France, because, as Thomas Hobbes observed, 'Glory is like honour, if all men have it, no man hath it, for they consist in comparison and precellence; neither doth the society of others advance any whit the cause of my glaring myself' (cited in Markey 2000, 354).

As it turned out, France dismissed Thailand's propositions. To the Thais, the demanded territories were stolen by France in the past, and reluctance to return them to a rightful owner was deemed contemptuous of Thailand's identity as an equal nation. As a result, the Thai public expressed their indignation towards France by protesting on the streets. The public outcry became widespread throughout the nation. The core message was pertinent to how France disregarded Thailand's identity as a nation with equal status. One of the prominent discourses that the Thais utilised to justify the use of force was how France in the nineteenth century unjustly preyed upon the then weak and inferior Siam. The Thai people in the Phibun era, however, saw themselves as a more developed nation, and hence France would be required to respect their stature.

With the people's pressure, the government's inaction would be the equivalent of inferiority. Therefore, the government became involved in projects to portray themselves as a civilised place and to encourage the Laotian and Cambodian residents under the French protectorate to rise up against France. Enhancing a civilised image of Thailand would enthral the Laotians and Cambodians to immigrate to Thailand and would further justify the government's territorial campaigns. Moreover, more populations and territories could be a great trajectory to become a great power, which could heighten the status and prestige of the nation.

While Thailand preserved the use of force as a last resort, France's provocative actions along the borders further worsened the festering relationship between the two nations. Inaction would confirm the nation's inferiority. The only viable option to reaffirm Thailand's status was to declare war against France. The discourses of the Thai elites after Thailand's victory over France indicated that Thailand's status and prestige were greatly enhanced following the skirmishes.

In the case of Japanese-Thai relations (1941–1944), Thailand's proactive behaviours were a result of its status anxiety vis-à-vis Japan. From the outset, it seems fairly convincing for the flexible foreign policy approach and Schweller's model to explain Thailand foreign policy towards Japan in the wartime period. For instance, Thailand's sway towards the Japanese orbit could match the description of a bamboo bending towards the prevailing wind. Similarly, Thailand's entry into the alliance with Japan could be due to its limited, revisionist aspiration to reclaim the territories from Britain and France. In fact, Japan simply needed Thailand as a hub and not as an ally. The Thais were given a choice to maintain their independent position without jeopardising the integrity of neutrality. This choice would be optimal because, if Japan won the war, Thailand could claim that it assisted the victor power, whereas if the Allied powers won, Thailand could gain international sympathies.

Nonetheless, on closer inspection, historical evidence reveals that the reason Thailand became the Japanese ally was due to the concern about its status. The Thai leaders were agitated by the chance that Japan would designate Thailand as one of the Japanese colonies. In order to preserve honour, a deal with the devil was a necessary evil. Yet, it would be undeniable that such descriptions still correspond to the flexible foreign policy approach and Schweller's categorical explanation. However, these two approaches could not holistically make sense of Thai behaviours in the following years. Japan would prefer to limit Thailand's involvement in the war to the minimum level in order to prevent Thailand's entanglement with the imperial grand strategy. Additionally, Thailand's best course of action would be to remain passive in relation to Japan in order to hedge between the Axis and the Allies.

Contrary to what IR scholars would expect, Thailand was persistent to become part of the war for the purpose of reaffirming status and securing recognition from Japan. The Thais did not want to be regarded as a Japanese stooge. Hence, the Thai government pursued a number of strategies to exemplify Thailand's equal partnership in the alliance. For example, it unnecessarily declared war on the Allies without Japan's permission to show that it did not receive an instruction from anyone. Thailand's non-declaration of war would be a strategic advantage for Japan because the enemies would be reluctant to bombard Thailand, which would be perceived as an enemy-occupied territory. To further exhibit an identity as an equal partner, the Thai leaders circumvented the Japanese in seeking the Axis membership. This scheme was secretly executed to prevent the others from seeing Thailand as Japan's satellite nation. Becoming an Axis member would mean Thailand would be on par with Japan, Italy, and Germany.

Although Tokyo disapproved of Thailand's Axis ambition, the Thais remained ardently obdurate to elevate their national standing vis-à-vis Japan by negotiating with the Japanese SAA to dispatch the Thai troops into Burma. Despite approximate shortcomings in the terms of the agreement, in financial resources, and in strategic senses, the Thai government secured the deal with Japan to send the Thai troops into Burma in May 1942. The military campaign in Burma was operationalised to seek ontological security as the evidence in Chapter 6 suggested. Such an operation in Burma was of unimportance to Thailand considered from material and rationalist perspectives. Japan had frequently been reluctant to allow Thailand to participate in matters of foreign and military affairs. Moreover, Thailand's dispatch of the troops into the Shan states was not a guarantee that Japan would return those territories. As such, Thailand's military campaign could be considered an irrational miscalculation from the viewpoints of the flexible foreign policy approach and from Schweller's model.

Additionally, Thailand turned against Japan in less than a year of the alliance. The reason was not because of Japan's bleak situation in the war. It was due to how the Japanese treated Thailand as one of her colonies on several occasions. For Phibun, once the Japanese gradually demoted Thailand as part of the *Greater East Asia Co-prosperity Sphere*, or in other words, once the Thai-Japanese relations became unequal in late 1942, he turned against the Japanese (Terwiel 1980, 21). In response to Japan's imperious practices, Phibun tried to establish contact with China, relocated the capital city to the mid-part of the country, and re-launched cultural engineering programmes in order to enhance Thailand's civilised status. All in all, Thailand's proactive behaviours from 1941 to 1944 were governed by its concerns about status and recognition.

Policy implications

The cases of Thailand on which this research focused might bring doubts to practitioners with regard to the issue of policy implications. Yes, it was undoubtedly true that international politics is commonly dominated by great powers. However, there are contemporary cases in which small states can pose problems and dangers to international security. And sometimes those questions of the small states could not be solved by carrot-and-stick measures.

One of the noticeable cases, which could be a tipping point to the outbreak of the war, is the case of North Korea. The North Korean leaders and their provocative behaviours in nuclear missiles testing have been a thorny alarm to East Asian security for decades. Their leaders rationally realise that they could be toppled from power if the US lands on their soils. They also understand that their confrontational actions would rile China, which is their only ally.

Not only North Korea, but how would practitioners understand the case of the State of Palestine? The small number of Palestinians has been incessantly fighting and provoking Israel for almost five decades. Despite Israel's on-going expansionism into Palestine to the extent that the Palestinians were reduced to *de facto* residents within the Israeli-cum-Palestinian sovereignty, it would be more sensible for Palestine to halt any acts of provocation given a huge difference in military capabilities between the two states. Nevertheless, there have been sporadic military offences from the Palestinian areas.

Another relevant case involves the Filipinos and their President Rodrigo Duterte. It has been common knowledge that the Philippines has been involved in the South China Sea disputes since the Cold War period, and it has no reservations when it comes to territorial issues. To guard against the Chinese military threat, the Filipinos have been dependent on the American security umbrella. This has been their nation's foreign policy code of conduct for a long time. Nevertheless, when Duterte came to power in 2016, he openly raised an anti-American tone. His defiance reached the level where he pledged to renounce the American aids. At the same time, his presidency also maintains an adamant position as regards the conflicts in the South China Sea.

How would any policy-makers make sense of such nuancing misdemeanours displayed by small states such as North Korea, Palestine, and the Philippines? If the existing approaches fail to explain these cases, would it more tenable to throw new light on these puzzling events? It could be the cases that all of the three states are simply concerned about their psychological existence. Hence, they have pursued wild foreign policies in order to gain recognition and to confirm their existence.

Any potential researchers could further delve into these questions to offer policy options for practitioners. If status and recognition are of influential elements, the policy-makers could, for example, introduce necessary arrangements which could meet with these states' intangible interests. For example, diplomatic platforms could be organised for the purpose of recognising the importance of these states' status in order to diffuse feuds (Renshon 2017, 270).

Possible weaknesses

Although the preceding section briefly discussed different cases in order to provide the external validity of the approach employed in this thesis, it is not without identifiable weaknesses. This book embarks on the two events of Thai foreign policy during the Second World War. The approach traces the development of Thailand's sense of ontological insecurity in the nineteenth century and verifies how Thailand's concerns for status and recognition loomed large even after the end of absolute monarchy. These factors subsequently shaped Phibun's foreign policy-making when the Thais dealt with France and Japan.

In order to replicate the approach undertaken in this book, researchers must be able to have access to primary resources. Language skills become an indispensable element in this route of research. Defying any existing case studies which approvingly obsess about material and rationalist explanations is possible. However, such a possibility is not the equivalent of convenience. If a research conduct relies on secondary sources, there is a likelihood that the researchers could be clouded by the existing literature, which mostly places an emphasis on material factors.

Secondly, utilising primary resources and relevant historical documents could improve the research validity. Because status concerns and recognition could sometimes run against rational policy options, public speeches delivered by elites usually cover genuine intents of politicians. Hence, sole reliance on public and official documents could encounter questions of validity claims. On the contrary, the utilisation of primary, private, and secret documents offers more opportunities to establish arguments that certain intangible components do matter to policy outcomes (Larson 1985, 60–61).

From this angle, a language barrier and clearance to confidential sources could be a strength and weakness of the approach in question. The strength is observable. The use of archival documents reinforces the rigour of the arguments. And there is a strong tendency that the researchers could pioneer new findings in the field. The weakness that could appear is for any researchers who work on comparative cases. It would be difficult for those concentrating on three or four comparative cases to be authorised clearance to primary sources. This is not to mention the issue of proficiency in several different languages. Jonathan Renshon (2017), a scholar whose interest lies in status and conflicts, recognises this problem. He supplements his research mission by operationalising an experimental research methodology to prove how status matters for policy-makers and constructing quantitative measures to assess how status deficits could be influential to state behaviours.

Concluding remarks

This book has tackled the puzzle of Thailand's behaviour during the Second World War. It highlighted the significance of intangible elements such as ontological security, status concern, and recognition in determining foreign policies of small states. As the preceding sections suggested, there are also other prospective cases that could be analysed through a similar framework. IR has been criticised for its excessive focus on great powers and its preference for material and rationalist explanations over ideational ones. In fact, the majority of states in the international system are either small or middle powers, which should receive more attention in the discipline. As such, the usage of the case of Thailand, which was considered a small state during the Second World War, could partly display how the small states could behave anything beyond being passive in foreign relations.

Moreover, there has been a recent surge of interest in IR scholarship in turning towards ideational explanations in international phenomena. The emotive, ontological, practice turns are emerging in the field of IR, and these so-called turns bring about theoretical repertoires which require further empirical assessments to substantiate their potentially rigorous claims. This book combines these two trends, namely, the trend in small- or middle-sized state studies and the trend in employing ideational elements' factors of theories, with the hopes that this research project could be a part of a larger contribution to the growing study of non-Western states in IR through the dimensions of ideational theories.

Although the book might fill the gap of the IR literature, it is equally essential to address further empirical puzzles in the case of Thailand. As this book has thoroughly argued, ontological and status anxieties had been part of Thailand's mode of foreign policy considerations since the European powers expanded into Asia in the nineteenth century. Even though the book has painted a picture of how the Siamese-Thai elites had been constantly worried about their nation's standing in international society from the days of their first encounter with the West to the end of the Second World War, another potential question that could arise from Thai studies academics would be whether Thailand would continue to be affected by ontological and status apprehensions after the war and whether the psyches would last. Such questions are greatly important for both Thai studies and IR. That is, despite an increasing interest in ontological security and status-concern approaches, there is an inadequate research project to elucidate the temporal termination of the social anxieties in the international arena. These two questions would require further research in order to provide a well-rounded answer in the upcoming future.

Bibliography

Archival sources

Foreign Relations of the United States [FRUS]

FRUS 1941 Vol. 5

Document 136 'Memorandum of Conversation, by the Secretary of State'
Document 191 'The Minister in Thailand (Grant) to the Secretary of State'
Document 239 'The Minister in Thailand (Grant) to the Secretary of State'
Document 411 'The Minister in Thailand (Peck) to the Secretary of State'
Document 416 'The Secretary of State to the Ambassador in the United Kingdom (Winant)'
Document 429 'The British Embassy to the Department of State'

The Magic of Pearl Harbor [MPH]

MPH Vol. 1: 14 February 1941–12 May 1941

Document 413 Page A-217

MPH Appendix Vol. 3

Document 1122 Page A-569

MPH Appendix Vol. 4

Document 1105 Page A-504
Document 1137 Page A-515
Document 1150 Page A-520
Document 1175 Page A-529

The National Archives, Kew [TNA]

Government Communications Headquarters (HW)

HW-1/571

FO 371: Far Eastern [Siam 40]

FO371/16261, F5846/4260/40 'Siamese Affairs'
FO371/16261, F5917/4260/40 'Political Events in Siam'
FO371/16261, F6564/4260/40 'Political Situation in Siam'
FO371/19379, F2639/2639/40 'Siamese Legal Codes'
FO371/21052, F1496/164/40 'Defence of Siam'
FO371/21052, F2269/14/40 'Broadcast Speech by Siamese Minister of Defence'
FO371/22207, F4339/113/40 'Political Situation in Siam,'
FO371/22207, F4660/113/40 'Irredentist Movement in Siam'
FO371/22207, F7178/113/40 'Political Situation in Siam'
FO371/22207, F10005/113/40 'Irredentist Movement in Siam'
FO371/22207, F10006/113/40 'Political Situation in Siam'
FO371/22207, F10430/113/40 'Siamese and Japanese Designs against French Indo-China'
FO371/22207, F10968/113/40 'Situation in Siam-Indo-China Frontier District'
FO371/22214, F10000/1391/40 'Siamese Foreign Relations'
FO371/22215, F5586/2113/40 'Attitude of Siam in the Event of a War in the Far East'
FO371/23595, F4252/1850/40 'Siamese Policy in Event of European War'
FO371/23595, F10315/1860/40 'Siamese Attitude to European War'
FO371/23595, F19040/43/40 'Notes on Siam, July-August 1939'
FO371/23596, F11457/1860/40 'Siamese Neutrality'
FO371/23596, F11460/1860/40 'Proposed Siamese Pacts of Non-aggression with Great Britain and France'
FO371/23596, F11516/1860/40 Proposed Siamese Pacts of Non-aggression with Great Britain and France'
FO371/24751, F2819/19/40 'British and French Non-Aggression Pacts with Thailand'
FO371/24751, F3326/19/40 'British and French non-Aggression Pacts with Thailand: Japanese Proposals to Thai Government'

National Archives of Thailand [NAT]

Headquarters of the Commander-in-Chief of the Thai Armed Forces (BokoSungsut)

BokoSungsut-1/103
BokoSungsut-1/155
BokoSungsut-1/157
BokoSungsut-1.8/6
BokoSungsut-1.9/1
BokoSungsut-1.12/45
BokoSungsut-1.12/141

BokoSungsut-1.12/192
BokoSungsut-1.12/201
BokoSungsut-1.12/212
BokoSungsut-1.16/3
BokoSungsut-1.16/71
BokoSungsut-2/67
BokoSungsut-2.4.1.2/1

Office of Prime Minister (SoRo)

SoRo-0201.8/99
SoRo-0201.20/2
SoRo-0201.20/3
SoRo-0201.24/46
SoRo-0201.25/109
SoRo-0201.25/772
SoRo-0201.25/821
SoRo-0201.33/11
SoRo-0201.33/12
SoRo-0201.33/14
SoRo-0201.33/28
SoRo-0201.33/45
SoRo-0201.33/53
SoRo-0201.35/1
SoRo-0201.35/2
SoRo-0201.35/6
SoRo-0201.35/8
SoRo-0201.35/11
SoRo-0201.35/26
SoRo-0201.37.6/18
[2] SoRo-0201.4/13
[2] SoRo-0201.4/18
[2] SoRo-0201.21.3/1
[2] SoRo-0201.21.3/5
[2] SoRo-0201.45/7
[2] SoRo-0201.86/17
[2] SoRo-0201.86/45
[2] SoRo-0201.86/91
[2] SoRo-0201.86/129
[2] SoRo-0201.86/133
[2] SoRo-0201.92/13
[2] SoRo-0201.92.1/4
[2] SoRo-0201.92.1/6
[2] SoRo-0201.92.1/7
[2] SoRo-0201.92.1/8
[2] SoRo-0201.97.3/7

[2] SoRo-0201.98/2
[2] SoRo-0201.98/9
[2] SoRo-0201.98/19
[2] SoRo-0201.98.1/6
[2] SoRo-0201.98.1/13
[2] SoRo-0201.98.2/1
[2] SoRo-0201.98.3/3
[3] SoRo-0201.2.7/49
[3] SoRo-0201.55/7
[3] SoRo-0201.55/8
[3] SoRo-0201.55/16
[3] SoRo-0201.55/19
[3] SoRo-0201.55/21
[3] SoRo-0201.55/24
[3] SoRo-0201.55/44
[3] SoRo-0201.55/45
[3] SoRo-0201.55/47

Ministry of Education (SoTo)

SoTo-0701.9.5.1/13
SoTo-0701.23.1/6
SoTo-0701.28/29
SoTo-0701.29/1
SoTo-0701.29/4
SoTo-0701.29/5
SoTo-0701.41.1/26
[2] SoTo-15.3/42

Ministry of Foreign Affairs (KoTo)

KoTo-73.2.4.1/17
KoTo-80/325
[2] KoTo-1.1/17
[2] KoTo-1.1/23
[2] KoTo-1.1/20
[2] KoTo-1.1.5/6
[2] KoTo-1.1.5/9
[2] KoTo-1.1.5/11
[2] KoTo-1.1.1.1/1
[2] KoTo-1.1.1.1/2
[2] KoTo-1.1.1.1/3
[2] KoTo-1.1.1.1/4
[2] KoTo-1.1.1.1/5
[2] KoTo-1.1.1.1/6
[2] KoTo-1.1.1.1/7
[2] KoTo-2.4/65
[2] KoTo-2.4.1/76

[2] KoTo-2.4.1/82
[2] KoTo-2.4.1/83
[2] KoTo-2.4.1/93
[2] KoTo-2.4.1/99
[2] KoTo-2.4.2/90
[2] KoTo-2.1.6/10
[2] KoTo-2.7/29
[2] KoTo-3.6.3/1
[2] KoTo-7.1/6
[2] KoTo-7.1/10
[2] KoTo-7.1/11
[2] KoTo-8.1.1/27
[2] KoTo-8.1.1/29

Ministry of Interior

MoTo-0201.2.1.14/1
MoTo-0201.2.1.14/3

Undisclosed Document Receiving from Ministry of Foreign Affairs in Twenty Years (KoTo 0202/61)

KoTo-0202/61-Washington-38/233

Personal Documents donated to the National Archives (SoBor)

SoBo-9-Eak-Weesakul

Office of the Secretary of the National Assembly

Thai Parliament's Minutes of Proceedings (Raignan Kanprachum Sapha Phuthaen Ratsadorn)

TPMP 1/1932, 28 June 1932
TPMP 46/1932, 9 December 1932
TPMP 20/1934 [1935], 14 February 1934 [1935]
TPMP 3/1938, 26 December 1938
TPMP 4/1940, 18 July 1940
TPMP 10/1940, 29 August 1940
TPMP 14/1940, 19 September 1940
TPMP 1/1941, 9 June 1941
TPMP 4/1941, 23 December 1941

Office of the Secretariat of the Cabinet

Thailand's Minutes of Cabinet Meeting (Raignan Kanprachum Khana Rattamontri)

TMCM 4/1937, 12 May 1937
TMCM 1/1938, 20 December 1938
TMCM 10/1938 [1939], 13 February 1938 [1939]
TMCM 4/1939, 8 May 1939

TMCM 11/1939, 5 June 1939
TMCM 47/1939, 2 September 1939
TMCM 72/1939, 27 December 1939
TMCM 73/1939 [1940], 3 January 1939 [1940]
TMCM 74/1939 [1940], 10 January 1939 [1940]
TMCM 83/1939 [1940], 13 March 1939 [1940]
TMCM 1/1940, 15 April 1940
TMCM, 2/1940, 17 April 1940
TMCM 11/1940, 5 June 1940
TMCM 12/1940, 11 June 1940
TMCM 18/1940, 17 July 1940
TMCM 20/1940, 7 August 1940
TMCM 22/1940, 21 August 1940
TMCM 24/1940, 4 September 1940
TMCM 25/1940, 11 September 1940
TMCM 27/1940, 25 September 1940
TMCM 29/1940, 9 October 1940
TMCM 30/1940, 16 October 1940
TMCM 31/1940, 23 October 1940
TMCM 33/1940, 30 October 1940
TMCM 36/1940, 13 November 1940
TMCM 38/1940, 27 November 1940
TMCM 3/1941, 22 January 1941
TMCM 4/1941 25 January 1941
TMCM 5/1941, 29 January 1941
TMCM 6/1941, 3 February 1941
TMCM 8/1941, 12 February 1941
TMCM 10/1941, 26 February 1941
TMCM 13/1941, 12 March 1941
TMCM 14/1941, 17 March 1941
TMCM 26/1941, 14 May 1941
TMCM 47/1941, 23 August 1941
TMCM 49/1941, 30 August 1941
TMCM 52/1941, 10 September 1941
TMCM Special Cabinet Meeting, 7–8 December 1941
TMCM Special Cabinet Meeting, 8 December 1941
TMCM Special Cabinet Meeting, 10 December 1941
TMCM Special Cabinet Meeting, 11 December 1941
TMCM 16/1942, 18 March 1942
TMCM 15/1942, 29 April 1942
TMCM 27/1942, 13 May 1942
TMCM 28/1942, 20 May 1942
TMCM 36/1942, 22 July 1942
TMCM 47/1942, 25 September 1942
TMCM 50/1942, 14 October 1942
TMCM 1/1943, 2 January 1943

TMCM x/1943, 8 September 1943
TMCM x/1943, 29 September 1943

Manuscript Room, University of Cambridge's Library

MS Scott (James)

MS-Scott UL1.55.9

Newspapers

Bangkok Times

Bangkok Times 12 June 1940

Lakmuang

Lakmuang 4 October 1940
Lakmuang 5 October 1940

Prachachat

Prachachat 4 November 1938

Nikorn

Nikorn 13 January 1941
Nikorn 2 April 1941
Nikorn 11 April 1941

Srikung

Srikung 15 May 1937
Srikung 2 September 1937

Thai Rashdra

Thai Rashdra 11 November 1940

Notebook

Civilian Commanding Notebook of Field Marshal Phibunsongkhram 1 June-13 August 1943
Cultural Commanding Notebook of Field Marshal Phibunsongkhram 6 March 1943–25 July 1944
Military Commanding Notebook of Field Marshal Phibunsongkhram 20 January-4 May 1943

English-language secondary sources

Aldrich, R. J. (1988). A question of expediency: Britain, the United States and Thailand, 1941–42. *Journal of Southeast Asian Studies*, *19*(2), 209–244.

Aldrich, R. J. (1993). *The Key to the South: Britain, the United States, and Thailand During the Approach of the Pacific War, 1929–1942*. Oxford: Oxford University Press.

Alexander, J. (2004). Toward a Theory of Cultural Trauma. In J. Alexander, R. Eyerman, B. Giesen, N. J. Smelser, & P. Sztompka (Eds.), *Cultural Trauma and Collective Identity*. Berkeley: University of California Press.
Allison, G. T. (2017). *Destined for War: Can American and China Escape Thucydides's Trap?* London: Scribe Publications.
Allison, G. T., & Zelikow, P. (1999). *Essence of Decision: Explaining the Cuban Missile Crisis* (Vol. 2). New York: Longman.
Anderson, B. (1978). Studies of the Thai State: The State of Thai Studies. In E. Ayal (Ed.), *The State of Thai Studies: Analyses of Knowledge, Approaches, and Prospects in Anthropology, Art History, Economics, History, and Political Science*. Athens: Ohio University Centre for International Studies.
Anderson, B. (2006). *Imagined Communities: Reflections on the Origin and Spread of Nationalism*. London: Verso Books.
Baker, C., & Pasuk, P. (2014). *A History of Thailand*: Cambridge: Cambridge University Press.
Barmé, S. (1993). *Luang Wichit Wathakan and the Creation of a Thai Identity*. Singapore: Institute of Southeast Asian Studies.
Barnhart, J. (2016). Status competition and territorial aggression: Evidence from the scramble for Africa. *Security Studies*, *25*(3), 385–419.
Barston, R. P. (1973). Introduction. In R. P. Barston (Ed.), *The Other Powers: Studies in the Foreign Policies of Small States*. New York: Barnes and Noble.
Batson, B. A. & Hajime, S. (1990). *The Tragedy of Wanit: A Japanese Account of Wartime Thai Politics*. Singapore: National University of Singapore.
Bauman, Z. (2000). *Liquid Modernity*. Cambridge: Polity Press.
Baylis, J., Smith, S., & Owens, P. (2008). *The Globalization of World Politics: An Introduction to International Relations*. Oxford: Oxford University Press.
Becker, D. J. (2014). Memory and trauma as elements of identity in foreign policymaking. In E. Resende & D. Budryte (Eds.), *Memory and Trauma in International Relations: Theories, Cases and Debates* (pp. 57–73). New York: Routledge.
Bell, D. (2006). Introduction. In D. Bell (Ed.), *Memory, Trauma and World Politics: Reflections on the Relationship between Past and Present* (pp. 1–29). New York: Palgrave Macmillan.
Berger, T. (2002). The power of memory and memories of power: The cultural parameters of German foreign policy-making since 1945. In J.-W. Müller (Ed.), *Memory and Power in Post-War Europe: Studies in the Presence of the Past* (pp. 76–99). Cambridge: Cambridge University Press.
Bhabha, H. (1994). *The Location of Culture*. London and New York: Routledge.
Booth, K. (1997). Security and self: Reflections of a fallen realist. In K. Krause and M. C. Williams (Eds.), *Critical Security Studies* (pp. 83–119). London: University of Minnesota Press.
Bourdieu, P. (1984). *Distinction: A Social Critique of the Judgement of Taste*. Cambridge, MA: Harvard University Press.
Brah, A., & Coombes, A. (2000). Introduction: The conundrum of 'Mixing'. In A. Brah & A. Coombes (Eds.), *Hybridity and Its Discontents: Politics, Science, Culture* (pp. 1–15). London and New York: Routledge.
Browining, C. (2015). Nation branding, National self-esteem, and the constitution of subjectivity in late modernity. *Foreign Policy Analysis*, *11*(2), 195–214.
Brown, M. E., Lynn-Jones, S. M., & Miller, S. E. (1995). *The Perils of Anarchy: Contemporary Realism and International Security*. Cambridge, MA: MIT Press.

Bull, H. (2012). *The Anarchical Society: A Study of Order in World Politics*. Palgrave Macmillan.
Bull, H., & Watson, A. (1984). *The Expansion of International Society*. Oxford University Press.
Buszynski, L. (1982). Thailand: The erosion of a balanced foreign policy. *Asian Survey, 22*(11), 1037–1055. doi:10.2307/2643978
Buzan, B. (1993). From international system to international society: Structural realism and regime theory meet the English school. *International Organization, 47*(3), 327–352.
Caruth, C. (1996). *Unclaimed Experience: Trauma, Narrative, and History*. Baltimore: Johns Hopkins University Press.
Carvalho, B., & Neumann, I. (2015). Introduction: Small states and status. In B. Carvalho & I. Neumann (Eds.), *Small State Status Seeking: Norway's Quest for International Standing* (pp. 1–21). New York: Routledge.
Chaiyan, R. (1994). *The Rise and Fall of the Thai Absolute Monarchy: Foundations of the Modern Thai State from Feudalism to Peripheral Capitalism*. Bangkok: White Lotus.
Chakrabongse, C. (1960). *Lords of Life: The Paternal Monarchy of Bangkok, 1782–1932, with the Earlier and More Recent History of Thailand*. London: Alvin Redman.
Charivat, S. (1985). *Thai Foreign Policy, 1932–1946*. Bangkok: Thai Khadi Research Institute, Thammasat University.
Charnvit, K. (1974). The first Phibun government and its involvement in world war II. *The Journal of the Siam Society, 62*, 25–64.
Charnvit, K. (2000). Siam/civilisation – Thailand/globalization: Things to come? *Thammasat Review, 5*(1), 114–133.
Christensen, T. J. (1996). *Useful Adversaries: Grand Strategy, Domestic Mobilization, and Sino-American Conflict, 1947–1958*. Princeton, NJ: Princeton University Press.
Coast, J. (1953). *Some Aspects of Siamese Politics*. New York: International Secretariat, Institute of Pacific Relations.
Coicaud, J.-M. (2015). A brief case study of Germany and Japan: Emotions and passions in the making of world war II. *Japanese Journal of Political Science, 16*(3), 227–247.
Corrine, P. (1999). *Thailand's Foreign Policies: The Four Decades after the Second World War (1945–1989)*. Bangkok: Faculty of Political Science.
Crosby, J. (1945). *Siam: The Crossroads*. London: Hollis & Carter ltd.
Dafoe, A., Renshon, J., & Huth, P. (2014). Reputation and status as motives for war. *Annual Review of Political Science, 17*, 371–393.
Deighton, A. (2002). The past in the present: British imperial memories and the European question. In J.-W. Müller (Ed.), *Memory and Power in Post-War Europe: Studies in the Presence of the Past* (pp. 100–120). Cambridge: Cambridge University Press.
Direk, J., & Keyes, J. G. (1978). *Siam and World War II*. Bangkok: Social Science Association of Thailand Press.
East, M. A. (1973). Size and foreign policy behavior: A test of two models. *World Politics, 25*(4), 556–576. doi:10.2307/2009952
Edkins, J. (2002). Forget trauma? Responses to September 11. *International Relations, 16*(2), 243–256.
Edkins, J. (2003). *Trauma and the Memory of Politics*. Cambridge: Cambridge University Press.

Elias, N. (1997). *The Germans*. New York: Columbia University Press.

Elias, N., & Scotson, J. L. (1994). *The Established and The Outsiders: A Sociology Enquiry into Community Problems*. London: Sage Publications.

Elman, C., & Elman, M. F. (1997). Diplomatic history and international relations theory: Respecting difference and crossing boundaries. *International Security, 22*(1), 5–21.

Elman, C., & Elman, M. F. (2008). The role of history in international relations. *Millennium-Journal of International Studies, 37*(2), 357–364.

Elman, M. F. (1995). The foreign policies of small states: Challenging neorealism in its own backyard. *British Journal of Political Science, 25*(2), 171–217.

Erikson, E. H. (1950). *Childhood and Society*. New York: W.W. Norton.

Fanon, F. (2008). *Black Skin, White Masks*. London: Pluto Press.

Ferrara, F. (2015). *The Political Development of Modern Thailand*. Cambridge: Cambridge University Press.

Fierke, K. M. (2004). Whereof we can speak, thereof we must not be silent: Trauma, political solipsism and war. *Review of International Studies, 30*(4), 471–491.

Fierke, K. M. (2007). *Critical Approaches in International Security*. Cambridge: Polity Press.

Finnemore, M. (1996). *National Interests in International Society*. Ithaca: Cornell University Press.

Flood, E. T. (1969). The 1940 Franco-Thai border dispute and Phibuun Sonkhraam's commitment to Japan. *Journal of Southeast Asian History, 10*(2), 304–325.

George, A. L. (1979). The causal nexus between cognitive beliefs and decision-making behavior: The 'Operational Code' belief system. In L. Falkowski (Ed.), *Psychological Models in International Politics*. Boulder, CO: Westview Press.

Gerring, J. (2006). Single-outcome studies A methodological primer. *International Sociology, 21*(5), 707–734.

Giddens, A. (1984). *The Constitution of Society: Outline of the Theory of Structuration*. Berkeley and Los Angeles: University of California Press.

Giddens, A. (1990). *The Consequences of Modernity*. Stanford: Stanford University Press.

Giddens, A. (1991). *Modernity and Self-Identity: Self and Society in the Late Modern Age*. Stanford: Stanford University Press.

Gilady, L. (2018). *The Price of Prestige: Conspicuous Consumption in International Relations*. Chicago: University of Chicago Press.

Gildea, R. (2002). Myth, memory and policy in France since 1945. In J.-W. Müller (Ed.), *Memory and Power in Post-War Europe: Studies in the Presence of the Past* (pp. 59–75). Cambridge: Cambridge University Press.

Gilpin, R. (1983). *War and Change in World Politics*. Cambridge: Cambridge University Press.

Gilpin, R. (1988). The theory of hegemonic war. *The Journal of Interdisciplinary History, 18*(4), 591–613.

Goffman, E. (1963). *Stigma: Notes on the Management of Spoiled Identity*. New York: Simon & Schuster.

Goldstein, J., & Keohane, R. O. (1993). Ideas and foreign policy: An analytical framework. In *Ideas and Foreign Policy: Beliefs, Institutions, and Political Change* (pp. 3–30). Ithaca: Cornell University Press.

Gong, G. W. (1984). *The Standard of Civilization in International Society*. Oxford: Oxford University Press.

Greenfeld, L. (1995). *Nationalism: Five Roads to Modernity.* Cambridge, MA: Harvard University Press.

Hall, D. G. E. (1968). *A History of South-East Asia* (3rd ed.). London: Palgrave Macmillan.

Handel, M. I. (1981). *Weak States in the International System.* London: Cass.

Herman, C. F. (1972). Policy classification: A key to the study of comparative foreign policy. In J. N. Rosenau, V. Davis, & M. A. East (Eds.), *The Analysis of International Politics: Essays in Honor of Harold and Margaret Sprout.* New York: Free Press.

Herzfeld, M. (2002). The absent presence: Discourses of crypto-colonialism. *The South Atlantic Quarterly, 101*(4), 899–926.

Hobson, J. (2004). *The Eastern Origins of Western Civilisation.* Cambridge: Cambridge University Press.

Holsti, O. (1969). *Content Analysis for the Social Sciences and Humanities.* Reading, MA: Addison-Wesley.

Honneth, A. (1996). *The Struggle for Recognition: The Moral Grammar of Social Conflicts.* Cambridge, MA: MIT Press.

Honneth, A. (2014). The international politics of recognition. In B. Carvalho & I. Neumann (Eds.), *The International Politics of Recognition.* New York: Routledge.

Hopf, T. (1998). The promise of constructivism in international relations theory. *International Security, 23*(1), 171–200.

Hutcheon, L. (2006). *A Theory of Adaptation.* London and New York: Routledge.

Huysmans, J. (1998). Security! What do you mean? From concept to thick signifier. *European Journal of International Relations, 4*(2), 226–255.

Innes, A., & Steele, B. (2014). Memory, trauma, and ontological security. In E. Resende & D. Budryte (Eds.), *Memory and Trauma in International Relations: Theories, Cases, and Debates.* London: Routledge.

Jackson, P. (2010). Afterword. In R. Harrison & P. Jackson (Eds.), *The Ambiguous Allure of the West: Traces of the Colonial in Thailand* (pp. 187–205). Hong Kong: Hong Kong University Press.

Jeshurun, C. (1970). The Anglo-French declaration of January 1896 and the Independence of Siam. *Journal of the Siam Society, 28*(2), 105–126.

Jeshurun, C. (1977). *The Contest for Siam 1889–1902: A Study in Diplomatic Rivalry.* Kuala Lumpur: Penerbit Universiti Kebangsaan Malaysia.

Jones, F. C. (1954). *Japan's New Order in East Asia: Its Rise and Fall, 1937–45.* Oxford: Oxford University Press.

Katzenstein, P. J. (1996). *The Culture of National Security: Norms and Identity in World Politics.* New York: Columbia University Press.

Keene, E. (2002). *Beyond the Anarchical Society: Grotius, Colonialism and Order in World Politics.* Cambridge University Press.

Khong, Y. F. (1992). *Analogies at War: Korea, Munich, Dien Bien Phu, and the Vietnam Decisions of 1965.* Princeton, NJ: Princeton University Press.

Kinnvall, C. (2002). Nationalism, religion and the search for chosen traumas: Comparing Sikh and Hindu identity constructions. *Ethnicities, 2*(1), 79–106. doi:10.1177/1469682002002001523

Kinnvall, C. (2004). Globalization and religious nationalism: Self, identity, and the search for ontological security. *Political Psychology, 25*(5), 741–767.

Kislenko, A. (2002). Bending with the wind: The continuity and flexibility of Thai foreign policy. *International Journal,* 537–561.

Kitchen, N. (2010). Systemic pressures and domestic ideas: A neoclassical realist model of grand strategy formation. *Review of International Studies*, *36*(1), 117–143.

Kobkua, S.-P. (1995). *Thailand's Durable Premier: Phibun through Three Decades, 1932–1957.* Oxford: Oxford University Press.

Kristeva, J. (1989). *Black Sun: Depression and Melancholia*. New York: Columbia Press.

Kullada, K. M. (2004). *The Rise and Decline of Thai Absolutism*. New York: Routledge Curzon.

Laing, R. (1969). *The Divided Self: An Existential Study in Sanity and Madness.* Penguin.

Lapid, Y., & Kratochwil, F. V. (1996). *The Return of Culture and Identity in IR Theory.* Cambridge University Press.

Laplanche, J., & Pontalis, J.-B. (1967). *The Language of Psychoanalysis.* New York: W.W. Norton.

Larson, D. W. (1985). *The Origins of Containment: A Psychological Explanation.* Princeton, NJ: Princeton University Press.

Larson, D. W., Paul, T. V., & William, C. W. (2014). Status and world order. In T. V. Paul, D. W. Larson, & W. C. Wohlforth (Eds.), *Status in World Politics* (pp. 3–29). Cambridge: Cambridge University Press.

Larson, D. W., & Shevchenko, A. (2019). *Quest for Status: Chinese and Russian Foreign Policy.* New Haven: Yale University Press.

Larsson, T. (2008). Western imperialism and defensive underdevelopment of property rights institutions in Siam. *Journal of East Asian Studies*, 1–28.

Lebow, R. N. (2008). *A Cultural Theory of International Relations.* Cambridge: Cambridge University Press.

Lebow, R. N. (2010). *Why Nations Fight: Past and Future Motives for War.* Cambridge University Press.

Likhit, D. (1964). *Siam and Colonialism, 1855–1909: An Analysis of Diplomatic Relations.* Bangkok: Thai Watana Panich.

Likhit, D. (1974). Thailand's foreign policy determination. *The Journal of Social Sciences*, *11*(4).

Lindemann, T. (2011). *Causes of War: The Struggle for Recognition.* Colchester: ECPR Press.

Lobell, S. E., Ripsman, N. M., & Taliaferro, J. W. (2009). *Neoclassical Realism, the State, and Foreign Policy.* Cambridge: Cambridge University Press.

Loos, T. (2006). *Subject Siam: Family, Law, and Colonial Modernity in Thailand.* Ithaca, NY and London: Cornell University Press.

Loos, T. (2010). Competitive colonialisms: Siam and the Malay Muslim South. In R. Harrison & P. Jackson (Eds.), *The Ambiguous Allure of the West: Traces of the Colonial in Thailand* (pp. 75–91). Hong Kong: Hong Kong University Press.

Lysa, H. (1984). *Thailand in the Nineteenth Century: Evolution of the Economy and Society.* Singapore: Institute of Southeast Asian Studies.

Lysa, H. (2004). 'Stranger within the Gates': Knowing semi-colonial Siam as extraterritorials. *Modern Asian Studies*, *38*(2), 327–354.

Mattern, J. B., & Zarakol, A. (2016). Hierarchies in world politics. *International Organization*, 1–32.

McSweeney, B. (1999). *Security, Identity and Interests: A Sociology of International Relations* (Vol. 69). Cambridge: Cambridge University Press.

Mitzen, J. (2006a). Anchoring Europe's civilizing identity: Habits, capabilities and ontological security 1. *Journal of European Public Policy, 13*(2), 270–285.
Mitzen, J. (2006b). Ontological security in world politics: State identity and the security dilemma. *European Journal of International Relations, 12*(3), 341–370.
Morgenthau, H. J. (1948). *Politics Among Nations: The Struggle for Power and Peace* (1st ed.). New York: A. A. Knopf.
Murashima, E. (1988). The origin of modern official state ideology in Thailand. *Journal of Southeast Asian Studies, 19*(1), 80–96.
Murashima, E. (2002). The Thai-Japanese alliance and the Chinese of Thailand. In P. H. Kratoska (Ed.), *Southeast Asian Minorities in the Wartime Japanese Empire.* London: RoutledgeCurzon.
Murashima, E. (2005). Opposing French colonialism Thailand and the independence movements in Indo-China in the early 1940s. *South East Asia Research, 13*(3), 333–383.
Murashima, E. (2006). The commemorative character of Thai historiography: The 1942–43 Thai military campaign in the Shan States depicted as a story of national salvation and the restoration of Thai Independence. *Modern Asian Studies, 40*(4), 1053–1096.
Murray, M. (2014). Recognition, disrespect, and the struggle for Morocco: Rethinking imperial Germany's security dilemma. In T. Lindemann & E. Ringmar (Eds.), *The International Politics of Recognition.* New York: Routledge.
Murray, M. (2019). *The Struggle for Recognition in International Relations: Status, Revisionism, and Rising Powers.* Oxford: Oxford University Press.
Nossery, N., & Hubbell, A. (2013). Introduction: Transmitting the unspeakable through literature and art. In N. N. El & H. Amy (Eds.), *The Unspeakable: Representations of Trauma in Francophone Literature and Art* (pp. 1–19). New Castle: Cambridge Scholars Publishing.
Nuechterlein, D. E. (1965). *Thailand and the Struggle for Southeast Asia.* Ithaca, NY: Cornell University Press.
Organski, A. F. K., & Kugler, J. (1980). *The War Ledger.* Chicago: University of Chicago Press.
Palmer, G., & Morgan, T. C. (2011). *A Theory of Foreign Policy.* Princeton, NJ: Princeton University Press.
Pashakhanlou, A. H. (2017). Fully integrated content analysis in international relations. *International Relations, 31*(4), 447–465.
Pavin, C. (2010). *Reinventing Thailand: Thaksin and His Foreign Policy.* Singapore, Chiang Mai, Thailand: Institute of Southeast Asian Studies and Silkworm Books.
Peleggi, M. (2002). *Lords of Things: The Fashioning of the Siamese Monarchy's Modern Image.* Hawaii: University of Hawaii Press.
Pensrinokun, K. (1988). Adaptation and appeasement: Thai relations with Japan and the Allies in world war II. In E. B. Reynolds & C. Kamchoo (Eds.), *Thai-Japanese Relations in Historical Perspective* (pp. 125–159). Bangkok: Innomedia Co., Ltd. Press.
Pettman, R. (2000). *Commonsense Constructivism, or, The Making of World Affairs.* ME Sharpe.
Prizel, I. (1998). *National Identity and Foreign Policy: Nationalism and Leadership in Poland, Russia and Ukraine.* Cambridge: Cambridge University Press.
Renshon, J. (2016). Status deficits and war. *International Organization, 70*(3), 513–550.

Renshon, J. (2017). *Fighting for Status: Hierarchy and Conflict in World Politics.* Princeton, NJ: Princeton University Press.

Resende, E., & Budryte, D. (2014). Introduction. In E. Resende & D. Budryte (Eds.), *Memory and Trauma in International Relations* (pp. 1–11). New York: Routledge.

Reynolds, B. E. (1991). Imperial Japan's cultural program in Thailand. In G. K. Goodman (Ed.), *Japanese Cultural Policies in Southeast Asia During World War 2* (pp. 93–116). London: Macmillan Press.

Reynolds, B. E. (1994). *Thailand and Japan's Southern Advance, 1940–1945.* London: Macmillan Press.

Reynolds, B. E. (2004). Phibun Songkhram and Thai nationalism in the fascist era. *European Journal of East Asian Studies, 3*(1), 99–134.

Ringmar, E. (1996a). *Identity, Interest and Action: A Cultural Explanation of Sweden's Intervention in the Thirty Years War.* Cambridge: Cambridge University Press.

Ringmar, E. (1996b). On the ontological status of the state. *European Journal of International Relations, 2*(4), 439–466.

Rose, G. (1998). Neoclassical realism and theories of foreign policy. *World Politics, 51*(1), 144–172.

Rosenau, J. N. (1969). *Linkage Politics: Essays on the Convergence of National and International Systems.* New York: Free Press.

Rosenau, J. N. (1971). *The Scientific Study of Foreign Policy.* New York: Free Press.

Rosenau, J. N. (1974). *Comparing Foreign Policies: Theories, Findings, and Methods.* Beverly Hills, CA: Sage Publications; distributed by Halsted Press.

Rosengren, K. E. (1981). *Advances in Content Analysis.* London: Sage.

Rothstein, R. L. (1968). *Alliances and Small Powers.* New York: Columbia University Press.

Sampson, M. W. (1994). Exploiting the seams: External structure and Libyan foreign policy changes. In J. A. Rosati, J. D. Hagan, & M. W. Sampson (Eds.), *Foreign Policy Restructuring: How Governments Respond to Global Change.* Columbia, SC: University of South Carolina Press.

Sasley, B. (2014). Remembering and forgetting in Turkish identity and policymaking. In E. Resende & D. Budryte (Eds.), *Memory and Trauma in International Relations: Theories, Cases, and Debates* (pp. 138–152). New York: Routledge.

Saurette, P. (2006). You dissin me? Humiliation and post 9/11 global politics. *Review of International Studies, 32*(3), 495–522.

Schia, N. N., & Sending, O. J. (2015). Status and sovereign equality: Small States in multilateral settings. In B. Carvalho & I. Neumann (Eds.), *Small State Status Seeking: Norway's Quest for International Standing* (pp. 73–85). New Yok: Routledge.

Schweller, R. (1994). Bandwagoning for profit: Bringing the revisionist state back in. *International Security, 19*(1), 72–107.

Schweller, R. (1998). *Deadly Imbalances: Tripolarity and Hitler's Strategy of World Conquest.* New York: Columbia University Press.

Schweller, R. (2004). Unanswered threats: A neoclassical realist theory of underbalancing. *International Security, 29*(2), 159–201.

Schweller, R. (2006). *Unanswered Threats: Political Constraints on the Balance of Power.* Princeton, NJ: Princeton University Press.

Siffins, J. W. (1975). *The Thai Bureaucracy: Institutional Change and Development.* Westport, CT: Greenwood Press.

Snyder, J. (2013). *Myths of Empire: Domestic Politics and International Ambition*. Ithaca: Cornell University Press.

Sorasak, N. (2010). *The New History of the Seri Thai Movement*. Bangkok: Institute of Asian Studies, Chulalongkorn University.

Chanintira, N. T., Soravis, J., & Jittipat, P. (2019). Introduction. In N. T. Chanintira, J. Soravis, & P. Jittipat (Eds.), *International Relations as a Discipline in Thailand: Theory and Sub-fields* (pp. 1–18). New York: Routledge.

Spivak, G. (2000). Deconstruction and cultural studies: Arguments for a deconstructive cultural studies. In N. Royle (Ed.), *Deconstructions: A User's Guide* (pp. 14–43). New York: Palgrave Macmillan.

Stanton, E. F. (1954). Spotlight on Thailand. *Foreign Affairs*, *33*(1), 72–85. doi:10.2307/20031076

Steele, B. J. (2005). Ontological security and the power of self-identity: British neutrality and the American civil war. *Review of International Studies*, *31*(3), 519–540.

Steele, B. J. (2008a). Ideals that were really never in our possession': Torture, Honor and US identity. *International Relations*, *22*(2), 243–261.

Steele, B. J. (2008b). *Ontological Security in International Relations: Self-Identity and the IR State*. New York: Routledge.

Stowe, J. A. (1991). *Siam Becomes Thailand: A Story of Intrigue*. Hawaii: University of Hawaii Press.

Subotic, J., & Zarakol, A. (2013). Cultural intimacy in international relations. *European Journal of International Relations*, *19*(4), 915–938.

Subotic, J. (2016). Narrative, ontological security, and foreign policy change. *Foreign Policy Analysis*, *12*(4), 610–627.

Subrahmanyan, A. (2015). Education, propaganda, and the people: Democratic paternalism in 1930s Siam. *Modern Asian Studies*, *49*(4), 1122–1142.

Suhrki, A. (1971). Smaller-nation diplomacy: Thailand's current dilemmas. *Asian Survey*, *11*(5), 429–444. doi:10.2307/2642980

Suzuki, S. (2005). Japan's socialization into Janus-faced European international society. *European Journal of International Relations*, *11*(1), 137–164.

Suzuki, S. (2009). *Civilization and Empire: China and Japan's Encounter with European International Society*. New York: Routledge.

Swan, W. L. (1987). Thai-Japanese relations at the start of the pacific war: New insight into a controversial period. *Journal of Southeast Asian Studies*, *18*(2), 270–293.

Sztompka, P. (2000). Cultural trauma the other face of social change. *European Journal of Social Theory*, *3*(4), 449–466.

Tarling, N. (1960). Siam and Sir James Brooke. *Journal of the Siam Society*, *48*(2), 43–72.

Taylor, C. (1995). *Philosophical Arguments*. Cambridge, MA: Harvard University Press.

Tej, B. (1977). *The Provincial Administration of Siam 1892–1915: The Ministry of the Interior under Prince Damrong Rajanubhab*. Kuala Lumpur: Oxford University Press.

Terwiel, B. J. (1980). *Field Marshal Plaek Phibun Songkhram*. St. Lucia Australia: University of Queensland Press.

Terwiel, B. J. (1991). The Bowring Treaty: Imperialism and the indigenous perspective. *Journal of the Siam Society*, *79*(2), 40–47.

Terwiel, B. J. (2011). *Thailand's Political History: From the 13th Century to Recent Times*. Bangkok: River Books.

Thamsook, N. (1977). *Thailand and the Japanese Presence, 1941–45*. Singapore: Institute of Southeast Asian.

Thamsook, N. (1978). Pibulsongkram's Thai nation-building programme during the Japanese military presence, 1941–1945. *Journal of Southeast Asian Studies*, *9*(2), 234–247.

Thompson, V. (1940). Thailand irredenta – Internal and external. *Far Eastern Survey*, *9*(21), 243–250. doi:10.2307/3021985

Thongchai, W. (1994). *Siam Mapped: A History of the Geo-body of a Nation*. Hawaii: University of Hawaii Press.

Thongchai, W. (2000). The quest for "Siwilai": A geographical discourse of civilizational thinking in the late nineteenth and early twentieth-century Siam. *The Journal of Asian Studies*, *59*(3), 528–549.

Thongchai, W. (2011). Siam's colonial conditions and the birth of Thai history. In V. Grabowsky (Ed.), *Southeast Asian Historiography Unravelling the Myths: Essays in Honour of Barend Jan Terwiel* (pp. 20–43). Bangkok: River Books.

Thorun, C. (2009). *Explaining Change in Russian Foreign Policy: The Role of Ideas in Post-Soviet Russia's Conduct Towards the West*. New York: Palgrave Macmillan.

Varenne, A. (1938). Indo-China in the path of Japanese expansion. *Foreign Affairs*, *17*(1), 164–171. doi:10.2307/20028911

Vella, W. F. (1955). *The Impact of the West on Government in Thailand*. Berkeley: University of California Press.

Vella, W. F. (1957). *Siam under Rama III, 1824–1851*. Locust Valley, NY: JJ Augustin.

Vella, W. F., & Vella, D. B. (1978). *Chaiyo! King Vajiravudh and the Development of Thai Nationalism*. Hawaii: University of Hawaii Press.

Vieira, M. A. (2016). Understanding resilience in international relations: The non-aligned movement and ontological security. *International Studies Review*, *18*(2), 290–311.

Vieira, M. A. (2018). (Re-)imagining the 'Self' of ontological security: The case of Brazil's ambivalent postcolonial subjectivity. *Millennium*, *46*(2), 142–164.

Viraphol, S. (1976). *Directions in Thai Foreign Policy* (Vol. 40). Singapore: Institute of Southeast Asian Studies.

Viraphol, S. (1977). *Tribute and Profit: Sino-Siamese Trade, 1652–1853* (Vol. 76). Cambridge, MA: Harvard University Press.

Vital, D. (1971). *The Survival of Small States: Studies in Small Power/Great Power Conflict*. London and New York: Oxford University Press.

Volkan, V. D. (1997). *Bloodlines: From Ethnic Pride to Ethnic Terrorism*. New York: Farrar, Straua and Giroux.

Waever, O. (1996). The rise and fall of inter-paradigm debate. In S. Smith, K. Booth, & M. Zalewski (Eds.), *International Theory: Positivism and Beyond*. Cambridge: Cambridge University Press.

Waltz, K. N. (1979). *Theory of International Politics*. Reading, MA and London: Addison-Wesley.

Wang, Z. (2014). *Never Forget National Humiliation: Historical Memory in Chinese Politics and Foreign Relations*. New York: Columbia University Press.

Ward, S. (2017). *Status and the Challenge of Rising Powers*. Cambridge: Cambridge University Press.

Watson, A. (1984). European international society and its expansion. In H. Bull & A. Watson (Eds.), *The Expansion of International Society* (pp. 13–32). Oxford: Clarendon Press.

Wendt, A. (1992). Anarchy is what states make of it: The social construction of power politics. *International Organization*, *46*(2), 391–425.
Wendt, A. (2003). Why a world state is inevitable. *European Journal of International Relations 9*(4), 491–542.
Wendt, A. (2004). The state as person in international theory. *Review of International Studies*, *30*(2), 289–316.
Wohlforth, W. (1993). *The Elusive Balance: Power and Perceptions During the Cold War*. Ithaca: Cornell University Press.
Wolf, R. (2011). Respect and disrespect in international politics: The significance of status recognition. *International Theory*, *3*(1), 105.
Wyatt, D. K. (1969). *The Politics of Reform in Thailand: Education in the Reign of King Chulalongkorn*. New Haven: Yale University Press.
Wyatt, D. K. (2003). *Thailand: A Short History* (2nd ed.). New Haven, CT: Yale University Press.
Zakaria, F. (1998). *From Wealth to Power: The Unusual Origins of America's World Role*. New Jersey: Princeton University Press.
Zala, B. (2017). Great power management and ambiguous order in nineteenth-century international society. *Review of International Studies*, *43*(2), 367–388.
Zarakol, A. (2010). Ontological (in) security and state denial of historical crimes: Turkey and Japan. *International Relations*, *24*(1), 3–23.
Zarakol, A. (2011). *After Defeat: How the East Learned to Live with the West*. Cambridge and New York: Cambridge University Press.
Zarakol, A. (2014). What made the modern world hang together: Socialisation or stigmatisation? *International Theory*, *6*(2), 311–332.
Zehfuss, M. (2001). Constructivism and identity: A dangerous liaison. *European Journal of International Relations*, *7*(3), 315–348.
Zehfuss, M. (2004). Writing war, against good conscience. *Millennium*, *33*(1), 91–121.
Zehfuss, M. (2007). *Wounds of Memory: The Politics of War in Germany*. Cambridge: Cambridge University Press.

Published English documentary sources

Ike, N. (1967). *Japan's Decision for War: Records of the 1941 Policy Conferences*. Palo Alto: Stanford University Press.
Togo, S. (1975). Foreign minister Togo opposes the greater East Asia ministry. In J. Lebra (Ed.), *Japan's Greater East Asia Co-Prosperity Sphere in World War II: Selected Readings and Documents*. Kuala Lumpur: Oxford University Press.

English-language theses and dissertations

Asadakorn, E. (1980). *Foreign Policy-making in Thailand: ASEAN Policy, 1967–1972*. PhD Diss., State University of New York at Binghamton.
Battye, N. A. (1974). *The Military, Government and Society in Siam, 1868–1910*. PhD Diss., Cornell University.
Bhansoon, L. (1986). *Thailand's Foreign Policy Under Kukrit Pramoj: A Study in Decision-making*. PhD Diss., Northern Illinois University.
Busbarat, P. (2009). *Embracing Proaction: The Role of Self-perception in Thailand's Post-Cold War Foreign Policy*. PhD Diss., Australian National University.

Chai-Anan, S. (1971). *The Politics of Administration of the Thai Budgetary Process*. PhD Diss., University of Wisconsin.

Copeland, M. (1993). *Contested Nationalism and the 1932 Overthrow of the Absolute Monarchy in Siam*. PhD Diss., Australian National University.

Corrine, P. (1980). *Thailand in Southeast Asia: A Study of Foreign Policy Behavior (1964–1977)*. PhD Diss., University of Hawaii.

Flood, E. T. (1967). *Japan's Relations with Thailand, 1928–1941*. PhD Diss., University of Washington.

Hall, S. (2007). *Siam and the League of Nations: Modernization, Sovereignty, and Multilateral Diplomacy, 1920–1940*. PhD Diss., Leiden University, Leiden.

Hell, S. (2007). *Siam and the League of Nations: Modernization, Sovereignty and Multilateral Diplomacy, 1920–1940*. PhD Diss., Leiden University.

Kislenko, A. (2000). *Bamboo in the Wind: United States Foreign Policy and Thailand During the Kennedy and Johnson Administrations 1961–1969*. PhD Diss., University of Toronto.

Markey, D. S. (2000). *The Prestige Motive in International Relations*. PhD Diss., Princeton University.

Muhamad, A. F. (2008). *The Struggle for Recognition in Foreign Policy: Malaysia under Mahatir 1981–2003*. PhD Diss., London School of Economics and Political Science.

Murray, M. (2008). *The Struggle for Recognition in International Politics: Security, Identity and the Quest for Power*. PhD Diss., University of Chicago.

Oblas, P. (1974). *Siam's Efforts to Revise the Unequal Treaty System in the Sixth Reign (1910–1925)*. PhD Diss., University of Michigan.

Pongphisoot, B. (2009). *Embracing Proaction: The Role of Self-perception in Thailand's Post-Cold War Foreign Policy*. PhD Diss., Australian National University.

Puli, F. (2013). *Constitutions and Legitimisation: The Cases of Siam's Permanent Constitution and Japan's Postwar Constitution*. PhD Diss., Cambridge University.

Reynolds, E. B. (1988). *Ambivalent Allies: Japan and Thailand, 1941–1945*. PhD Diss., University of Hawaii.

Smairob, S. (1980). *A Strategy for Survival of Thailand: Reappraisal and Readjustment in her Alliances (1969–1976)*. PhD Diss., University of Oklahoma.

Snidvongs, N. (1960). *The Development of Siam's Relations with Britain and France in the Reign of King Mongkut, 1851–1868*. PhD Diss., University of London.

Strate, S. (2009). *The Lost Territories: The Role of Trauma and Humiliation in the Formation of National Consciousness in Thailand*. PhD Diss., University of Wisconsin-Madison.

Vinita, K. (1975). *The Politics of Pibul: The National Leader, 1932–1944*. PhD Book, American University.

Wilson, C. M. (1970). *State and Society in the Reign of Mongkut, 1851–1868: Thailand on the eve of Modernization*. PhD Diss., Cornell University.

Zarakol, A. (2007). *After Defeat: Turkey, Japan, Russia and the Grand Strategy of Assimilation*. PhD Diss., University of Wisconsin-Madison.

Thai-language secondary sources

Atthachak, S. (1995). *Kanplianplaeng Lokkathat Khong Chonchan Phunam Thai Tangtae Ratchakan Thi 4-Po.So. 2475 [Transformation of the Thai Elite's World View from the Fourth Regin to 1932]*. Bangkok: Chulalongkorn University.

Charnvit, K., Thamrongsak, P., & Vigal, P. (Eds.). (2001). *Chomphon Po. Phibunsongkhram Kup Kanmueang Thai Samai Mai [Field Marshal Phibunsongkhram and Modern Thai Politics]*. Bangkok: The Foundation for the Promotion of Social Sciences and Humanities Textbooks Project.

Kobkua, S.-P. (1989). *Nayobai Tangprathet Khong Ratthaban Phibunsongkhram, Po.So. 2481–2487 [Thai Foreign Policy of the Phibunsongkhram Government, 1938–1944]*. Bangkok: Sathaban Thaikhadisuksa, Mahawitthayalai Thammasat: Chatchamnai doi Sun Nangsu Mahawitthayalai Thammasat.

Krairiksh, N. (2008). *Kanmueang Nok 'Phongsaowadan' Ratchakan Thi 5: Bueanglang Phrabatsomdetphrachunlachomklaochaoyuhua Sadet Praphat Yurop [Politics Beyond Chronicles during the Reign of King Rama V: Behind King Chualongkorn's European Voyage]*. Bangkok: Matichon.

Manij, C. (1979). *Thai Kup Songkhram Lok Khrang Thi Nueng [Thailand and the First World War]*. Bangkok: Pittayakarn Press.

Manit, N. (1997). *Kanmueang Thai Yuk Sanyalak Rat Thai [Thai Politics in the Era of the Symbol of the Thai State]*. Bangkok: Rungruang Printing.

Murashima, E., & Sorasak, N. (1986). Phaen Kan Buk Khong Yipun Kup Botbat Nayokratthamonthri Chompon Po. Phibunsongkhram [Japanese Plan and Role of Marshal Pibulsongkhram]. *Silpawattanatham*, *7*(9), 82–91.

Nakarin, M. (1989). Rabop Ratthaniyom Chompon Po. Phibunsongkhram: Kan Ko Rup Khong Khwamkit Lae Khwammai Thang Kanmueang [The State Convention Regime of Field Marshal Phibunsongkhram: The Formation of Political Thought and Meaning]. *Ratthasartsarn*, *3*(15), 228–274.

Nakarin, M. (2010). *Kanpathiwatsayam Po.So. 2475 [The Revolution of Siam in 1932]*. Bangkok: Samnakphim Fadiaokan.

Nakarin, M., Puli, F., Sarunyou, T., & Natthapol, C. (2018). *Yak Luem Klup Cham [Want to Forget, but Still Remembering]*. Bangkok: Matichon Press.

Naruemit, S. (1981). *Samphanthaphapthangkanthut Rawang Thai Kap Sathannaratprachachonchin [Diplomatic Relations between Thailand and the People's Republic of China]*. Bangkok: Thaiwattanapanich Press,.

Pensri, D. (1984). *Kantangprathet lae Amnat Athippatai Khong Thai Tangtae Samai Ratchakanthisi thueng Sin Samai Ratbanchompon Po. Phibunsongkhram [Thai Foreign Affairs and Sovereignty from King Rama IV to the end of Field Marshal Pibul Songkhram]*. Bangkok: Chaopraya.

Prayoon, P. (1974). *Banthuek Rueang Kanpleanplangkanpokkhrong 2475 [Records of the 2475Revolution]*. Bangkok: Phuangaksorn Press.

Prayoon, P. (1975). *Chiwit Ha Phandin Khong Kaphachao [My Life in Five Reigns]*. Bangkok: Bannakij.

Rome, B. (2009). *Songkhram Lae Khwamkhaen Thai-Farangset [War and Grudge between Thailand and France]*. Bangkok: Siambanthuek Press.

Sang, P. (1944). *Suek Thai Nai Roi Pi, 2385–2485 [Thai war in the Hundred Years between 1842–1942]*. Bangkok: Thai Khasem Press.

Somsak, J. (2004a). Prathet Thai Aayu Krop 65: Komun Mai Keawkup Kan Plianchue Prathet Pi 2482 [Thailand 65 years: New evidence on the name changing of the country in 2482 B.E.]. *Silpawattanatham*, *25*(8).

Somsak, J. (2004b). Prawattisat Wan Chat Thai chak 24 Mituna Tueng 5 Thanwa [History of the National day from 24 June to 5 December]. *Fah Deaw Kan*, *2*(2), 70–122.

Supamit, P. (2007). *Khwamsamphanrawangprathet: Phatthanakan Lae Khwamkaona Khong Ongkhwamru [International Relations: Development and Progress of a Body of Knowledge]*. Bangkok: National Research Council of Thailand.

Thamrongsak, P. (1990). Kanriakrongdindaen Po.So. 2483: Pitcharana Patchai Pai-nai Choeng Kam Athibai [Territorial Retrocession in 1940: A Consideration of Internal Factors]. *Samut Sangkomsart, 12*(3–4).

Thamrongsak, P. (2009). Kanriakrongdindaen Po.So. 2483 [Territorial Retrocession in 1940]. In T. Petchlertanan (Ed.), *Sayamprathetthai kap dindaen nai Kamphucha lae Lao [Siam-Thailand and Territories in Cambodia and Laos]* (pp. 83–220). Bangkok: The Foundation for the Promotion of Social Sciences and Humanities Textbooks Projects.

Thamsook, N. (1978). *Mueang Thai Samai Songkhram Lok Krang Thi Song [Thailand in the Second World War]*. Bangkok: Dungkamol.

Toshiharu, Y. (1985). *Ratthaban Chompon Po. Phibunsongkhram Lae Songkhrampaesifik [The Phibul Regime and the Pacific War]* (Athon, F. Trans). Bangkok: The Foundation for the Promotion of Social Sciences and Humanities Textbooks Projects.

Published Thai documentary sources

Ananda, P. (1975a). *Chomphon Po Phibunsongkhram Lem 1 [Field Marshal Phibunsongkhram Vol. 1]* (Vol. 1). Bangkok: Montri Press.

Ananda, P. (1975b). *Chomphon Po Phibunsongkhram Lem 2 [Field Marshal Phibunsongkhram Vol. 2]* (Vol. 2). Bangkok: Montri Press.

Chai-Anan, S., & Kattiya, K. (1989). *Ekkasan Kanmueangkanpokkhrong Thai 2411–2475 [Documents on Thai Politics and Administration 1868–1932]*. Bangkok: Social Science Association of Thailand.

Chira, W. (1979). *Gnan Phraratchathan Phloengsop Pol Aek Chira Wichitsongkhram [Commemorative Funerary Volume of General Chira Wichitsongkhram]*. Bangkok: Damrong Press.

Damri, P. (1938, April). Nayobai Thang Ruea Khong Siam Kup Kongtapruea [Maritime Policy of Siam and the Navy]. *Nawikasart, 4*, 858–906.

Khana-Yoowasarn. (1934). *Siam RorSor 112 [Siam and RorSor 112]*. Bangkok. Yong Li Press.

Konthi, S. (1984). *Kan Withesobai Khong Thai Rawang Po.So. 2483–2495 [Thai Foreign Affairs from 1940–1952]*. Bangkok: Post Publishing.

Luang Saranuchit. (1979). *Thiraluek Nai Ngan Phraratchathanphloengsop Ponthri Luang Saranuchit [Commemorative Funerary Volume for Maj. Gen. Luang Saranuchit]*. Bangkok: Bualuang Press.

Nakamura, A. (1991). *Pu Banchakan Chao Phut: Banthuek Pu Banchakarn Kongthapyipin Pracham Prathet Thai Kiaokup Songkhramlokkhrangthisong [The Bhuddist Commander: A Memoir of the Japanese Commander in Thailand during the Second World War]* (E. Murashima & M. Nakarin, Trans.). Bangkok: The Foundation for the Promotion of Social Sciences and Humanities Textbooks Project.

Netr, K. (1967): *Chiwit Nai Phon [The Life of the General]*. Phra Nakorn: Phuang Aksorn.

Office of Prime Minister. (1990). *Nangsuewian Khanaratthamontri Nai Suan Ti Kiao Kup Kotmai Waduai Rabiap Karatchakan Ponlaruean (2475–2525) [Circulars from the Cabinet as Regards Law on Regulations for Civil Servants (2475–2525, B.E.)]*. Bangkok: Office of the Civil Service Commission.

Publicity Bureau. (1940a). *Khaokhosanakan*. Phranakorn: Publicity Bureau.
Publicity Bureau. (1940b). *Pramuan Kum Prasai Lae Suntharapojna Khong Nayokratthamontri [Collections of Words and Speeches of Prime Minister]*. Phranakon: Publicity Bureau.
Publicity Bureau. (1941a). *Khaokhosanakan*. Phranakon: Publicity Bureau.
Publicity Bureau. (1941b). *Mueang Thai: Nangsuephap [Thailand: A Photobook]*. Phranakorn: Publicity Bureau.
Publicity Bureau. (1941c). *Prathet Thai Rueang Kan Dai Dindaen Kuen [Thailand and the Lost of Territories]*. Phranakorn: Publicity Bureau.
Publicity Bureau. (1942). *Khaokhosanakan*. Phranakorn: Publicity Bureau.
Sa-nguan, I. (1938, November). Khongkhwan Khong Chat [Gift of the Nation]. *Nawikasart, 11*, 2554–2565.
Saeng, C. (1993). *Kromrotfai Kup Korani Pipat Indochin Farangset Lae Songkhrammahaaechiaburapha [The Railway Department: the French Indo-China Dispute and the Greater East Asian War]*. Bangkok: Darnsutha Karnpim.
Sub-committee of Maintaining the Military of the Naval Unit. (1937, December). Khwam Samkan Khong Kamlang Thang Ruea [The Importance of the Navy]. *Nawikasart, 20*, 3183–3197.
Thepphasatsathit. (1904). *Phumisat Lem 2 [Geography Volume 2]*. Bangkhunphrom: Kromsuksathikarn.
Wan, W. (1943). *Prawat Kanthut Khong Thai [Diplomatic History of Thailand]*. Phranakorn: Office of Prime Minister.
Wichit, W. (2003). *Phathakatha Lae Kanbanyai Lem 2 [Speeches and Lectures Vol. 2]*. Bangkok: Sangsan Books.

Thai-language theses and dissertations

Darunee, B. (1977). *Botbat Khong Thai Samai Songkhramlokkhrangthisong [The Role of Thailand during WWII]*. MA Thesis, Srinakarinwirot University.
Kongsakon, K. (2002). *Kan Sang Rangkai Phonlamueang Thai Samai Chompon Po. Phibunsongkhram Po.So. 2481–2487 [Constructing the Body of Thai Citizens during the Phibun regime of 1938–1944]*. MA Thesis, Thammasat University.
Nattapoll, C. (2009). *Kanmueang Thai Samai Chomphon Po. Phibunsongkhram Phaitai Rabiaplok Lhong Saharat Amerika [Thai Politics in Phibun's Government Under the U.S. World Order (1948–1957)]*. PhD Thesis, Chulalongkorn University.
Nipaporn, R. (2002). *Khwamsamphan Thang Watthanatham Rawang Thai-Yipun Po.So. 2475–2488 [Cultural Relationship between Thailand and Japan, 1932–1945]*. MA Thesis, Thammasat University.
Somchoke, S. (1981). *Khwamsamphan Thang Thahan Rawang Thai Kup Yipun Nai Songkhrammahaaechiaburapha Po.So. 2484–2488 [Military Relations between Thailand and Japan in the War of Greater East Asia 1941–1945]*. MA Thesis, Chulalongkorn University.
Sumet, S. (1980). *Nayobaitangprathet Khong Thai Samai Chomphon Po Phibunsongkhram [Thai Foreign Policy during Field Marshal Phibul Songkhram]*. MA Thesis, Srinakarinwirot University.
Supaporn, B. (2003). *Kan Riakrong Dindaen Ti Dai Kuen Chak Farangset Po.So. 2483–2491[Demands for the Retrocession of Territories from the French and their Subsequent Administration, 1940–1948]*. MA Thesis, Chulalongkorn University.
Suraphan, B. (1978). *Kan Sang Than Amnat Thang Kanmueang Khong Luangphibunsongkhram: Suksa Chapo Korani Kan Kwatlang Porapak Thang Kanmueang*

Nai Pi Po.So. 2481 [The Political Power Consolidation of Luang Pibulsongkram: With Special Reference to the Liquidation of Political Opposition in B.E. 2481]. MA Thesis, Chulalongkorn University.

Thanee, S. (1982). *Khwamsamphan Rawang Thai Kap Satharanaratprachachonchin: Vikhro Naew Nayobaitangprathet Khong Thai Thi Mi To Chin Po.So. 2949–2515 [The Sino-Thai Relations: An Analysis of Thai Foreign Policy Toward China 1949–1972]*. MA Thesis, Thammasat University.

Index